The Royal Navy Wasp

An Operational and Retirement History

The Authors: Wing Commander Terry Martin RAF (Retd) left and Commander Larry Jeram-Croft RN (Retd), standing in front of Terry Martin's Wasp, XT 787, June 2017.

The Royal Navy Wasp

An Operational and Retirement History

Larry Jeram-Croft and Terry Martin

Pen & Sword
AVIATION

First published in Great Britain in 2018 by
PEN AND SWORD AVIATION
an imprint of
Pen and Sword Books Ltd
47 Church Street
Barnsley
South Yorkshire S70 2AS

ISBN 978 1 52672 114 3

Printed and bound in India by Replika Press Pvt. Ltd.

Typeset in Ehrhardt MT Std 11.5/15 by
Aura Technology and Software Services, India

Pen & Sword Books Ltd incorporates the imprints of Pen & Sword
Archaeology, Atlas, Aviation, Battleground, Discovery,
Family History, History, Maritime, Military, Naval, Politics, Railways,
Select, Social History, Transport, True Crime, Claymore Press,
Frontline Books, Leo Cooper, Praetorian Press, Remember When,
Seaforth Publishing and Wharncliffe.

For a complete list of Pen and Sword titles please contact
Pen and Sword Books Limited
47 Church Street, Barnsley, South Yorkshire, S70 2AS, England
E-mail: enquiries@pen-and-sword.co.uk
Website: www.pen-and-sword.co.uk

Contents

Foreword

Foreword by Admiral Sir George Zambellas:
This book needed to be written. For aficionados of the mighty Westland Wasp HAS Mk1 - the aircrew, Flight maintainers, ground crew, helicopter controllers, Flight Deck Officers as well as aviation enthusiasts - a proper and authoritative reference was very much needed. Larry and Terry have achieved that magnificently.

Yet, in truth, the Wasp was a source of very much more than evolutionary naval helicopter capability. It was the basis for thousands of lessons, some cruel, about single-engined rotary capability, and a million dits. To be a Wasp pilot, was to join a band of truly unusual people, hugely proud of the privilege of mastering the strengths and weaknesses of obviously one of the most elegant and beautiful flying machines ever invented. It took courage to carry out a hydraulics-off deck landing in the day, never mind at night, or to believe that a downwind engine-off at 400 feet over the sea was survivable. It took even more courage to be the aircrewman in such circumstances.

But, courage we had. And fun. There are so many stories. It was my privilege to be a Waspie, and the source of a few dits.

George Tanser

Lt Zambellas and
LACMN Cunningham
HMS ROTHESAY
Flight 1985-1987.

By LJC:

The first helicopter I ever flew in was a Wasp. I had been lucky enough to be awarded a Flying Scholarship through my school's Combined Cadet Force and was learning to fly Piper Cherokees at the Oxford Air Training School in Carlisle. A ship's Flight aircraft popped in for fuel and the pilot offered some of us a quick trip. What a contrast to a light aircraft! It was noisy, cramped and vibrated. However, it could also belt around at ground level at silly speed as well as manage some quite hair-raising 'aerobatics'.

I was soon reacquainted with the machine two years later when serving as a Midshipman in HMS *Sirius*. Although, as an officer under training, I had to spend time with all the ship's departments, I spent as much time as I could in the hangar and Flight Deck and managed to scrounge more than my fair share of time in the aircraft. I even managed to get into the left-hand seat and play around with the AS 12 missile sight mounted above me.

Many years later, after I had qualified as a naval aviator and completed two front line tours on the Sea King and Lynx, I also converted to the Wasp. This was so that I could test fly the aircraft as part of my duties as the resident test pilot at HMS *Osprey*, the Naval Air Station at Portland in Dorset. Converting onto a first generation machine after the others I was more familiar with was 'interesting'. The Wasp was simple and limited. It also needed a great deal of concentration to fly, and it could bite very hard if you abused it. That said, as a machine to enjoy for pure piloting pleasure it was a delight, as you had to master it every second you were in the air. It did have a rudimentary Auto Stabilisation and Flight Control system but I (like many others) actually found it easier to fly with it switched out. Although it had a system to automatically control the rotor speed, it could also be flown in manual control, which was hard work. In my opinion, the absolute pinnacle of flying skills for a helicopter pilot is being able to land without the use of an engine. 'Engine offs' were practiced in all single engine aircraft and I had originally learned how to do them when learning to fly in the Gazelle helicopter. The difference to the Wasp was chalk and cheese. A Wasp descending in autorotation has the aerodynamics of a house brick. When you arrive at one hundred and fifty feet there is absolutely no margin for error when you flare the aircraft and plonk it onto the runway – pure pilot s***!

It's quite amazing to realise that this machine flew from small ships all around the world, often in atrocious conditions, with one pilot and virtually no navigation aids. It had limited endurance, especially when carrying the various weapon loads it was capable of delivering and limited power to leave and recover to a heaving and pitching deck.

The reason for its existence was to solve the problem of attacking a submarine well outside the range of the ships own weapons. Other navies tried various solutions, but the Royal Navy solved the problem first, and in the process became a world leader in small ship aircraft operations. The Wasp was the first of a long line of aircraft and it's a tribute to the soundness of the design that it stayed in service for so long.

By TM:

I remember the very first time I saw a Wasp helicopter. I was 13 years old and it was displayed in the static line up at 'Daedalus Air Days' in 1967. HMS *Daedalus* was a Naval Air Station at Lee-on-Solent in Hampshire, which closed in 1996. I recorded the tail number of that first Wasp. It was XT789. I could never have imagined that I would one day be the proud and privileged owner of its sister, XT787.

However, I can't say that I took much interest in this little helicopter at the time, and even going to navy air shows didn't convince me to join the Royal Navy (RN) as a career. I did want to fly though, but I was destined to fly wearing a light blue uniform. The twist to this tale was that I couldn't decide whether to follow a career in medicine or in flying, so I elected to do both. During my early medical career in the Royal Air Force (RAF), and after my primary training in fixed wing aircraft, I was stationed at RAF Shawbury, the home of RAF rotary wing training, where I learned to fly the Gazelle. You could say this was a life changing event. Unlike my predecessors who became Medical Officer Pilots (MOPs) and flew the Hunter and then the Hawk, I gave up this route so that I could continue in the rotary wing world.

I spent twenty-four years in the RAF and only saw a Wasp once in all that time. I was stationed at the RAF Support Unit in Belize and a Wasp was flying in for repairs. However, it wasn't flying under its own power, it was dangling beneath an RAF Westland/Aerospatial Puma, having been lifted from the Caribbean guard ship. It had been a victim of a heavy landing resulting in damage to the landing gear.

On the other hand, during a Taceval (tactical evaluation) exercise at RAF Shawbury in 1985, I did fly in a Scout, albeit for only forty minutes. I recall thinking, 'what a wonderful rugged and compact machine' but, again, even in my wildest dreams, I didn't think I'd ever have a licence and rating to fly one myself.

Leap forward to 1999 and suddenly there are Scouts and Wasps for sale on the civilian market, and at an affordable price! This was very tempting, especially when I was offered the opportunity to buy a 50% share of Westland Wasp G-RIMM, formerly HAS1 XT435 in the RN and NZ3907 in the Royal New Zealand Navy

(RNZN). So it was in this striped 'stinger' tailed Wasp, XT435, that I cut my teeth and learned to fly a real beast of a helicopter. It may have only one engine, but that Nimbus 103 has a lot of power, and the agility of this cumbersome looking machine surprised me immensely. I was very lucky to receive excellent tuition, partly on the Scout (ex-Army Air Corps instructors), but mostly on the Wasp (ex-RN Fleet Air Arm instructor), and I learned to respect these machines with their small rotor disc, rapid rate of descent in autorotation, and their propensity to run out of tail rotor authority.

Respect was the word, but practice was the process. Endless autorotation after autorotation, manual throttle, hydraulics out, engine-off landings, practice tail rotor failures and every other conceivable emergency possible to practice. This was all a challenge but one which I happily faced. Achievement was reward in itself, and, in time, flying the Wasp became second nature. She was a delight to fly and it was 'real' flying. No autopilot, no height hold, no stabilisation. None of the 'add-ons' that were there for the RN pilots. Just pure piloting skills, but the Wasp demands the pilot's attention continuously, second by second, and rewards me with agility, responsiveness and the excitement of flying a rugged jet-engined brute which turns heads and draws admirers wherever I go.

To bring the story up to date, I should mention my current aircraft, Westland Wasp HAS1 G-KAXT, formerly XT787 in the RN, and NZ3905 in the RNZN. Bought from Kennet Aviation in 2012, this superb machine retains its RN markings and is dressed in the South Atlantic camouflage scheme as worn by the ship's Flight Wasp, XS527, during the attack on the Argentine submarine, the *Santa Fe*, in 1982. XT787, of HMS *Endurance*, is now a frequent sight at UK air shows and other events, and I fly and display her in respect of the crews that flew Wasps in the Cold War years and during the Falklands conflict. It is a privilege to keep the history of this wonderful and significant helicopter alive.

Authors' Profiles

Larry Jeram-Croft spent thirty years in the Royal Navy. He trained as an aircraft engineer and then as a helicopter pilot. He was awarded a Queen's Commendation for search and rescue duties and flew the Lynx off HMS *Andromeda* during the Falklands War. He then became the Maintenance Test Pilot at RNAS Portland for four years flying the Lynx and the Wasp. Retiring from the Royal Navy in 2000 as a Commander, he worked in industry for seven years before retiring for a second time. He then bought a yacht and lived in the Caribbean with Fiona, his wife, before returning to the UK to write books. He now lives in Somerset, where apart from writing he continues to fail to hit a golf ball with any skill whatsoever.

Apart from this book, he has a similar book about the Lynx helicopter published with Pen and Sword. He also currently has thirteen novels available on Amazon. Nine of these are the 'Jon Hunt' series that have been described as the 'British Top Gun' and cover the career of a modern naval officer in current times starting from the Falklands and covering events thereafter. Based on his own military experience they are regularly praised for a degree of authenticity rarely found in military fiction.

Terry Martin, despite growing up in Portsmouth and in a navy family, never had the ambition to go to sea. As a child he was drawn to aviation, but also wanted a career in medicine! It seemed that the option of being a Medical Officer Pilot in the RAF would make it possible to learn to fly and be a doctor. Terry studied medicine at University College London and initially learned to fly at the University of London Air Squadron. He qualified as a pilot (PPL) and as a doctor within two months of each other in 1981 and then spent the next ten years on active RAF duty, followed by a further seventeen years as a reservist in the Royal Auxiliary Air Force. Terry became a Flight Medical Officer and was fortunate to receive training in the De Havilland Chipmunk, Scottish Aviation Bulldog, British Aircraft Corporation Jet Provost and, eventually, he flew the two seater British Aerospace Harrier T4A. It was the Harrier flight that convinced Terry that VTOL, STOL and hovering, where much more fun than flying fast! Realising that he was past his sell-by date for Harrier training, he learned to fly the Westland Aerospatiale Gazelle at RAF Shawbury, followed by later hands-on experience on the

Westland Aerospatiale Puma with 230 Squadron at Gütersloh in Germany and 1563 Flight (33 Squadron) in Belize as the squadron 'doc'. During his twenty-seven years in the Royal Air Force, Terry reached the rank of Wing Commander and, in addition to aerospace medicine, he specialised in emergency medicine, intensive care medicine and aeromedical evacuation. He now works as a consultant in anaesthesia and critical care as well as being the Medical Director of an international air ambulance company based in the heart of 'Wasp country', the south-west of England. Terry has privately owned and flown several Wasps since 2000 and still flies as a display pilot in the UK.

Acknowledgements

Many people have helped us produce this book. Indeed it would not have been possible without them. Individual contributors have already been given acknowledgement against their respective articles. However, we would like to thank all those who have given their time, dug out old photos, and trawled through their records to remember things that happened, in many cases quite a long time ago. Apart from those contributors, we would also like to acknowledge the particular input and help we received from the following:

AgustaWestland Ltd (Now Leonardo Helicopters): Dave Gibbings.
The Fleet Air Arm Museum: Barbara Gilbert.
The RN Flight Safety Centre: Commanding Officer, Commander Ben Franklin.
Royal Navy Media Communications Staff at Whale Island for approval to use articles from the RN '*Cockpit*' and '*Flight Deck*' magazines.
The supply of *Flight Deck* magazines: Courtesy of the National Museum of the Royal Navy.

Finally, we would like to apologize to all those who flew this marvelous aircraft whose stories we have not been able to include. In such a long period of time there would be far too many anyway. Hopefully, those we have chosen provide sufficient evidence as to what a fantastic machine the Wasp has been.

The views and opinions expressed are those of the authors' alone and should not be taken to represent those of Her Majesty's Government, MOD, HM Armed Forces or any government agency.

Cartoons:

'Steev' is Steve George, a retired RN Air Engineer who has nothing better to do with his time than try to draw mildly amusing pictures. He's been cartooning since childhood, and has expanded his work to include illustrating children's books. He takes most (misplaced) pride in producing cartoons for the Fleet Air Arm's '*Cockpit*' magazine, the publication he was first inspired by when just five. He is an unabashed lover of naval aviation and the people he was lucky enough to work with. (Except for pilots, who should on no account be allowed to breed further.)

Steev takes commissions from a variety of customers, and can be reached at *wismageorge@me.co* if you are desperate enough to want him do some work for you.

LJ-C
TM

Section One

WASPS IN ROYAL NAVY OPERATIONAL SERVICE

Chapter 1

The Military Need

To understand why the Royal Navy became a world leader in helicopter operations from small ships one has to understand some of the issues of anti-submarine warfare that were concentrating the minds of naval officers in the post-war period.

Anti-submarine warfare is and has always been a game of cat and mouse with the balance constantly shifting as technology advances on both sides. The Second World War saw the start of a step change that continues to this day.

Active sonar is where a loud sound is transmitted into the water and any reflection off a large object can be detected. By the fifties, the systems were becoming very effective. However, for the submarine, the sound could be heard before the ship could receive a viable echo and so warn the submariner that he was being hunted before the ship knew he was there.

Passive sonar is simply a system that listens to noise in the water. Submarines always try to use it so as not to give their presence away. It didn't come into common use in the surface fleet until the seventies. For the submarine, surface ships with their loud machinery and spinning propellers are inherently noisy and can be detected and identified from a long way away. The only down side is that it is impossible to accurately assess a target's range from passive information, so a significant amount of time is needed to calculate distances from shifts in target bearing. Also, in the fifties, submarines were all still battery powered underwater and were extremely quiet, but they needed to regularly run their diesels to charge them. By now they could do this at periscope depth using a snorkel device. However, this in turn made the quiet submarine noisy and also possible to detect using radar.

So, in order to attack a target, the submarine needed full batteries and had to sneak up submerged on its prey and try to avoid detection by any surface units until it was in range with its own torpedoes. On the surface, the ships would be trying to detect the submarine before this could happen. If a submarine was detected it could be attacked. Originally this was with depth charges, which were simply a large explosive device set to detonate at a pre-set depth. However, this required the ship to steam over the top of the target. With the submarines own weapons increasing in range this was not a good option. By the fifties, mortar systems had been developed that could fire large anti-submarine depth charges over greater distances, but they still required to detonate very close to the submarine to be effective. The maximum range of the Royal Navy's Mortar Mark 10 system was 1000 yards, which was only really good enough for a close-in, last ditch encounter.

Using aircraft to prosecute submarines was nothing new. Even in the First World War they were used in this role. However, detection was purely by using the 'Mark One Eyeball' and the attack was with simple bombs. By the Second World War, things had moved up a gear and both naval and RAF aircraft were used to good effect. However, they all needed to catch the submarine on the surface to prosecute an attack.

By the mid-fifties there were several new ways to use aircraft in the anti-submarine role. Firstly, they were now able to detect submerged submarines themselves. Fixed wing aircraft such as the Shackleton Maritime Patrol Aircraft (MPA) and the Mark One Gannet carrier borne aircraft were capable of deploying sonar buoys. These devices, when dropped in the water, would drop a hydrophone below them and listen for a submarine then radio the results back to the aircraft. By dropping a barrier of several buoys across the submarines expected line of attack there was a good chance that it would pass between two of them and provide a degree of localisation. There were even some active sonar buoys that could be deployed to provide even greater localisation accuracy. With the introduction of helicopters even more accuracy and responsiveness could be achieved. The Mark 7 Whirlwind helicopter could lower an active sonar ball into the water and 'ping' for submarines and then move quickly to a new location to either continue to hunt or prosecute a target.

However, there was still the need for a more effective method of attack. The chances of calling up a surface unit to do this were slim as the ranges the aircraft operated meant that they would probably be too far away. Depth charges could be carried by aircraft and, in fact, are still even to this day, but they are more effective at putting a submariner off his aim rather than actually doing any damage. To this end the Americans developed a homing anti-submarine torpedo (the Mark 44) that could be carried by aircraft. When dropped in the vicinity of a submarine it could use its own active sonar to track and then attack the target, thus decreasing the need for extreme accuracy in localising the submarine.

There still remained several problems. If the hunting aircraft carried weapons, it was at the expense of fuel and hence time on task. This was particularly true of the early helicopters. Also, one could not necessarily rely on an MPA being on task when needed. So, it was not unusual for a warship to have detected a submarine but have no way of attacking it as it was just too far away and someone else's aircraft were not available. Consequently, giving a warship an autonomous weapon system to attack submarines and also be able to supplement other ASW helicopters as a weapon carrier started to become a priority.

In the mid-fifties, the Royal Navy started to consider whether a small helicopter could be operated from destroyers and frigates for just this purpose. The system would come to be known as MATCH. The Manned Anti-Submarine Torpedo Carrying Helicopter system and the aircraft would be the WASP Helicopter Anti-Submarine (HAS) Mark 1.

Chapter 2

The Early Days

The Wasp can trace its ancestry directly back to the early machines of Juan de la Cierva
(or even earlier). *Steve George.*

The Westland Aircraft Works was a division of Petters Limited and was formed in 1915 to construct aircraft under licence for the First World War. In 1935 it became Westland Aircraft Limited. During the Second World War they took over Spitfire repair and overhaul when the Supermarine facility in Southampton was heavily bombed and were largely responsible for developing the aircraft into the naval variant, the Seafire. In addition they produced their own designs. The most successful was the Lysander monoplane, well known for taking agents into wartime France. However, their twin engined Whirlwind fighter might well have made a difference in the early years of the war as it was fast - it would leave a Spitfire standing - and armed with four 20 millimetre cannon which would have outgunned any aircraft during the Battle of Britain. Unfortunately, problems and delays in procurement of the Rolls Royce Peregrine engines, plus other issues, meant it entered service too late and saw little action. Just after the end of the war, the company produced the Wyvern, a heavy, fast naval fighter with contra rotating propellers powered by an Armstrong Siddeley

Python gas turbine. In all, eight naval squadrons operated the aircraft and it saw service during the Suez crisis, but its performance was overshadowed by the introduction of early jets. It also had problems with its technology, particularly the engine, which had an unreliable propeller control system and a habit of flaming out on take-off due to the accelerations of a catapult launch.

In the fifties, there were a large number of aircraft manufacturers producing everything from long-range bombers to fighters. Because of the growing threat from the USSR and other conflicts like Korea and Suez, the British Government continued to sponsor new designs. It was a golden age for the British aircraft industry. Many innovative ideas that are still being used today sprang from this time. Britain was a world leader. However, the country was almost bankrupt and by the mid-fifties something had to be done. The Government commissioned a White Paper to review the situation. It was led by the then Minister of Defence, Duncan Sandys.

The report was instrumental in forcing fundamental change, although some of its assumptions, for example, that manned aircraft would not be needed in the future as missiles would replace them, were more than a little premature.

On the commercial side, the report concluded that many of the aircraft companies should merge. The incentive to do so was that only these groups would be liable to receive further government contracts. Consequently, by 1960, the British Aircraft Corporation (BAC) was formed out of English Electric, the Bristol Aeroplane Company, Hunting Aircraft and Vickers Armstrong. Hawker Siddeley took over de Havilland, Blackburn and Folland having already taken over Armstrong Whitworth, AVRO, Gloucester and Hawker before the war.

Once the Second World War was over, Westland made a decision to concentrate on rotary wing aircraft. It was a brave decision, but not universally approved, and the Chief Designer W. Petter left to form the aircraft division at English Electric. Amongst his post-war designs were the Canberra, Lightning and Gnat aircraft. Westland made several unsuccessful proposals for new helicopters in various categories, but in the end made an agreement with Sikorsky in the United States to build some of their designs under licence. These included the very successful Whirlwind, Wessex and Sea King helicopters which were heavily re-engineered versions of the originals.

Rotary wing aircraft, although in their infancy, were starting to be developed by several companies. Westland, cash rich from their Sikorsky licence, were seen to be the main lead and so they took over Saunders Roe, Fairy Aviation and the helicopter division of the Bristol Aeroplane Company.

One of the projects that Saunders Roe took with them was the Saunders Roe P531, a small single turbine engined helicopter. It first flew in July 1958, but when Westland re-engineered it, two versions emerged, the Scout for the army and the Wasp for the navy.

The P531

To understand the gestation of this machine one can go all the way back to the pre-war years and the work of who was a Spanish Count, a civil engineer, pilot and aeronautical engineer, and he invented the autogyro aircraft as early as 1920. An autogyro, whilst looking like a helicopter, actually needs a propulsion engine for forward thrust, the resultant forward airflow spins up the rotors and they provide lift. The rotor system works in the same way that a normal helicopter does in autorotation. In 1923, Cierva developed the articulated rotor and this resulted in the first successful flight of a stable rotary wing aircraft with his C4 prototype.

The Cierva C4, the first stable rotorcraft.

Cierva's initial work was conducted in Spain, but in 1925 he brought his C5 machine to Britain to successfully demonstrate it to the Air Ministry. As a result of these trials Cierva attracted the interest of James Weir, a rich Scottish industrialist, and together they formed the Cierva Autogyro Company.

Cierva himself concentrated on design of the rotor systems and made a partnership the A.V. Roe Company for the supply of airframes. A series of development aircraft then followed with the technology of controlling rotors becoming established with full cyclic and collective controls being developed. The first production variant, the C30, was produced by AVRO and also Loire et Olivier in France and more notably Focke-Wolfe in Germany.

Cierva's main aim had been to produce an aircraft that couldn't stall like a fixed wing machine, but by the mid-thirties was starting to accept the advantages of powering the main rotor, in other words the helicopter. In 1936, his company tendered for a military specification and offered a Gyrodyne machine because he felt it would be simpler and more reliable than a helicopter. This machine would use a powered rotor for take-off and landing, but rely on small wings and the main rotor acting as an autogyro in forward flight. However, it only reached the study stage, although patents for the concept were granted in the UK and US. The idea was never successful until the late fifties when the Fairey Company produced the Rotodyne, which although it flew successfully, never made it into production, not the least because of the noise it made from its tip jet propulsion. It is interesting to note that these ideas are now being revisited now that the technology has matured to overcome many of the limitations of helicopters, not the least being the inability to fly faster than about 200 Knots.

In December 1936, Cierva himself was killed when the Dutch DC-2 that he was travelling in from Croydon crashed in fog during take-off. However, he solved many of the basic problems of controlling rotor systems that remain in use to this day. After his death, his company was revived by G&J Weir and became their aircraft division, although in 1943 it was reconstituted back to being the Cierva Autogyro Company.

Post-war, the company concentrated initially on helicopters like the W9 and the Cierva Air Horse, which at the time was the world's largest machine. Unfortunately, in 1948, the Air Horse crashed, killing the company's manager and chief test pilot as well as the rest of the crew and Weir withdrew their investment. All contracts were transferred to Saunders Roe by 1951.

The Cierva W9 helicopter. The aircraft used ducted air rather than a conventional tail rotor and had other innovative ideas, some of which are only just being reconsidered today. It was destroyed in an accident in 1946, but parts of the rotor system were used in the W14 Skeeter prototype. As will be seen later this is a direct link to the eventual design of the Wasp.

The Cierva W.11 Air Horse. The loss of this aircraft caused the closure of the Cierva Company and all contracts being transferred to Saunders Roe.

One of the designs that transferred to Saunders Roe was for the W14 Skeeter, a small two seat machine designed for military and civil use as an observation aircraft. It was powered by a Jameson piston engine of 110 horsepower and first flew in 1948. The engine proved unreliable and significant redesign was undertaken, as well as replacing the engine with the well proven 145 hp Gipsy Major. This machine, the Skeeter 2, had severe ground resonance issues and was destroyed in testing in 1950.

Saunders Roe now had full responsibility for the machine and even though the government withdrew funding they continued with its development at their own cost. Final solutions to the ground resonance issue were a redesigned undercarriage and revised blade friction dampers. The final version was the Skeeter 6 with a 215 hp Gipsy Major engine and sixty-four were ordered by the British Army.

The SARO (Saunders Roe) Skeeter 6. (*Ruth AS*)

Saunders Roe initially looked at replacing the engine in the Skeeter with a small gas turbine as a private venture. These engines produce far more power for a given size and weight and so are extremely suitable for helicopters and they were now becoming available. So, using the Skeeter airframe as the basis and a Blackburn Turbomeca Turmo 600 engine, they came up with the design for the P531.

The SARO P531, its predecessor the Skeeter and its successor the Wasp can clearly be seen in the design. *(WHL)*

The Fairey Ultralight

Saunders Roe were not the only company looking at small agile helicopters with military applications in the fifties. A military requirement had been issued for a small observation aircraft for the army. In the end the Skeeter was selected, but Fairey also then proposed the ultralight for the navy and some sea trials were carried out.

The aircraft was revolutionary in concept. The engine was a Palouste gas turbine which only produced compressed air which was fed up through hollow rotor blades to tip jets at the end of each blade. By powering the rotor this way the need for complicated transmissions and anti-torque tail rotors was completely removed. It was extremely manoeuvrable, but due to its size not really suitable for the navy with the need to lift two homing torpedoes. With the merging of the companies and the P531 having significant more performance, the Ultralight was shelved.

Not everything was lost however, and several of the technologies went on to be incorporated in the Fairey Rotodyne as mentioned previously.

The Fairy Ultralight. *(WHL)*

It was a fascinating era of development for rotary wing aircraft. Much of the technology became 'standardised' in that the basic configuration of one main rotor, driven by one or more gas turbines, with a tail boom and tail rotor to counteract torque, was pretty much universally adopted. It is interesting to see that some of the early unsuccessful ideas are now coming back. Ducted air systems (NOTAR) are now used on several types, and compound aircraft like the Rotodyne are also being considered.

Initial Naval Trials
The navy had been keeping a keen eye on the P531 as it clearly had the potential to fulfil the need for a machine that could operate from small ships.

700 Royal Naval Air Squadron has been in existence since 1940, but in 1955 it was reformed as a 'Fleet Requirements Unit' and took on responsibility for initial testing of prototype or new production aircraft before they entered service. It continues its work to this day as it is the designated squadron number for all Intensive Flying Trials Units (IFTU) which put an aircraft through its operational paces before entering service. Normally, a letter in brackets is added after the number to indicate which aircraft it is

operating, for example the Lynx IFTU was 700 (L). For some reason, when testing the P531 it was designated 700 (X) from 1959 until 1961.

Below is an extract from the book '*On the Deck or in the Drink*', written by Lieutenant Brian Allen, one of the trials pilots on 700 Squadron responsible for conducting the first naval trials. (This book is also available from Pen and Sword.)

'*In eager anticipation after the Christmas break of 1960 I entered the squadron offices 700 Squadron at Yeovilton. After I had made my number with Tony Shaw the commanding officer he introduced me to the other helicopter pilots on the squadron. After the formalities, Colin took me over to the hangar to show me the aircraft that we would be using to evaluate new equipment prior to any contract been placed with the manufacturer. In the helicopter section we were to fly a variety of Whirlwind marks. There were also three other small helicopters of a type I had never seen before. Colin explained that they were P531s, a prototype, and we would be carrying out extensive trials together with testing equipment to suit the roles in which they were expected to perform, it was anticipated that they would operate from small ships to provide an extended range to the ships attack systems, both anti-submarine and surface systems. They still carried the prototype numbers allocated by Saunders Roe as they had developed them for their prospective users the Royal Navy and the Army Air Corps. Subject to the admiralty decision after a valuation by 700 Squadron, if they were eventually purchased by the services, they were to be named the Wasp in the naval role and the Scout for the army.*

'*After some initial trials on the Whirlwind helicopter, my next task was to familiarise myself with the P531. Colin took me up for an introduction flight on 23 January 1961, followed by a solo flight forty minutes later. The P531 was a feisty little helicopter, mostly a Plexiglas cabin, the two aircrew seated side by side. The small fuselage also housed a Blackburn turbo jet engine. It would have reminded any pilot who had trained on the little Hiller helicopters of being in an advanced version of that sporty, exciting machine. Being destined for use on small frigates its development schedule revolved around suitable equipment, mainly for hunting submarines and associated weaponry. Evolving an acceptable landing gear, suitable for the limited landing area available on the stern of a frigate were the considerations at present. The particular problems to be solved initially related to landing the helicopter safely from every flight on the severely restricted confines of the stern area. Obviously, any serious slippage could easily lead to the aircraft toppling over the side of the frigate and possibly causing injury to deck crew in the worst instance. It was therefore imperative that some sort of undercarriage, that would give a safe and positive adhesion on a slippery, possibly violently moving deck, was needed, and we were the pilots to slip and slide until a suitable solution was accepted.*

The first selections brought forth were for non-slip pads, thought to be suitable. They were now being designed and were shortly to be available for practical testing. We had a date for a trial at sea with HMS Undaunted, *a frigate with a converted stern, able to take a helicopter. They were to take place at the end of April into May, and we were to prepare earlier than that with two days rehearsal at the Royal Aircraft Establishment Bedford, making use of their 'rolling deck'. If the dry runs were successful, we would cross the Irish Sea with one P531 to RAF Ballykelly. There we would refuel the aircraft before flying on to land on HMS* Undaunted. *Colin and I were to be the pilots.*

'I should point out that, as trials and development pilots, we were only required to test equipment and its suitability for use by a future operational pilot. Observers evaluated any equipment pertaining to the observer role, but they always needed drivers.

'I had to get to know the P531 well before the trials. In addition to this I had other tasks, mostly testing new equipment for use by observers using our Whirlwinds and a lone Dragonfly we had to play with.

'The P531 proved to be a feisty little helicopter. Powered by a turbo jet engine, it was easier to start than piston engine models and once in the air it was surprisingly quiet and smooth to fly, just a high-pitched scream coming from the power unit. Being small and with the cockpit having a bubble glass around it, it gave excellent all round vision and a feeling that you were suspended in the air. The aircraft was very nippy and as responses by the aircrafts appeared to take place so quickly, the mind and reflexes were not surprisingly, concentrated. It was more akin to a racing car than a military project. Of course at this stage, it was a pure rotary wing aircraft such as a disc jockey or A-list celebrity might purchase. The only modifications made to the P531 as a military aircraft were those that allowed us to quickly install or remove the various items of equipment that we were assessing for a particular task; once fitted out for the roles expected of it at sea, its increased weight would inevitably slow it down. I resolved to enjoy the sensation of unencumbered flight while I could. The racehorse could rapidly become a carthorse in the military aviation world; every aeronautical designer had something they wish to hang on any new aircraft.

'One thing slightly worried me. I was told that Saunders Roe, the manufacturers, had been reluctant to release the helicopter to the navy for trials use, as the three helicopters had all nearly reached the end of their programmed flying life. They had been extensively flown by Saunders Roe on demonstrations and at air shows. Somehow, a way around this hurdle had been found and now, possibly past their sell by date, here they were for us to play with. Naturally, Saunders Roe were interested in the various trials that we had scheduled for their prototype and provided us with all the help they could to maintain the P531.

'After a week or so, my general flying practice and familiarisation was complete and I was deemed qualified to undertake any trial that was considered necessary

in the process of acceptance of a production model into fleet service. Meanwhile, there were other calls on our time to complete trials on various devices fitted into Whirlwinds. I was in my element flying different aircraft on such a variety of tasks.

'At the end of April 1961, Colin and I took the P531 up to RAE Bedford for the initial rolling deck trial. The Royal Aircraft Establishment had created a mock-up of an area the size of a frigate's deck and mounted the platform on a frame that looked like scaffolding. They had devised an ingenious motorised system that rolled the platform in a similar way to the stern of a frigate. Seen from the ground it looked alarming when gyrating around; the platform, our flight deck, being about 35 feet above the ground and rocking and rolling like some fairground ride. The P531 was fitted with what the boffins had dreamed up as the answer to the problem of stopping slippage after landing on a very restricted, probably wet, violently moving deck. On each skid there were two circular plates containing ridged rubber discs. All Colin and I had to do was to carry out thirty-six deck landings each on the rolling deck, for the inventors to see if it was a viable answer before repeating the trial on board a real frigate, moving on a hopefully boisterous, real sea. The powers that be had already decided that HMS Undaunted *would be the frigate, and the usually frisky Irish Sea off Londonderry the venue.'*

The P531 on the rolling deck. It was later used for similar trials with the successor to the Wasp – the Lynx. (*RNFSC*)

'Landing on the Bedford deck was a novel experience. Once over the deck there was little visible reference available to the heaving platform below. A slow descent from the hover, until some part of the skid touch the deck and then a decisive landing worked well, although both Colin and I noted that the P531 could waltz about on its rubber pads at first contact. It was advisable to be ready for a quick lift off if the movement became too pronounced. However, our thirty-six landings satisfied the assembled inventors who, incidentally, stood well away from the heaving contraption to observe the experiment. The trip to HMS Undaunted was confirmed that early May. The really interesting part of the trial was yet to come.

'In early May we joined HMS Undaunted with P531 and a ground crew, and on the fifth started our deck landing trials. The weather was extremely disappointing. Unusual for the Irish Sea, it was flat calm, with a sluggish swell. Nevertheless, I managed a few deck landings with no trouble at all. It was rather inconclusive as the ship was so steady, I could have been landing ashore and having the ship's superstructure to refer to it was certainly easier to land on than the deck at Bedford. After conferring with the Captain, it was decided they would try to induce a more realistic movement by going at full speed and making the ship role by continually reversing the helm. From the air, it looked as if the man at the wheel was drunk and it must have been uncomfortable for all on board. Colin and I made several approaches to the now rolling deck and landed on. The waltzing of the aircraft across the deck noted at Bedford was far more evident but not dangerous.'

The P531 (Sea Scout) in RN colours with the rubber pads fitted to skids. (*WHL*)

'Over the next few days we continued the trial and discovered that the bouncing around was becoming much more evident and at times alarming. It was discovered that the movement, together with the slip resistant gritty paint on the flight deck, had badly eroded the rubber pads on the skids. With a wet deck, there was hardly any adhesion at all. Disappointed, we completed other trials relevant to future small ship operations before returning to Yeovilton to discuss alternative, more durable undercarriages for the helicopter. A tethering device was mooted that once attached, winched the aircraft down onto the deck and caster like wheels could be locked at an angle and so prevent any wayward movement on landing. Of course these methods were not immediately available and although I was not to know it, my deck landing days with the P531 were soon to cease for ever.

'For the present, however, we had other trials to occupy our time back at Yeovilton. Much later, in 2008, at the 815 Squadron gathering at Yeovilton, I met a pilot who had served in a frigate with an operational Wasp. He declared it to be the finest little helicopter he had ever flown in. I felt proud to have been involved in its development.

'The next project for the P531 was the evaluation of some submarine detection equipment. Another Colin, Lieutenant McClure, an Observer, was to carry out the trial while I did the flying. The device entails towing a small, light glider-like receiver at the end of a long cable streamed from the back of the aircraft. Colin faced backwards alongside me, operating the display. We had been told that this lightweight and compact apparatus have been developed by the American oil industry to discover oilfields from the air. The US Navy had realised its military potential and much to the oil firm's chagrin and their own reluctance, allowed us to borrow one of the valuable kits to carry out our own tests in our lightweight helicopter. Its rarity and value had been stressed and its safe return emphasised by our American allies. If we could operate it successfully, it would make an ideal submarine detection package for the new P531. The preliminary trials proceeded satisfactorily and Colin McClure and I detached from Yeovilton to Portland in late June 1961, to carry out further trials to locate known wrecks lying in the seas off Chesil Beach. The seabed was liberally scattered with well charted wrecks and our hopes were high. If we could not find them, the project would be considered a failure.'

This equipment became to be known as a Magnetic Anomaly Detector, or MAD for short. The U.S. Navy continued to develop it with great success. In the mid-70s several equipments were borrowed from America and fitted to both Sea King and Lynx helicopters and trialled by the navy. Although the trials showed that the equipment could be very useful, it was never fully integrated into Fleet Air Arm aircraft. However, on this occasion all the equipment was successfully returned to the U.S. Navy. One has to wonder had these trials been successful whether the Wasp would have had a method of detecting submarines from the outset. It would have greatly enhanced its overall capability.

'We had been flying several days in June without getting the positive results we had hoped for. Although there had been enough to encourage further testing and Colin and I took off at midday to fly down Chesil Beach towards Charmouth. The area was strewn with known wrecks. It was perfect weather on 19 July 1961 and, as was fairly usual with helicopter crews, we flew relaxed in our uniforms instead of the regulation flying suit. Colin was sitting at his controls operating the equipment facing backwards as we flew out to the tip of Portland Bill, maintaining 300 feet. Turning onto a westerly course, I streamed the receiver on its cable, behind the aircraft. I settled on the course given to me by Colin and, as is usual when working gear, we remain silent except for any flight alterations required by Colin. I casually noted a frigate close to inshore by the beach passing down my starboard side. It was virtually stationary and I assumed it must be taking a break from its exercises to carry out the more important 'up spirits', when rum is issued.

'There was a slight bang and my controls went slack, immediately the helicopter reared up and rolled over out of control. Realising that we were in serious trouble, I quickly called a Mayday. By now we were descending fairly rapidly and whirling round and round, gyrating violently as we did so. I thought that the tail rotor must have failed in some way, as the fuselage was now trying to equate with the main rotor revolutions by spinning madly in the opposite direction. I ordered Colin to jettison his side door and in case he was still in doubt, told him we were about to ditch. As we were pitching and rolling so much, the sea view only occasionally passed by the windscreen followed by blue sky and glimpses of land flashing by. I fought to try and regain some form of control. I had read of a similar incident that had been resolved by keeping the helicopter in forward flight, airflow keeping it relatively stable. It was painfully apparent that the P531 had never read this article.

'Inevitably, we finally ditched into the sea with a teeth-jarring crash and, I should think, a huge splash. Without the doors we sank immediately, filling swiftly with water, but at least with the doors jettisoned, it was possible to unstrap and roll sideways out of the wrecked helicopter, now sinking rapidly, intent in joining the *rusting hulk's that we had been seeking only a minute or so ago. Totally immersed, I rolled free of the helicopter, by now well down into the dark depths. Disorientated and not knowing the way to the surface, I inflated my life saving waistcoat and floated to the surface. Thanks to all the adrenaline, I was unaware of any injuries. Once at the surface, I looked around for Colin and was dismayed to see no sign of my friend. With only your head floating at the surface it is often difficult to see beyond the next wave and I desperately hoped I would see his head bobbing nearby. As I turned around seeking him, I saw a rescue boat approaching me from the frigate. They of course had been astounded to witness the whole event. They hauled me into the boat and onto a stretcher, with me anxiously telling them of the missing Colin and asking them to search. The sea was fairly calm but they could find nothing on the surface.*

'While the ship hastily returned around to the bill to Portland the surgeon on board the ship, armed with a pin, check to find out whether I still had feeling in my legs. My affirmative through teeth now clenched with pain reassured him and me that there was no paralysis. Little enough comfort as I thought of my lost observer Colin, but by now the intense steadily increasing pain in my back was taking most of my attention.'

The accident had damaged two vertebrae in Brian's back and although they eventually healed he would never fly with the Royal Navy again.

'The next day I was told that the wreck of the P531 had been located and salvaged. Colin was sadly still with the aircraft, it was thought that the equipment we were testing had broken loose from its temporary mountings on impact and stunned him; facing backwards his foot had also been trapped in the helicopter structure.

'However, the whole aircraft, including the jettisoned doors, detached tail rotor and the gear we were towing had been brilliantly and totally recovered in very difficult conditions. Unfortunately, the sea had consumed nearly every bit of the equipment and I was told that our unhappy American cousins taken back only a handful of brass gear wheels. Later, when I saw the wreckage of the P531, I noted the cause of my injury; on impact with the sea, my seat had collapsed to the floor. Beneath the seat there was a large metal joint connecting several controls together. This irregular shaped joint about the size of a grapefruit had driven through my seat pan like an armour piercing shell. The seat cushion and dinghy pack had prevented any actual wounding from the torn metal, but the impact of been transmitted up the spine causing the compaction.

'A few days later, a group of Saunders Roe experts and naval advisers gathered around my bed to discuss, and listen to a bent pilot's views on a possible resolution to any future accident where a Wasp or Scout might ditch. I listened in dawning horror as they proposed fitting flotation bags behind the cockpit and just under the main rotors. An immersion switch would automatically inflate them once in the water and keep what was left of the aircraft afloat, while the hapless crew evacuated the partially submerged goldfish bowl of a cockpit. It occurred to me immediately the position of the bags under the rotors would in the first instance, according to sod's law, inflate and damaged the main rotor while the aircraft was airborne and going peaceably about its business. Of course this was a mere pilot's view, and all but me insisted that this would never happen. They did say however, that they would consider my opinion and I'm glad to say that production models had flotation bags attached to the undercarriage. Better to float upside down on the surface, rather than fall from several hundred feet without main rotors, remains my humble end users view.'

Brian is correct in that the initial production P531/Wasp had flotation gear on the undercarriage, however, this was soon deemed unsuitable as it still allowed the aircraft to roll inverted. As will be seen later in the book large clamshell fittings were mounted just below the rotors and allowed the aircraft to float level, albeit with the pilot's nose just underwater. He could then escape through the jettisonable roof panel. Although Brian's concerns about inadvertent inflation in flight proved incorrect, the effect on the aerodynamics of the aircraft was significant. The flotation gear caused enormous drag and had a profound effect on the handling of the helicopter.

The trials continued without Brian Allen, but unfortunately in January, whilst attempting a heavy take off out of wind, a second aircraft was lost. As it transited from the deck it lost height and the port landing pad hit the deck causing the aircraft to nose over and topple inverted into the water. The pilot, Lieutenant Commander Shaw, escaped uninjured, but his observer, Sub Lieutenant Fraser, was hurt. The aircraft sank in twenty-four fathoms of water but was subsequently salvaged. It now resides along with the sole intact surviving airframe at the Fleet Air Arm museum at Yeovilton.

However, the trials taught the navy and Westland helicopters a great deal about ship operations. The undercarriage idea of using rubber pads was even taken further when air bled from the engine was used to make them 'suck' the aircraft onto the deck. The air could be reversed and so produce an air cushion for moving the aircraft around. Unfortunately, the decks of ships proved too uneven to make a good enough seal and the idea was dropped in favour of a wheeled undercarriage. Other ideas which were included in the design of the Wasp was a deck tie down arrangement of some sort and the possibility of putting the rotors into negative pitch to help keep the aircraft firmly on deck once there. It is of note that both these ideas not only appeared in the design of the Wasp, but were taken even further in its successor, the Lynx.

Chapter 3

The Wasp

Modern procurement processes for developing and buying military equipment are a far cry from earlier years. In depth analysis of requirements, collating lessons learnt from previous machines, scoping studies, assessment studies, the list is long and while it may result in exactly what the services need, it is very time consuming. Some might say because of this, by the time the system has entered service it is so long since the original requirement was written that it no longer fulfils a current need!

The SARO P531 was a private venture, although there was an emerging requirement for an improved Skeeter for the army and the navy were looking for a shipborne weapon carrier. However, one does have to wonder in those days, how much the military requirements were actually generated by what the various desk officers were seeing that was available, rather than being generated by a formal requirements analysis.

Also, these machines were all relatively simple compared to modern helicopters and consequently the design and build timescales were much shorter. Even so, the time to produce the first 'Sea Scout' - soon renamed the Wasp - was remarkably short.

The P531 first flew in July 1958 and trials continued until 1961, by which time the SARO team had been incorporated into Westland. The first order for the 'Sea Scout' was placed in September 1961 and the first Wasp flew in October 1962, only thirteen months later. 700(W) - the Wasp IFTU - formed in June 1963 and operated until March 1964 when 829 Squadron took them over and they became operational. Two and half years to go from ordering a new aircraft to being introduced into service would be unthinkable in these days. As an illustration, the Lynx, which replaced the Wasp, took four times as long. It was ordered in 1967, flew in 1971 and entered service in 1977.

The lessons from the P531 trials and the emerging requirement from the navy quickly resulted in the final design of the aircraft. Brian Allen, in his article in the previous chapter, makes the observation that the racehorse he was flying could soon become a carthorse once the navy started hanging things off it. In fact the new design would more than compensate for this and the new machine would have far better performance than its predecessor.

Airframe. The Maximum All Up Weight increased from 3,800 to 5,500lbs and the speed from 100 to 120 miles per hour. The airframe was enlarged and strengthened, with a larger rear cabin. The main difference for shipboard operations was the landing gear. The P531 trials had experimented with various ideas, but in the end a four wheel undercarriage with long stroke oleos was decided upon. This allowed the aircraft to be landed 'firmly' and gave good deck adhesion. The wheels could be castored to different angles. At sea they were set so that the aircraft could rotate while on deck into the relative wind for take-off. To aid this procedure tie down system from the centre of the aircraft to the deck was provided. The aircraft could then be safely rotated on deck and the tie down released by the pilot just prior to launching. When operating from ashore the front wheels were aligned fore and aft and the rears were toed in. This was because if the aircraft had to be run on with forward speed in an emergency the scrubbing of the rear wheels provided a braking effect. The Wasp did not have brakes as such. Each wheel had a manually operated wheel lock which could be used to ensure that the wheels were completely fixed for stowage at sea.

The Wasp's long stroke undercarriage. The wheels are configured for shore operations. At sea the rear two would be toed out and the fronts toed in to allow the aircraft to swivel around them. *(LJC)*

Power. To lift the larger machine a new power plant was required. The original Turmo engine in the P531 only produced 325 hp, whereas the Nimbus in the Wasp could produce just over a 1000. However, it was actually limited to 685 hp due to the aircraft's transmission. In fact, after the completion of the navy trials, SARO produced two more aircraft, designated the P531-2, one of which was powered by the Nimbus, but the other had a Rolls Royce Gnome, also de-rated, but to 635 hp. Although not selected, the Gnome went on to be fitted to the later marks of Whirlwind, the Wessex mark 2 and 5 and all marks of Sea King. The reason for the selection of the Nimbus was based on its simple and rugged design. In comparison, the Gnome was a 'Swiss watch' with multiple external links to variable guide vanes on the compressor and was very intolerant of ingesting anything through the intake. It really needed to be fully enclosed and have a clear intake path.

The rugged and relatively simple Nimbus. Derated from 1050 to 685 shaft horsepower. *(LJC)*

The Nimbus was in fact a French design. Based on the Turmo of the 1950s it was developed under licence, initially by Blackburn aircraft and then Bristol Siddeley. Later on it was taken over by Roll Royce. It is a simple design with a two stage axial and single stage centrifugal compressor. The compressor feeds an annular combustion chamber followed by a two stage turbine. Behind that is a single stage free power turbine which drives a two stage reduction gearbox. The drive to the main rotor gearbox is then taken forward from this gearbox underneath the engine while the drive to the tail rotor is taken off the rear. The engine is mounted on the transmission deck behind the main gearbox and makes for a compact and neat installation. It is also very easy to access as there are no panels to remove to examine and maintain it.

There were two variants of the engine. The Mark 103/503, which was used in the RN and mainly differed from the other variant, the 103/502, in that it had a twin caliper rotor brake, whereas the 103/502 only had a single caliper system. A rotor brake on a helicopter is similar to a car disc brake and is used to hold the rotors stationary once the engine has been started, and quickly slow the rotors once the engine had been shut down. With the Wasp, being able to stop the rotors quickly was important when operating at high wind speeds on a ship's deck, hence the bigger caliper. It is also worth noting one very clever and simple element of the design of this system. Should the brake not be fully disengaged it is quite possible for the disc to overheat and catch fire. Indeed, two of the later Merlin helicopters were both lost due to rotor brake fires. With the Wasp system, behind the brake pads were large lumps of solder. Should the heat rise in the brake, the solder would melt and the pads fall away from the disc, thus ensuring that the brake would cool down. Added to that, two metal pins were set in pads and it could be seen whether the solder had actually melted from the position of the pins. It was a simple foolproof design that did the job. I should know, as one day I took off with the brake partially on (no excuse – but it was a long time ago). I couldn't get away with the error of course because when I returned it was immediately noticeable to the ground crew on the post flight inspection.

The simple and fail safe rotor brake caliper on the Wasp. The arrows show where the pins are that indicate that the brake has not been overheated. The disc itself can be seen above and below the caliper. *(LJC)*

For aerodynamic reasons, helicopters need the speed of the rotor to be kept relatively constant. In the case of the Wasp this was a nominal 400 rpm. With most previous early helicopters, adjusting the engine power to maintain rotor speed as the collective lever was adjusted to change lift was done with a manual throttle on the collective lever. As the collective was raised the twist grip throttle would be opened. The Nimbus was fitted with an engine governor so that once the throttle had been fully opened it automatically maintained the rotor speed for the pilot. This was a great leap forward for pilots and made flying far less demanding and allowing him to concentrate on other things. However, should the governor fail, the throttle could be partially closed and the aircraft flown manually. That's not to say that students learning to fly the machine spent too much time with it in the governed range!

Transmission. As already mentioned, the Nimbus was derated from 1000 hp to 685 hp this was because the transmission in the aircraft could not take all the power that the engine could provide. The reason for this was that the design was an uprated version of that used in the P531. For the Scout and the early Wasp this was quite sufficient to achieve the required flight envelope. However, for the Wasp, once the flotation gear had been fitted and it was at Maximum All Up Weight (which it was when weapons were loaded) it meant that the aircraft was quite marginal in terms of power in hand.

The main rotor gearbox ahead of the engine and with the spider flying controls operating through the centre of the gearbox itself. *(LJC)*

So that a pilot knows the limits of his transmission, helicopters tend not to use power as a unit of measurement. The factor that limits the amount of power that can go through a gearbox is Torque. This is a measure of how much 'twist' is being put on to the various gears and shafts. At a constant speed, power and torque are directly proportional. However, as the rotor speed can vary to some extent, a gauge showing Torque is of much more practical use. It is also easy to measure as there is normally somewhere in a helicopters transmission where it can be directly measured. In the Wasp, this was initially by using a hydraulic system. The basic idea was that as the torque increased on the gears in the turbine reduction gearbox, the pressure of oil needed to supply them would increase. After some years of operation it was felt that this system was not sufficiently accurate and replacement was incorporated using strain gauges to actually measure the twist of the tail rotor drive shaft. An audio warning was given to the pilot when the maximum figure (103.5%) was reached, which led to the Wasp pilot's mantra when taking off from the deck of 'pull to the bells'. In fact, the weak link in the system was the flexible couplings in the tail rotor drive shaft. However, had there been a move to redesign the transmission to take more power, it would have required a major programme which wasn't deemed cost effective at the time. That said, had anyone asked a Wasp pilot whether he would have liked the other 300 hp that engine could give, there is no doubt what he would have said!

Rotor system. The flying controls in the P531 were 'manual' i.e. the pilot's muscle power was required to move the rotor control systems through a series of mechanical rods and links. With the heavier Wasp, hydraulic actuators were introduced to make the aircraft easier to fly. The aircraft can be flown with the hydraulics turned off, but it is very heavy on the controls and requires considerable effort. Once again, flying 'hydraulics out' was commonplace during training and adding the loss of the engine governor into the mix made the aircraft quite a handful.

One of the three flying control servo jacks which made the aircraft light and easy to fly, although it could still be flown with the hydraulics switched off. *(LJC)*

Another innovation that can be traced back to the designs of Cierva was the method used to change the pitch of the rotor blades both cyclically and collectively. At some point the flying controls of a helicopter, one has to transmit the pilot's control inputs, which are 'static', onto the rotating rotor system. Many helicopters use a swash plate system. Three control rods, often hydraulically actuated are attached to a fixed plate, the fourth corner rod is held by a flexible scissor arrangement. The rotor blades all have a small rod attached to their roots (pitch control rods) which can be pushed and pulled to change the pitch of the blade. These rods are attached to a similar plate to the fixed one, but it rotates with the rotors. With a bearing in between, the two plates butt up against each other. Tilting or raising the fixed plate transmits the same movement across the rotating boundary and changes the rotor blade pitch as required by the pilot when he moves his controls. The system is relatively complicated and somewhat bulky.

The Cierva spider system that was used in the Wasp (and its successors the Lynx and Wildcat) uses a more compact and simpler system. The rotor head is mounted on top of the gearbox on one bearing. However, through the centre of the gearbox is a rod, and at the top four arms extend and are attached to the rotor blade pitch control rods. This whole assembly rotates. On the bottom of the rod is a bearing and this is then attached to the flying controls which then either raise or lower the rod to apply collective pitch, or tilt it laterally to apply cyclic pitch.

The Wasp spider flying controls. The horizontal arms are controlled by a rod coming up inside the gearbox and then operating each pitch change rod to alter blade pitch. *(LJC)*

The main rotor blades of the Wasp were made of metal. This may seem fairly obvious these days, but those of its predecessor the Skeeter were actually made out of plywood. Consequently, the Wasp blades were far stronger and less prone to being damaged. However, the tail rotor blades were originally still made of wood. There is a story that eventually there remained only two engineers at Westland who could make these and they went on strike for more money. Consequently, Westland redesigned them out of metal. More likely is that the wooden blades had limited aerodynamic thrust and it was actually possible to stall the tail rotor. This normally occurred when flaring the aircraft hard to come in to land beside a ship. Some ships would carry two pilots, the second one (the P2) would normally be a junior pilot carried to gain experience and it was more often the P2 who got caught out. When the tail rotor stalled, the aircraft would start to spin and with one exception ended up in the water. Consequently it was known as 'P2 death spiral'. The new metal blades had a different aerofoil and effectively solved the problem.

The two types of tail rotor blade. On the left is the earlier wooden version and on the right the later metal blade. Close examination shows that the wooden blade is smaller, slightly tapered, with a smaller surface area and was hence less effective. *(LJC)*

An account of this frightening experience is recounted below by Lieutenant (later Commodore) Tony Hogg:

Surviving the 'P2 Death Spiral'
'The logbook simply says 7 September 1976, self and Aircrewman Cockerill – DIDTACS – 55 minutes, but there was a lot more to the sortie than this.

'I was eighteen months into my role as second pilot in HMS *Andromeda* flying the Wasp helicopter. I had 550 flying hours. I knew it all!

'It was a warm, clear and balmy morning in the Mediterranean. The time was about 0500 and I was returning from a DIDTACS sortie. I could smell the bacon as I approached the ship to land on.

'It had been a friendly night for night flying and I felt euphoria as I approached to hover on the port side of the flight deck. It just felt right to arrive with bags of panache and a big flare. But I had forgotten two important things: first, there was very little relative wind (not much lift) and second, that I was in a first generation Wasp with a wooden tail rotor and notoriously little tail rotor thrust to maintain direction in the hover. As I levelled the aircraft ready to move right over the flight deck, and putting in loads of left boot to counteract main rotor torque, suddenly there was a big fat zero to maintain directional control. I moved right, rotating right as I went, across the flight deck and out to the ship's starboard quarter. For reasons I don't recall now I failed to put the nose down and pick up speed and un-stall the tail rotor, instead, I fell into an uncontrolled spot turn, 10 to 15 feet above the water (so said the accident report). Bizarrely, with the fair *Andromeda* trickling through the water at slow speed 100 yards away, I continued my uncontrolled manoeuvre: there was the ship - there it was again - and again and again as we continued our unauthorized pirouette. By now I had certainly drawn an audience on the ship. I remember very clearly not feeling any sense of fear or panic. What I do remember, as I glanced left, was the colour of my aircrewman's face – a sort of gangrenous green!

'I was fit; I was a diver, I enjoyed the dunker and I felt no fear of entering the water. The challenge was more of a puzzle to solve. There we were, entirely stable: neither climbing nor sinking and in a fairly steady rotation to the right with periods of about three or four seconds. So... What to do? Of course I was too "green" to have had erudite discussions as to the correct immediate actions in this scenario - applying opposite boot to uninstall the tail rotor.

'What I did was instinctive: I tried to widen the circle by applying left cyclic to try to widen the turn, both to slow the rate of rotation and pull out of the spot turn. Twice I nearly made it. I must have picked up a gust of wind on the third attempt, and entirely cross controlled, I staggered out of the spot turn. Still fairly calm I then executed a normal deck landing, but with a little less panache this time! I was greeted in two ways: the first was the receipt of a very nice chocolate sweet from the senior maintenance rating; the second, once I had left the aircraft, was to receive an almighty bollocking from my Flight Commander: "you must've over-torqued that aircraft massively, P2, if you think I'm going to f'"ing fly it now, you've got another thing coming!!"

'Of course after all the over-torque checks, we carried on flying and, I "learnt about flying from that". I believe I was the only P2 to recover from a stalled tail rotor in this way. With the benefit of years more experience, I should have been awarded a Green Endorsement for bringing the aircraft back - but such is life…'

Stowage. Another innovation was to be able to fold the tail of the aircraft as well as the rotor blades to enable the aircraft to fit into the very small hangars of the warships of the day. Unlike larger machines like the Sea King, the blades were small enough to be folded manually, although it could still be pretty challenging with strong winds over the deck.

HMS *Hecla's* aircraft in the folded configuration in the process of being ranged on deck. *(WHL)*

Flotation. In Chapter 2, Brian Allen's account of his ditching in the P531 gave rise to the SARO designers suggesting that flotation bags should be fitted. His comment was, 'I listened in dawning horror as they proposed fitting flotation bags behind the cockpit and just under the main rotors'. His main concern was what would happen if they inadvertently went off in flight. In fact, as it turned out, this was not an issue as can be seen in the photograph below.

A Wasp in flight with flotation bags inflated. As can be seen they are well clear of the rotors. *(RNFSC)*

However, the effect they had on aircraft performance when not inflated and their reliability when needed bears some discussion.

This article taken from *Cockpit* magazine was written by R.C. Maltby of Westland Aircraft Ltd, as part of the early development of the aircraft:

'From model tests carried out by Saunders Roe Ltd at Cowes it was evident that the Wasp helicopter would not have desirable ditching characteristics. The natural reaction after hitting the water appeared to be a roll to the inverted position followed by a nose down plunge after approximately six seconds. In consequence of this, design schemes were prepared and further tests carried out. With flotation bags attached in a position fairly low on the aircraft structure, the model turned upside down and remained in that position.

'A redesign was undertaken with inflatable bags mounted as high as possible on the aircraft structure. Light weight and speed of inflation were considered to be of the

greatest importance and an aspirated inflator was adopted. In this system a small air portal discharges into the throat of a pipe attached to the bag so entraining ambient air, which fills out the bag in approximately two seconds.

'With such a system it is not entirely satisfactory to leave the point of initiation of inflation until the aircraft touches the water because the aircraft will roll onto a partially inflated bag and arrest the action of inflation. The philosophy of operation with the Wasp system is therefore that the pilot shall inflate the system in flight, but that saline switches will be provided to inflate the bags automatically should he fail to do so.

'The flotation gear main components comprise two inflatable rubber bags, each bag being contained within a clam type light alloy shell. A light tubular framework fitted to both the port and starboard sides of the aircraft upon which the clam type shells are mounted, and a box section jury frame designed to encompass the cabin midsection. The jury frame providing attachment strong points for the forward tubular framework. Attachment points for the rear tubular framework are located adjacent to both engine servicing platforms and on port and starboard sides of the main rotor gearbox casing.

'Each clam upper shell carries an air inflation bottle together with the piping runs necessary for inflating the rubber bag and operating the pneumatic locking clamp release pin. The release pins are located at each end of the shell and control fulcrum client locking clamps which secure the upper and lower shelves together.

'In the event of a forced descent into the sea, a pilot controlled master switch is provided on the cyclic stick to operate the flotation gear. The switch being located below the pilot's handgrip. The photograph shows the flotation equipment in the inflated condition.

'In the event of the pilot being unable to operate the switch it can be activated by a submersion actuator, a device which, when immersed in salt water, will complete a circuit supplying electric current to the actuating coil of a relay. The relay contacts in turn close and permit current to flow to the air bottle solenoid valves which open and allow the air pressure to flow to the locking clamp release pins. The pins are then withdrawn pneumatically, releasing the lower clamshells which pivot downwards on the lower support struts; air then flows into the rubber bags by way of aspirators, two being fitted into the top of each bag. Two submersion actuators are installed on the aircraft and are wired in series with each other ensuring that both actuators must be immersed before the flotation gear will operate. The actuators are located beneath the centre after bay.

'This installation has been extensively tested in the tank at the Fairey Aviation Division of Westland Aircraft Ltd in conjunction with the Royal Aircraft Establishment. Coupled with the flotation equipment installation, two escape panels have been incorporated in the cabin roof as shown in the photograph. Flight testing both in the *deflated and inflated condition has been carried out by Westland Aircraft Ltd and the aircraft is now at Boscombe down for final clearance.*

'The tank tests and flight tests indicate that, provided the bags are fully inflated before ditching, a conscious pilot and crew will have no difficulty in making a safe escape through the panels in the canopy.

'The level of water within the cockpit immediately after ditching will, of course, depend on the extent of damage to the structure resulting from impact, but in all but the most severe cases will not be above the pilot's nose. Most important of all, the rollover and nose down natural ditching tendency has been countered and the problems of underwater disorientation of crew during escape will not arise.'

How it should have worked. (*RNFSC*)

This article gives the story of how the flotation gear was developed and also how good it should have been at keeping the aircraft stable and above water to allow escape. What it doesn't do is tell the story of the effect it had on the aircraft's flying characteristics. I flew the aircraft for over a year before I got to fly one with no flotation gear fitted on a delivery to the aircraft repair year at Fleetlands in Gosport. It was a revelation. The drag caused by the system meant that 90% torque was needed to do just about anything. You needed that much power to climb at 60 knots and if you lowered the nose you could just about stay straight and level at 90 knots. Getting to a maximum speed of 100 knots was just about possible with full power. Without the flotation gear the aircraft only need 70% torque to fly and could easily exceed 100 knots if desired.

On top of that it didn't take long for the 'Meccano' like supports to start to wear and as soon as the frames started to get any play in them it sent the vibration levels soaring.

Although with the system fitted, the aircraft was capable of meeting all the operational demands placed upon it. One does wonder how much more capable it could have been had a simpler and less agricultural system been developed.

Some months later, another article appeared in *Cockpit*, written by Lieutenant Commander D. Bridger, which gives more practical advice on the use of the equipment and also contradicts some of the confident assertions made by Westland and AEE for the system. It is entitled '*Ditching the Wasp*':

'The following report is based on the result of ditching trials of model and full-size Wasp aircraft conducted by the Westland Aircraft Company under conditions which cannot be regarded as entirely realistic. At the time of writing the views expressed should give some reasonable guidance to individuals so that they may take into account some of the factors which must be considered when planning the action they will take in the event of a ditching.

AIRCRAFT BEHAVIOUR ON DITCHING

1. *All doors on no flotation gear. - Aircraft floats for some time always inverts very quickly.*
2. *Doors off, no flotation gear. - Aircraft floats for a shorter period and inverts quickly.*
3. *All doors on, flotation gear fully inflated. - Aircraft may float for about 2 ½ minutes initially in a nose down attitude. Eventually the tail cone sinks and it is thought that the aircraft might sink completely thereafter. At all times the average size pilot's head is likely to be submerged. Aircraft will probably remain sensibly level laterally.*
4. *All doors off flotation gear fully inflated. - Much the same as 3 above, except that the nose is likely to settle down more rapidly.*
5. *Rear starboard door off, flotation gear fully inflated (a possible winching configuration) as for 4.*

Irrespective of speed, within a range of about 0 to 40 knots and with rates of descent up to about 500 ft/m, the aircraft tends to pitch nose down on entry into the water. Dynamic tests with models indicate that the aircraft is likely to roll to port into the inverted position. Static tests on a full size fuselage resulted in a role to starboard. All dynamic tests were done with no sideways drift at the point of touchdown.

Flotation gear

Although saline switches are fitted for automatic inflation it must be borne in mind that the system aspirates atmospheric air, moreover, water pressure on partially inflated bags may cause closing of flap valves which results in the exhausting of atmospheric air pressure. In consequence, the standard drill must be to select inflation manually. Full inflation will probably take about two seconds, but should not be initiated at speeds in excess of 60 knots or altitudes of 300 feet or more, or full inflation cannot be guaranteed. Incomplete inflation may increase the danger of damage to the flotation gear, particularly if the ditching is 'spectacular'.

Doors

If the doors are submerged, even partially, water pressure may prevent the doors from being opened or jettisoned. In this case opening the windows would help to equalise internal and external pressures as rapidly as possible. If jettison is selected any time, the door may continue to hang up at the latch. In this eventuality operate the normal door handle as well.

Escape hatches

To jettison the escape hatch in the cabin roof, pull handle and entirely remove the sealing strip, then give a sharp blow to the hatch near a corner. Considerable force may be necessary. Aircrew should practice escape hatch jettison drills regularly to become familiar with the technique and to ensure that the hatches do not bed down firmly. If the aircraft inverts it may not be possible to push off the escape hatch against external water pressure. Water pressure at depth may well force the hatch inwards. A possible modification which is being investigated is the fitting of a handle on the inside of the hatch which would permit the aircrew to pull the hatch inwards.'

The article continues to give procedural advice on flying techniques. However, it is interesting to note the difference between this and the previous article. There is direct contradiction as to whether the aircraft floats sufficiently high to keep the pilot's head/ nose above water and it is quite clear that jettisoning the roof panels was not as easy as first thought. Also, there seems to be quite a deal of concern about actually getting the bags to inflate correctly/fully. In fact for normal operation over the sea the aircraft was always flown with the doors removed and small wind deflectors fitted instead. There also seems to be conflicting data as to how the aircraft would react once in the water. It wasn't long before the RN introduced mandatory 'dunker' training for all aircrew to teach them how to escape from an uncontrolled ditching. In fact the Wasp - minus its doors - was probably the easiest aircraft in the inventory to escape from. One does have to wonder, given the detrimental effect the floatation gear had on aircraft performance, why it wasn't removed altogether.

It should be noted that when HMS *Endurance*, carrying two Wasps, headed back to the Falklands at the start of the war, the Flight Commander decided to remove the flotation gear from the aircraft to give him maximum range to search for potential surface targets. Weighing in at 400 pounds, the weight was better used for fuel, as well as much better fuel consumption due to less power required to fly.

Chapter 4

Roles and Weapons

Anti-submarine warfare (ASW)

When originally conceived, the Wasp as part of the MATCH system was seen as an extension of the ship's anti-submarine attack capability - pure and simple. It would also have secondary roles, i.e. passenger carrying, rescue, getting the mail etc. However, once at sea it quickly became clear it was also a major asset in identifying targets beyond visual range, although initially it had no attack capability of its own. In the ASW role it could carry ASW torpedoes, depth charges or a nuclear depth bomb (NDB). These weapons were heavy and consequently there was a trade off in the amount of fuel that could be carried, leading to greatly reduced endurance. Later on in its life it was fitted with an air-to-surface missile system which gave it an autonomous surface attack capability.

Depth charges.

The Mk11 Depth Charge. This is almost identical to the weapon used extensively in the Second World War and remains in service in all RN ASW helicopters to this day. It is effectively a large amount of explosive in a steel drum with a fuse, and a tail fin to allow it to drop cleanly. Simple it may be, but it can still cause damage. The Argentinian submarine *Santa Fe* was disabled by two of them dropped from the Wessex Mark 3 aircraft from HMS *Antrim* during the Falklands war. Just as importantly, it makes an enormous amount of noise. Any submarine commander relying on passive sonar information to make an attack is going to be significantly distracted if someone is dropping them, even quite far away.

A Mk 11 Depth Charge in its stowage cradle. This is a practice version, hence the blue colour of the main body. The live weapon weighs 300 pounds and the Wasp could carry two. It was primarily designed to attack submarines at shallow depths and on the surface. *(LJC)*

The WE177a nuclear depth bomb was also carried. This device was used both as an ASW weapon by helicopters, but also a ground attack bomb dropped in a variety of modes by fixed wing aircraft. Its efficiency as an anti-submarine device was much more limited than might be thought as the attenuating properties of water to shock waves is very high. That said and like the conventional Mk11, any submariner in the vicinity of one detonating near him was definitely not going to continue with his attack. There was also a school of thought that it was just as dangerous to the aircrew as anyone under the water. This wasn't in fact true and trials in the sixties showed that the blast did not actually breach the surface (at least that was what we were told!). Trouble for the enemy it may have been, but the administration and certification procedures to stow it in ships and load it onto aircraft probably made it more trouble for those given the thankless task of deploying with it.

A practice variant of the WE177a nuclear bomb, which in naval aircraft could be used as a depth charge, seen here at the armament museum in Gosport. Terry Martin's Wasp is in the background. *(TM)*

ASW homing torpedoes – the Mk44 and Mk46.

Submarine development continued strongly after the end of the Second World War - as did the various methods to counter them. While the Mk 11 depth charge was simple and old technology, it was soon clear that better methods were required. In the 1950s the Americans conducted a programme to select a new generation lightweight air launched anti-submarine torpedo. The result was the Mk 44. Original designs to use an internal combustion engine which would need a fuel that carried its own oxygen were shelved after an accident during development and an electric motor powered by a battery that became active once sea water flooded it was used. The weapon had a speed of 30 knots for six minutes and an active sonar in the nose to allow it to seek its target. The warhead was 75 pounds of high explosive and it weighed 432 pounds. The Wasp could carry two with limited endurance. In the aircraft it could be pre-programmed to have various initial search depths, floor depths, and run straight for the first 1000 yards, or dive immediately to depth before conducting its search for the target. However, it soon became clear that Soviet submarines of the era were getting too fast and could outrun and out dive the weapon. So, in 1960, a new requirement was raised for a replacement. This was the Mk 46.

The Mk46 was slightly heavier at 508 pounds and carried a bigger warhead of 97 pounds. It was faster at 40 knots and had almost double the range and had updated search modes to improve its effectiveness. In order to achieve this performance the use of an internal combustion engine was now necessary and it was powered by a liquid fuel called 'Otto fuel'. This brew of chemicals was toxic and highly inflammable, requiring special precautions to store the weapons, but nevertheless very effective. It is of interest that this weapon was later replaced by the all British Stingray torpedo which reverted once again to a sea water powered battery for propulsion. However, it came into service too late to be used by the Wasp. When flying with two of these weapons weighing over a thousand pounds the aircraft's endurance was severely limited.

Anti-surface warfare (ASUW).

One development in naval warfare that worried the navy was the deployment of small Fast Patrol Boats (FPBs) armed with surface-to-surface missiles. The Soviets had been developing the OSSA and KOMAR classes of FPB which carried the Styx missile ('Termit' in NATO designation) which had a range of about fifteen miles. These vessels posed a significant threat much greater than might be thought, especially in coastal warfare, where they could hide in the visual and radar shadow of the land and rapidly deploy for attack. This was all brought in very sharp focus in on the 21 October 1967.

Israel and Egypt had just fought the Six Day War and an uneasy truce was in place. The Israeli Navy were operating the destroyer *Eilat* off the coast of Egypt. *Eilat* was launched in 1942 as the Royal Navy Destroyer HMS *Zealous*, but had subsequently been sold to Israel. Both sides disagree about what happened next. The ship was off Port Said and according to Egyptian accounts, well inside their national waters. Whatever the rights and wrongs of the matter, two small patrol boats left the harbour and attacked as soon as they were clear of the breakwater. From a range of about ten miles, the first patrol boat fired two Styx missiles. Despite seeing the incoming missiles, turning away and increasing speed, the *Eilat* was hit by both. They hit amidships, one penetrating the engine room, and the ship started to burn and sink. An hour and half later, another patrol boat fired two more missiles. One malfunctioned, but the other hit the sinking ship's stern and finished her off. Fifty-seven men died and ninety-one were wounded.

The incident sent shock waves around the world's navies. The *Eilat* may not have been the most modern warship around, but the fact that a tiny patrol boat could inflict so much damage simply by slipping its lines and pointing its nose out of harbour was something to which there was very little defence. The Wasp needed an attack role.

The SS11 and AS 12 Missile systems.

Developed by the French company Nord Aviation and latterly Aerospatiale, the SS11 and AS 12 missiles were wire-guided weapons controlled through a visual site. The SS11 was primarily an army anti-tank and anti-personnel weapon and used in that role by the army, fitted to their Scout helicopters. The AS12 was configured to be used by helicopters against surface targets. Apart from the missiles themselves, the systems for carriage release and aiming in the helicopter were identical. Consequently, the Wasp was capable of firing both missiles.

The missiles had two solid fuel rocket motors. One was the initial booster rocket that burned for 1.2 seconds (SS11) or 2.2 seconds (AS12) and the second, a sustainer motor that burnt for either 20 or 30 seconds. The wings were positioned at an angle of one degree to the direction of flight so that the missile span to giving it stability. Two rearward-facing flares ignited on launch to make the missile more visible to the operator during flight.

The missiles steered using four metal vanes around the exhaust nozzle in a thrust vectoring system that directed the thrust of the sustainer motor. Steering signals were sent to the missile by means of two wires which paid out from two spools on the rear of the missile. The range of the SS11 was approximately 3500 metres and the AS12 double that at 7000 metres.

The optical sight for the missile was mounted in the roof above the co-pilots seat and operated by the Flight crewman. Two joysticks were required, one to keep the binocular sight on the target and one to control the missile in flight. As can be imagined, a good operator was required to make the missile effective.

As will be recounted later, this weapon was arguably the most effective ever deployed in this aircraft.

A Wasp with two AS12 missiles loaded, the visual sight can be seen
mounted in the left-hand cabin roof. *(WHL)*

With a missile that relied on visual control, there was clearly going to be an issue with operating it in the dark. Whilst the flares on the missile would be extremely visible, the same could not be said for the target. To this end the aircraft could carry 4.5 inch flares. The tactic would be to have two aircraft under positive control of a third party (a ship or radar equipped helicopter). One would drop flares at height behind the target to illuminate it, the other aircraft would then be able to see what it was firing at. Of course the target might just also be aware of what was going on, which put the aircraft, particularly the one dropping the flares, in an interesting position!

An interesting summary of the aircraft's developing capabilities appeared in *Flight Deck* magazine at the time:

'With the passing of the fixed wind world the variety of weaponry being attached to helicopters is assuming and ever increasing in variety and complexity. Nowhere is this more true than in the field of the small helicopter. The Wasp today is called upon to perform a far wider variety of tasks than it was designed to carry out. As initially conceived, the Wasp was purely an extension of the reach of a frigate's anti-submarine mortars and the object of its existence was to transport torpedoes or depth charges to sink a hostile submarine. As such the title of "Helicopter Anti-Submarine" was fully appropriate, designating the machine for a specific task.

'Today, however, the picture is not so simple. No longer is the Wasp merely an anti-submarine weapon carrier. At least one major new role has been placed on it in the shape of surface strike against missile-carrying FPBs. Here the Wasp, with the AS12 missile system, has, in the space of eighteen months, become the fleet's future front line defence against the threat from these formidable craft: the Wasp has adopted another role in addition to that of ASW.

'Reconnaissance is another common task for the aircraft. It can be launched to survey a jungle landing site, a beach for putting marines ashore, or for spotting for naval bombardment. It also has proved its worth as a pure reconnaissance vehicle (eg the Beira patrol) and in the internal security role the Wasp had a clear part to play: Anguilla is one recent example.

'What does this all add up to? It adds up to the fact that the Wasp is no longer a purely ASW weapon carrier and that as such the term "Helicopter Anti-Submarine" is no longer wholly applicable. Since naval aircraft are designated according to their tasks and since the Wasp combines reconnaissance, torpedo dropping and strike, the resurrection of the old title "TSR" seems more appropriate. Even if the aircraft is not re-categorised TSR1, which it ought to be, it is sincerely hoped that the title will be applied to future helicopters employed on similar duties.'

This short article is an interesting illustration of how the roles and capabilities of the machine had developed quickly once it had entered service. Unfortunately, the author's suggestion of re-designating the aircraft never happened. Indeed, its successor the Lynx was also originally designated as 'HAS', even though it had two primary the roles of ASW and ASUW from the outset. It was only when the Lynx was upgraded to the Mark 8 variant that the designation changed to Helicopter Maritime Attack 'HMA'.

A photograph of a Wasp with its full complement of 'teeth'. It's carrying three missiles on pylons. On the port carrier is an AS12. In service only two were carried, one on either side. The starboard weapons are the smaller SS11s, where four were carried, two on either side. There's another AS 12 on a box to the rear left. Two Mk 11 depth charges are on the extremities of the picture. The tall objects in front of the aircraft are 4.5 inch flares. The torpedoes in the trolleys are Mk 44s, with a WE177a nuclear depth bomb in the middle. The small objects in between the torpedoes and depth charges are smoke and flame floats and 'Signals Underwater Sound' which are small explosive charges dropped to simulate an attack on a submarine. *(Flight Deck)*

Once in service, tactics needed to be developed. The following *Flight Deck* article gives an insight into the initial thinking regarding the use of the weapon, as well as some probably over optimistic assessments of its capability:

'The second main role for the Wasp was introduced last year, when we purchased the AS12 wire-guided missile for use in the surface strike role. Despite usual teething difficulties, the

first ship to be so fitted is now at sea and yet another role is open to the Wasp. The first course of missile aimers joined 829 in September 1968 and, with the aid of a fiendish machine called a DX44 simulator, was indoctrinated in the intricacies of their art. All left-handed helicopter instructors and the Commanding Officer were immediately rejected as unsuitable for further training and by the end of the year the first missiles had been fired. The problems of procuring a target were largely overcome by destroying the only one in the country.

'This new task has opened up another field for aircrewmen. Apart from the necessary medical and educational qualifications, the aimer must also have the aptitude for missile control. The old adage of patting the head and stroking the tummy is even truer now for an aircrewman than it ever was for helicopter pilots! Combining these aiming skills with those of a Wasp maintainer, our steely eyed aircrewman is a most important man and a vital link in the chain of this new weapon system. Because of the complexity of the job, selection is through a very fine sieve and only the elite finally join the ranks of the AS12 missile aimers.

'However, having got this new toy from Father Christmas, how are we going to use it? The aircraft is fitted with a boom on either side and can carry four SS 11 or two AS 12 missiles. To assist the aimer there is an APX 260 gyro stabiliser sight fitted to the aircraft. This gives to magnifications times ten and times 2.5. The latter is used initially, and when the missile gets closer to the target, scale is changed to high magnification. Any of you who have tried to look through binoculars when in a helicopter will realise that the difficulties caused by vibration are considerable and the problem of designing the sight was a very thorny one.

'Although the SS 11 aimer did not really require the optical assistance it is essential when firing the AS12 missile with its much longer range. Target identification becomes a simpler problem and there is an additional bonus by using the sight when flying in a pure reconnaissance role. One of the snags that the army are facing is that there is no range finding attachment built into the sight. Since in the naval role it is envisaged that the helicopter will be under positive radar control, this is of no great consequence, although it would undoubtedly add to the flexibility of the system.

'By day the problem is simple: the Wasp is vectored to its target by a ship or an aircraft and launches the missiles as soon as the firing range is reached. This distance provides a distinct range advantage over all present close range gunnery systems, so there is no fear of it becoming a kamikaze attack.

'By night the problem is greater, as the target must be illuminated for the aimer to make a successful attack. There are nights on which this is not strictly necessary, when there is a full moon and a clear cloudless sky, but they are rare and can't be planned on. So to all intents and purposes some means of illumination is necessary. Those open to us

now ore star shell, 4.5 inch flares and surface burning in illuminants. Star shell is not really feasible as the attack will normally be carried out outside gunnery range. This leaves the flares as the best in service today. Its disadvantages are that it needs to be dropped from a great height and a low cloud base would therefore rule it out of court. We are then left with the Japanese wartime technique of using surface burning illuminants. This looks more promising. Another possible is the glow worm type weapon. However, 30 degrees nose up, which is necessary to launch the flare in a helicopter, is absolutely terrifying and until we can design a glow worm that does not hit the rotor blades and does not require you to stand on your tail, this solution will not work. Glossing quickly over that problem we are left with a relatively simple task of vectoring the missile aircraft into the kill with okay shouts of "Tally Ho", or other such calls. Being outside your parent ships radar coverage creates a small problem, but with the able assistance of a Wessex 3, who was probably dropping the flares anyway, all is not lost. Next question: can I have a radar set of my own? It will solve the ranging and the direction problem, however, the only set now available for installation in the Wasp does not have the necessary range.

'Despite some flippancy we now have a viable and potent new weapon at sea with the fleet. It adds considerably to the striking power of a frigate and there are obviously more roles than the pure anti-fast patrol boat one. As more experience is accumulated the armed Wasp will be the most lethal weapon in the fleet. Despite the demise of the fixed wing element, we shall still be able to strike back, using this time the sting of a Wasp.'

Secondary roles.

As alluded to in the previous *Flight Deck* article the aircraft took on more roles as its use at sea was developed, by the end of its service life it was capable of:

Stores and personnel transfers, whether internally or from an underslung load utilising a cargo hook on the belly of the aircraft.

Search and rescue.

A winch could be fitted for rescues and also personnel transfers, particularly to submarines and ships where there was nowhere to land.

Surface search/reconnaissance.

During the Falklands war some aircraft flew with a large radar reflector on one side to increase the aircraft's radar signature to help decoy Exocet missiles.

And of course it's most important role before satellites and the internet – collecting the ship's mail.

In addition to these formal roles, as will be seen from following chapters, it could be used in a multitude of useful and sometimes unofficial ways.

Chapter 5

Operations – The Early years

It didn't take long before the Wasp was operating all round the world. *(Steve George)*

As soon as the first RN prototype was ready, it was sent to sea for assessment trials. The following article appeared in the RN's flight safety magazine '*Cockpit*' in 1963:

Preliminary ship trials with WASP Mark one helicopter by Lieutenant Commander R. Leonard, MBE, DFC, AFC.

'*Flight handling and deck landing trials were made with the WASP Mark One helicopter on HMS* Nubian *during the period 25 February to 2 March 1963. Trials were jointly conducted by A and AEE Boscombe Down, RAE Bedford, and the aircraft manufacturer, under the control of a trials officer appointed by the*

Ministry of Aviation. The primary object of the trial was to assess the behaviour of the helicopter on a moving deck, to measure loads produced in the undercarriage and to determine the behaviour of the rotor during deck operations, also to assess the problem of night operations and the maximum wind speeds for starting and stopping rotors.

'*The Wasp used on the trials was the first prototype aircraft and was a derivative of the Scout helicopter to meet naval requirements. It differed externally in having a four wheeled undercarriage, and a half span tail plane to permit tail cone folding, an improved twin pad rotor brake, and anti-coning stops were fitted. Lashing posts were provided on the undercarriage, and a bomb slip was fitted under the fuselage for the attachment of a special tie down device. This device secured the helicopter to the deck, but permitted rotation of the helicopter so that it could be turned into wind, or any direction, as required. The wheels for deck operation were not castored but were arranged so that when the helicopter was rotated about its central tie down the wheels rolled and did not need to skid.*

'*The ship itself was provided with a helicopter hangar after the main superstructure and the hangar roof served as the flight deck. The flight deck was rectangular in shape with the long sides athwartships. With the helicopter arranged on the central tie down point, about 6 feet remained between the helicopter wheels and the forward and after deck edge.*

'*A Flight Deck Officers control position was provided forward of the flight deck.*

'*Before take-off, the helicopter was normally secured by four nylon lashings and the centre tie down. After start-up and when the rotor was engaged, the lashings were removed and the aircraft could then be rotated on the deck while still secured. This allowed the ship more freedom of manoeuvre as the helicopter could position itself to take off into the relative wind.*

'*Clearance to take off was received from the Flight Deck Officer and the collective was raised slightly so that the pull of the centre tie down could be felt, at this point the centre tie down was released by depressing a button on the collective pitch lever. The collective pitch was increased and the aircraft lifted cleanly off the deck, cleared the ship and transited in the up wind direction. This had the advantage of avoiding any turbulence on the lee side of the ship.*

'*The approach to the ship was made in two stages, the first part being the approach by the pilot to a position where the control of the helicopter could be assumed by the Flight Deck Officer, the second part being from this point onwards till the actual touchdowns. If the approach was made directly into the relative wind there was noticeable turbulence* in the air wake of the ship. This turbulence could be avoided by flying to one side or other of the turbulent areas. During the final stage of the approach the pilot was guided by the Flight Deck Officer who brought the aircraft to be positioned vertically over the deck.

'For the landing, the helicopter was held in the hover over the flight deck with brakes on. When cleared by the Flight Deck Officer the aircraft was landed firmly. Maximum relative wind conditions experienced during the trial were of the order of 35 to 45 knots with the maximum beam wind of 25 knots.

'Initially, all landings were made into the relative wind, but it was found that on certain headings, notably those of the beam, the pilot could see very little of the flight deck or ship and could not see the Flight Deck Officer. This made landings on these headings rather more difficult. Landings out of the relative wind were carried out and the helicopter landed along the fore and aft line of the ship. It was felt that the choice of whether to land with limited vision into the relative wind or to land with improved vision out of the relative wind depends on the individual pilot and the out of wind strength. In this respect the Wasp handles very well cross wind.'

The prototype Wasp secure on the deck of HMS *Nubian*.

'During this trial it was necessary to simulate rough sea states by destabilising the ship.
'By this means landings were made with the deck rolled to angles of up to 8°. From the piloting point of view no difficulty was experienced and in this phase of the trial the

undercarriage showed up particularly well as its main characteristic of been virtually dead beat with a long travel and no bounce made it particularly suitable for deck operations.

'Owing to the limited time available during the trial it was only possible to carry out one night sortie, this was sufficient to establish a technique that could be used for night operations and comment on the ship's lighting system.

'In general the technique used for night flying was similar to that used for the daylight flying, the main problem being during take-off and clearing the ship, a sudden transition was made from a lighted area to darkness, this transition required the pilot to fly sideways to clear the ship before initiating the climb away. The approaching descent was made using the glide path indicator, which was set at 3°, and the Horizon bar. The latter part of the approach was controlled by the Flight Deck Officer. Landings were made with and without the two red floodlights which are fitted to the forward edge of the flight deck facing aft.

'It was found that the illumination provided by the floodlights aided the pilot during the final approach and landing, but due to their brightness they tended to obscure the glide path indicator and thereby cause more difficulty on the approach. It was recommended that these lights be repositioned.

'These trials were carried out without the benefit of auto pilot / auto stabilisation equipment and without a radio altimeter; both of these items should greatly assist the operation of this helicopter from the ship.

'As a result of these trials it can be said that the undercarriage seems to be well adapted to deck landings, particularly on a rolling deck. Its non-bouncing characteristics were thought to be extremely good. In fact the helicopter appeared very suitable for the role. The only question still to be answered concerns positive securing of the helicopter immediately it touches down. At present nylon lashings are used for the immediate securing after touchdown, but it is felt there may well be sea state conditions which require a more positive method of securing.'

This may have been the first RN trial of the aircraft, but nearly everything that was trialled became standard procedure. The undercarriage and tie down arrangement in particular became the accepted standard.

The approach to the side of the ship and then moving across sideways has been standard RN procedure ever since for all helicopter types. However, it's interesting to note that many navies use a direct approach to the hover over the deck. In my opinion the RN technique is superior, as not only does it avoid any wake turbulence from the ships superstructure, but should an emergency overshoot be required the path ahead of the helicopter is not full of gyrating steel.

The use of red deck lighting was not adopted and hooded white lights are used, a cowl around the lights ensuring that they do not interfere with the light of the Glide Path Indicator.

Flying without stabilisation systems was not too much of a problem for the Wasp, but ship operations without an accurate Radar Altimeter, especially at night, were prohibited.

The author's final remark about needing a better way of securing the aircraft once landed never came to fruition and nylon lashings were the only method used for the Wasp, although it was given a limited amount of negative pitch to help it stick to the deck. The navy would have to wait for the next aircraft, the Lynx, before a viable system known as a deck harpoon was developed.

This prototype was not fitted with flotation gear, as can be seen in the photograph. Fitted to the rear undercarriage sponsons were two large balls. Many thought these were flotation canisters. In fact they were 'Luneburg lenses', which were a form of radar reflector, fitted to increase the aircraft's visibility on radar. They were not used operationally and a powered radar transponder was fitted to the tail instead (known as the bean can because of its shape).

Into Service - the Squadrons

The aircraft entered service on the 4 June 1963 at RNAS Culdrose when the Intensive Flying Trials Squadron 700(W) reformed to develop the MATCH concept and aircraft handling techniques. The first Wasp Flight for HMS *Leander* formed on the 11 November that year and other Flights soon followed: Dido, Penelope and Mohawk (a report of Mohawk's first embarkation is below). 700(W) disbanded on 4 March 1964 and re-commissioned as 829 Squadron as the headquarters unit for all the operational flights, while 706 Squadron took on the training task. The next Flights to form were Ashanti, Zulu, Euryalus and Galatea.

On 27 Nov 1964, 829 moved to RNAS Portland, as it was logical to base the aircraft in the same place as the ships that were working up there. However, 706 retained the training task until 703 Squadron formed, also at Portland and took over the role.

829 was the largest squadron in the FAA with forty-four Flights on its charge, plus four headquarters aircraft and a further two for the Ice Patrol ship HMS *Endurance* - a total of fifty aircraft. In addition, small numbers of Wasps were operated by 845 and 848 Commando helicopter squadrons as utility machines until 1973.

Crests of all FAA squadrons that operated the aircraft.

Getting started

Introducing aircraft of this sort into the fleet was a steep learning curve for all concerned. To operate an aircraft from a small ship required close cooperation between all departments and an understanding of the issues on all sides. That said, the aircraft soon fell into the classic definition of a 'force multiplier', as it immediately increased the capability of a Frigate or Destroyer in many ways, not just in its ability to drop torpedoes on a target. It could fly out and identify unidentified radar contacts, easily transfer personnel and equipment between ships, conduct rescues, later on it could attack surface contact with its own missiles, and in the days before the internet and satellite communications it could conduct the most vital task for a ship - it could collect the mail.

The following article appeared in *Cockpit* magazine and is a good example of the lessons very quickly learned in operating helicopters from small ships. In this case the article was submitted by the Flight Commander of a small ship's Flight:

> *'It is in the interest of all concerned that the Flight join the ship as early as possible, or in the event of this being impossible, as many of the Flight as possible should visit the new ship to acquaint themselves with the layout to check over the various compartments with*

a view to ensuring that all necessary items of equipment are available. First recovery and subsequent stowage of the aircraft can be just as harrowing for the maintenance crew as the first deck landing for the aircrew.

'Good communications and cross knowledge between the flight deck and command is an essential. Remember the flight deck of a destroyer or frigate is not directly visible from the bridge or compass platform.

'Safety factors to be borne in mind whilst handling include a sensible maximum of a 5° deck roll. It is well to bear in mind that it would take fifteen men to push a Wasp up the 5° slope. Wet and slippery decks, high winds, with the dangers of weather cocking and low temperatures add to this hazard.

'Blade spreading and folding is limited by wind speed, 30 knots being considered a safe maximum controllable by the maximum effective number of men. With no ship movement and the ship steady, absolute maximum of 35 knots can be accepted, but, with any appreciable role, 25 knots is the prudent maximum.

'On starting and shutdown it must be remembered that the pilot has very little control over the rotor and so cannot accept any latitude on the laid down acceptable wind limits. If, after permission to either engage or shut down is given, it is found, say, that a gust of wind takes conditions out of limits, it is much better to leave things as they are, turning the ship will make matters worse.

'For landings and take offs the ship's configuration is a more severe limitation than relative wind. When operating in marginal conditions it may well be necessary to remain in the hover over the deck for a long time awaiting a quiet period. In such prolonged hovers the pilot may well become too tense on the controls and would be advised to pull away from the deck for a few seconds. In such conditions deck landings may be a protracted process.

'Once airborne, the crew of the aircraft rely for their safety on proper control by the ship's operations room. Therefore, at all times the ship should keep the radar watch on the aircraft and inform the crew if the echo is no longer held. Regular radio checks at least every twenty minutes (whether the aircraft has been held or not) are advisable, as in the event of an engine failure there may well be no time to make a distress call. In addition, a listening watch on the guard frequency is most prudent and the ship must at all times inform the aircraft of any obstructions, including heavy cloud build up or the proximity of any other aircraft.

'Ships armament and missile systems should be carefully studied and well understood by all the ship's Flight, paying full attention to the dangers inherent to the aircraft and crews in the event of training or the firing of these systems.

'A good liaison between the maintenance crew and command is most essential and careful planning and thinking ahead will do much to save time and tempers by integrating maintenance requirements with the desired ships routine.

'As stores, usage stores anticipation and swift reader mounting of used items are essential, and whilst squirrelling must be avoided, small ship sensible demanding may well mean the difference between a full program and the aircraft remaining unserviceable.

'Passenger flying should be encouraged amongst the ship's company, especially those directly connected with aircraft operations, for example, helicopter control ratings, in order that they may better understand the aircrew task. At all times such passengers must be fully briefed on emergency drills and safety equipment. Block briefing of large numbers with a re-briefing immediately before flight would do much to save time and effort.'

It is almost impossible not to agree with every point made in this very short but extremely comprehensive report. Lessons learned in those days are still being learned again today. The point about getting ships staff airborne – particularly the helicopter control staff, was later taken to a deeper level when it was decided that the helicopter controller would actually become part of the Flight team rather than ship's company.

Below is a report from *Cockpit* magazine of the first embarkation of a Wasp in HMS *Mohawk* – the third Wasp Flight to go to sea:

'HMS Mohawk *is the first tribal class frigate to embark a Wasp for a general service commission in the Persian Gulf. The ship's Flight, which consists of the pilot and six ratings commissioned at RNAS Culdrose on 14 January 1964. The first aircraft given to the Flight resembled an initiative test. It stood in the corner of a hangar in pieces after being brought in from a turnip field where it landed in an emergency. When it was clear that the lack of modifications would delay the move to Portland for the workup, the present aircraft was handed over to the Flight.*

'On completion of the period of shore training at Portland the commanding officer of 737 Squadron sat in the passenger seat whilst the first deck landings on Mohawk *were conducted. These must have been a piece of cake, for after a short delay, to disembark his passenger, our pilot was back to his solo landings. It was at this stage that the first major problem was encountered, how to get the aircraft down the left into the hangar. The first attempt took ninety minutes. In addition to the Flight Deck Officer and the Flight there were four Royal Marine handlers all eager to learn the mysteries of using the four hand winches. These are positioned on each corner of the flight deck and by*

attaching wires to the oleos the Wasp can be manoeuvred. A suitable combination of movements has been devised now to allow for athwartships and fore and aft landings, this has cut the striking downtimes by more than half.

'Very early in the workup it was found necessary to change the aircraft's engine. This was because the starter generator drive had sheared twice, the second occasion giving the ship its first precautionary landing. The remarks of the ship's company are unprintable as they saw the Wasp been unloaded by crane and pushed along the jetty at Portland en-route to the helicopter base where the engine was replaced. This did not stop the ship operating a Wasp in any of the anti-submarine exercises, as Portland were kind enough to offer another aircraft to complete all sorties.

'When Mohawk's Wasp was again available it flew two and three times a day and remained a Condition One for long periods. This can produce humorous moments, as when in the heat of battle the Captain has to approve a request to go to Condition Two in order that the pilot can nip up to spring a leak.

'Throughout the workup, with the assistance of the Staff Aviation Officer to Flag Officer Sea training, we explored the operational ability of the Wasp. Flying was carried out in very strong winds and successful landings made with the ship pitching and rolling. A great advantage of the Wasp over the P531, the original Tribal helicopter with skids, is an undercarriage which allows the aircraft to stick to the deck on touchdown. Only on one occasion did we encounter blade sailing; this was immediately after land on when the tactical situation deemed it necessary to steam with over 40 knots of wind over the deck. The quickest turnaround achieved with rotor running refuelling was five minutes, whilst landing on to Condition One took a fraction longer. This involves moving the aircraft over the deck and positioning it on the centre tie down for start-up. Once on the tie down, the pilot is able to swivel the aircraft into the wind for launching. Landings are carried out into the wind with a final manoeuvre to touch down fore and aft or cross deck. For final stages of the landing, the Flight Deck Officer, who is in an excellent position, assists the pilot to touch down with flag signals.

'As in all aircraft carriers, flying is controlled from the bridge area. Mohawk's First Lieutenant wears the hat of commander (air), and selects flying courses for operations. Communications are very good, and with a system of Stop/Go lights, the bridge and Flight Deck Officer, there is a double safety factor. Ratings and Royal Marines from the ships company have been selected for training as handlers and firefighters and their enthusiasm and good humour has developed the whole flight deck party into an efficient unit, the operations room control of the Wasp is in the capable hands of the Chief Radar rating. The scramble times are such that the Command can virtually employ the aircraft as soon as a long-range sonar contact has been classified. When airborne,

the operations room takes the aircraft under positive control for Vectac and if necessary recovery can be by means of a ship controlled approach when the weather is poor.

'Many various sorties have been flown by the Wasp in the short time it has been embarked. They include flying a stretcher case to Portland, bombardment spotting, photographic and early warning against fighters attacking, the latter being a bonus whilst employed on another task.

'Being a guinea pig produces problems all round and not the least for the Supply Officer. He is often demanding air stores and no doubt will do so throughout the commission, but whether he can find somewhere to stow them is a different matter. All our predecessors have departed for the Gulf using the hangar as a naval store or cargo stowage. With space at a premium the pilot could be in the unenviable position of sharing a cabin with four spare rotor blades!

'On completion of the work up and a special refit at Chatham, we departed the Persian Gulf on 1 June and are looking forward to a successful twelve months commission East of Suez.'

It wasn't long before the aircraft was conducting operations worldwide. Below is an account from *Flight Deck* magazine by Lieutenant R.E. Smith, the Flight Commander of HMS *Ashanti* in 1965. On a historical note, the Beira patrol was an RN blockade of what was then Rhodesia, which had recently declared its independence from the UK. The crisis in Aden would quickly lead to our withdrawal from that region. The area known as 'Radfan' was part of Aden, near the border with The Yemen.

Middle East Wasp.

'The weather was dank. Warm front conditions, cloud on the deck and visibility down to something under half a mile. In fact, it was typical Culdrose weather and the met boys held out no hope of an improvement even for night flying. Thus it was that I found myself starting on my second point - one lunchtime in March 1965 - with a clear conscience and the rosy picture of a quiet afternoon in a crew room easy chair. Ten minutes later I was calling nervously for a third pint and struggling to readjust my thoughts. Mentally I reviewed the circumstances; one telephone call and all is changed; a way of life carefully built up over the years disintegrates. The call had been from "THEM", the appointers. How would you like to take a Wasp Flight? It had been a simple question, so simple that I had never considered it previously. Ill prepared excuses of; no previous anti-submarine experience, commando background, value as an instructor, promised another tour with 845, had all been blandly disregarded. The

soothing voice had relentlessly reiterated such blandishments as; own command, able to watch keep, keep abreast of the fleet, modern ships, and finally, will be going to…

'*The die was cast, there was no appeal from the sentence, and that is how I come to be writing this, sweltering in the heat of Bahrain as Flight Commander of 829 Squadron Ashanti Flight.*

'*It has been suggested that Ashanti Flight had an interesting time, had experienced boredom together with a fair share of excitement, but above all, have enjoyed themselves. All seven of us agree with these suggestions and it is to encourage anyone who finds himself in the position I was in that lunchtime, two and a half years ago, that I'm going to describe something of our time as a Middle East Wasp Flight.*

'*For the benefit of those unacquainted with small ship operations it would be fair to describe a Flight as a mobile and self-contained unit, carrying its own equipment but dependent upon its parent or foster parent's ship for stores and spares. The team is made up of a pilot, a Senior Maintenance Rating, three Petty Officers and two Junior Ratings, who between them cover the engine, airframe and radio equipment. In our case the team met as a unit for the first time at Culdrose in October 1965; by November we had moved to 829 Headquarters Squadron at Portland, and just before Christmas we received one brand-new and shiny Wasp directly from Fleetlands. Time spent at Portland was devoted to operational flying training for the pilot, practical experience in teamwork on their own aircraft for the ground crew, and an aircrewman's course for the Flight rating who volunteered for that duty, and of course, workup with our ship.*

'*Workup completed, we embarked in Ashanti at Devonport on 19 July and sailed for the Middle East on the twenty-fifth. A Persian Gulf commission these days is not what it was. Of the three frigates normally attached to the area two are now employed in the Beira blockade. Thus it was, that having transited the canal and left Aden behind, Ashanti steamed, or more accurately limped, towards Mombasa. On arrival it became apparent that repairs to the ship would take several weeks, a period during which the only flying possible would have been gentlemanly pleasure sorties from the civilian airport at Port Reitz. An excellent way to pass a month - or even two. Unfortunately, such employment seldom meets approval. HMS Zulu, a sister tribal frigate lacking a Flight of her own, was called upon to perform Ashanti's scheduled patrol and a temporary transfer to her was arranged.*

'*A transfer such as this is both interesting and challenging. One's "foster mother" may well be rusty in operational experience and an inspired guess is needed to decide what proportion of stores and "come in handy" items should accompany the Flight. All frigates without their own aircraft still maintain a full spares list and only major and short supply items such as a spare engine and rotor blades are lacking. Zulus workup was a scant six months behind her and in the interim she had cross-operated HMS Mohawk's Flight. The flight deck crew and helicopter control team were delighted to have an aircraft to play with, perhaps owing to the promise of something, anything, which offered a change from the monotony and tedium of lengthy patrols; whatever the reason, the loan period was a success. Within a week, we had covered day flying in all conditions and had graduated through dusk to full night operation. We had also arrived off Beira.*

'Much has been written about the Beira patrol following HMS Eagles marathon stint. During our period in the area the patrol was maintained by two frigates supported by an RFA tanker. The frigates took it in turns to man either the busy north or more restful south patrol lines and diligently challenged every vessel entering or leaving the area. A tanker, unless specifically mentioned on a declared innocence list, is always courteously requested to stop whilst instructions are obtained from London. Normally these instructions gave permission for the tanker to proceed into Beira, but on occasions a boarding party is ordered to carry out a careful scrutiny of the cargo consignment documents. This employment is extremely monotonous and the novelty of the helicopter enlivened proceedings – until of course the novelty wore off!

'The aircraft would be ranged at dawn, carry out an hour sortie in the forenoon, combining helicopter control exercises for the ships in company, with patrol flying, stores, mail and personnel transfers within the force and identification of distant radar contacts. During the afternoon Zulu would often anchor or drift and the serious business of fishing, or acquiring a tan, attended to (tropical routine is worked by all Persian Gulf frigates). Throughout daylight hours the aircraft would be at ten minutes readiness to launch to identify contacts and was thus able to prevent many instances of getting underway to intercept what turned out to be an innocent merchantman. Dusk or night flying took place on four nights a week.

'Zulu had been on patrol for three weeks when Ashanti appeared to relieve her. The Flight and stores were transferred in four helicopter lifts and we settled down to a crash programme of refreshing our natural mother's memory of flying operations. A seventeen day period during which the aircraft was unserviceable for a replacement hydraulic power pack occurred in the middle of October. It was fortunate that this period coincided with a visit to Mauritius, and with a grounded aircraft on our hands, full advantage of the opportunity for a run ashore was taken. Worldwide air stores backing was fully exercised in providing this replacement hydraulic unit; robbery off an aircraft at Singapore proceeded to dispatch by air from Singapore to Nairobi, in mid-flight, effort was made to intercept the unit for diversion to Mauritius, but from signals received it had already apparently gone missing, either in the Cocos Islands or

at Bangkok! When finally received, it was believed to have travelled by air to Aden, thence to Nairobi, and on to Mombasa, where it had to wait the sailing of the next frigate for the patrol area.

'Unfortunately, we left Mauritius at two thirds normal strength, as two of our Petty Officers were left behind for minor surgery. Once the hydraulic pack was replaced, three weeks intensive operating, so seriously undermanned, proved that six is the right number for prolonged periods of flying. On eventual return to Mombasa after an absence of sixty-six days, the aircraft had flown ninety hours in forty-nine days and the Flight had spent sixty-one days at sea. HMS Triumph *(an aircraft carrier converted to support ship) had arrived at Mombasa from Singapore to provide urgently needed support facilities for the overworked patrol frigates and we gratefully disembarked into her spacious Flight deck hangar. Ten days hard maintenance by a Flight now back to full numbers meant our responsibilities in that direction were fulfilled; to be in East Africa and not to go on safari would have been to miss the opportunity of a lifetime, and so all seven of us sallied forth in a hired minibus to see the sites and tour the Tsavo Game Park.*

'A further four weeks was spent on patrol before our final return to Mombasa at Christmas. During this period the Wasp's engine was changed at sea. The weather proved very helpful and in a surprisingly short time the spare was installed and ground tested; the outstanding problem was how and where to carry out a test flight. Caution and the book both suggested overland, but the only land at hand was Portuguese territory. The Portuguese authorities in Beira had always been most friendly on the occasions on which we had flown casualties ashore to hospital; so much so that the Captain invited the Commandant to lunch on board. The meal was a great success and the Commandant proved to have flown both with the RAF and RCAF and to hold strong views on the "stupidity of scrapping your TSR2 and not replacing your carriers"! On returning, our guest to the airport we were invited to shut down whilst a 20 gallon barrel of red wine was loaded into the back of the aircraft. A present from our oldest allies to the ships company.

'Banking on the good relations previously established we flew ashore, ostensibly to collect an RFA seaman released from hospital and on arrival carefully explained that engine performance had given us cause for concern on the way in and we would very much like to carry out a check Flight before returning. Nothing could have been simpler to arrange and with the Portuguese Lieutenant Colonel riding as an interested spectator in the rear seat, a full check test flight was completed. At all times the Portuguese behaved most correctly as befitted neutrals in the oil blockade, and at no time was bias or favouritism displayed. Hence, whilst waiting ashore for the return of a patient we

exchanged cheerful waves with the crews of Rhodesian Air Force DC 3s and on one occasion two RRAF Canberras and two Hunters were seen parked on the dispersal.

'Needless to say no one was sorry when, on the twenty-sixth of December, we sailed from Mombasa for the last time and turned north for Aden instead of south to Beira. Unfortunately, our progress northwards was marred by a failure of the ship's main blower and we limped into Aden on New Year's Eve in much the same manner as we had limped out four and a half months previously. This time the aircraft was in sympathy with the ship and suffered from a leaking tail rotor gearbox, so no flying took place for the next fortnight. These two weeks were a period of high excitement for, whilst a specialist survey team inspected the aircraft, discussions took place as to our employment during the two months repairs would take to effect on the ship. A proposal to return to HMS Zulu was vetoed when it was realised that she would be spending six weeks alongside in Bahrain. In the end we managed to convince people that a Wasp is basically the same beast as an army Scout and that we should therefore join up with an Army Air Corps Scout Flight.

'There are two Scout Flights at Falaise and they alternate roughly once every two months between aircraft maintenance coupled with internal security duties based at Falaise and direct support of the Radfan garrisons at Area West based on Habilayn (the old Fort Thumier). My good luck, as 8 Flight were about to move up country on 14 January. We flew to Habilayn to arrange accommodation, pre-position stores and generally discover what went on. Habilayn is an airstrip 2000 feet above sea level surrounded by hills rising to 5000 and 6000 feet. The runway surface is of oiled and rolled sand. On the western side of the strip and separated from it by the main Dhala road is the camp proper. Inside a perimeter of barbed wire which bristled with machine guns, mortars, wombats and armoured cars lived a British Battalion – later relieved by 45 Commando Royal Marines – a company of the Parachute Regiment, a Commando Artillery Battery, a Sapper Field Squadron an Armoured Car Squadron and Headquarters Area West. On the eastern side of the strip lie sandbagged sangars into which the aircraft can be pushed at night, the RCT, vehicle park and ammunition and fuel compounds. Scattered around the whole area are piquets, permanent positions atop commanding features armed with machine guns and in some cases wombats as well.

'During this visit we had a foretaste of our future employment when we were asked if we could take the medical officer of the Irish Guards to a village some 5000 feet up in the Jebel Radfan to visit a patient. The casualty proved to be an eighteen month old native boy in urgent need of an abdominal operation and he was flown to the hospital at Khormaksar. On 16 January, Petty Officers Jones and Alford and LAM Greatbatch were installed in tented accommodation at Habilayn and we flew an area reconnaissance *with Sergeant Blevins, Royal Marines, one of 45 Commando's Air Troop pilots acting as navigator. Despairing of ever making sense of a map in the mountainous country, I contented myself in identifying major features and within two days we were able to dispense with assistance and stagger around by ourselves. The resident AAC Flight upcountry works a seven-day week, daylight hours only, except for four nights a week and they provide a casualty evacuation aircraft; the remaining nights are covered by the RAF using a Wessex 2. We became fully integrated and worked a similar system; except that our numbers prevented a two watch routine. The original intention had been to change the upcountry team with those remaining on board every ten days, but in the event, both sections proved so contented with their individual roles that this idea was abandoned and the upcountry warriors remained on station for five weeks.*

'The first three weeks at Habilayn where noisy, on six consecutive nights the garrison was attacked by dissident tribesman using 61mm mortars, Blindicide rockets (a Czech version of a bazooka but simpler) and small arms. PO Alford considerably annoyed the army by remaining fast asleep throughout the first night's attack; not only did he fail to take an interest in the fireworks, but he actually snored!

'At night the aircraft were protected by being pushed into the sangars, but when the RAF left their casualty evacuation Wessex upcountry there was no room for the Wasp and one Scout which spent lonely nights sitting out on the dispersal. As a protection against small arms fire Stalwarts (armoured cars) were driven to positions around the aircraft to form an improvised rampart. On one occasion a Blindicide struck the ground a few feet from the aircraft, bounced, and exploded some 20 yards astern. We picked up shrapnel from around the tail next morning but miraculously there was not a scratch on the aircraft, the Scout was dented in the forward door by flying stone.

'A typical day would be, turn to at 0700, three forenoon sorties, a one hour break for lunch, three afternoon sorties, aircraft secured and sangared for the night by 1800, supper and to bed by 2100; the fresh air and altitude meant sound sleep and there was nothing to do in the evenings except on cinema nights. During our stay the ships Royal Marine detachment joined 45 Commando for a week and the Captain, Commander R. McCrum, took the opportunity to visit us all for twenty-four hours. Unfortunately, the dissidents did not oblige and there were no attacks that night. The Royal Marine detachment was picketing the heights overlooking the Dhala road, protecting parties of sappers repairing minor damage. The aircraft landed on the road and the Captain, pursued by a perspiring escort armed with an SLR rifle, proceeded to run up and down the Jebels (hills) in a horrifying manner!

'Flying in the Radfan is a unique experience, and with the impending loss of Aden, one that will not remain available to us for many months. Fortunately, we were present

in the cool season and temperatures upcountry rarely exceeded 30°C. The theatre of operations was, broadly speaking, a 40 mile radius around Habilayn and sorties to various outlying towns. One, Sanah, is only 3000 yards from a 27mm anti-aircraft battery in the Yemen and flights in and out were made at about 15 feet, taking care to keep the hill between us and any trigger-happy opposition. Initially we were very cautious and disregarding Scout experience worked up very slowly as time and trials proved the versatility of the Wasp in (for us) high altitude flight. Awabil is 6000 feet above sea level and many intermediate stages were taken before finally shutting down and relying on a battery start at that height. The aircraft was lightened by the removal of the flotation gear, Lunenburg lenses, and on occasions, the rear seat. Except when flying in the casualty evacuation role, all doors were removed. Thirty-six battery starts were made and on only two occasions was a second attempt necessary. Serviceability was excellent and very few snags were encountered; on one occasion on take-off with autopilot engaged the rudder pedals did not free with manoeuvre selected and the resultant upward twiddle to the right, whilst frantically searching for the release button, impressed the army considerably.

'Troop and ration convoys on the Dhala road are frequently ambushed by tribesmen using small arms from the heights on either side and it is standard practice for the convoys to have air cover in the form of a Scout armed with two forward firing and one waist mounted GPMG. During one period when Scout serviceability was zero it was necessary to provide armed convoy cover. The Wasp was 'volunteered'. The Scout waist mount fitted, tried dry, 800 rounds fired on the range and we took off with high hopes; perhaps fortunately, there was no requirement to use our new-found skill. During our stay we used the aircraft for troop transport, internal and underslung stores, ration and ammunition resupply, reconnaissance, armed convoy cover, gunfire spotting and casualty evacuation (nine days and one night). In thirty-five days upcountry the aircraft made 153 sorties, 407 landings, and carried 503 passengers ranging from Major Generals to expectant Arab mothers and completed 83 ½ hours flying in thirty-three flying days.

'Our period in Aden was perhaps the highlight of the commission; certainly it was a complete contrast to the preceding five months. However, it was not the end of the story; there are still places in the world where a helicopter is a comparatively rare beast and we have been called upon to consider undertaking a wonderful variety of missions. We have flown every ruler of the Trucial States bar one and he declined our offer on the grounds that helicopter flying might impair his virility! All varieties of casualty evacuation, searching for the wreckage of crashed aircraft, missing boats, lost land parties, and even making films, have come our way. Whatever an appointment to a *small ships Flight may bring, variety and interest are inevitable; as for enjoyment – that is surely up to you.'*

Meanwhile, on the other side of the world HMS *Gurkha* was having a rather better time of it as West Indies guard ship, as this article from *Flight Deck* describes:

'HMS Gurkha *left Bermuda for the UK on 3 December and completion of a six months deployment in the Caribbean. During this time the ship visited most of the Windward and Leeward Islands as well as Venezuela, Puerto Rico and the Dominican Republic and it has been a most interesting period for the ship's Flight despite some unserviceability, largely due to engine problems.*

'The ship left Rosyth early in July and arrived on station later in the month after a fuelling stop in the Azores. We called at Bermuda for a briefing by the senior naval officer West Indies (SNOWI) staff and at the same time picked up our Caribbean stores, the principal one of which, as far as the Flight was concerned, being the Bendix RT221 VHF radio which has proved invaluable during our time on the station. We will be sad to have to pass it on to HMS Sirius when we leave.

'After a visit to Freeport, the ship went for trials on the AUTEC range during which the wasp was called to the assistance of the pilot of a Cessna light aircraft which are carried out a forced landing following an engine failure. The pilot was rescued unhurt, but as the aircraft, which appeared undamaged, was in the middle of a mangrove swamp on Andros Island, it seemed unlikely that anything short of a heavy lift helicopter would be able to extract it.

'HMS Gurkha continued her way south, exercising with HMS Berwick on the way, but unfortunately the aircraft suffered a partial engine failure resulting in an engine change. As our spare engine also proved to be unserviceable, we were obliged to await the arrival of two replacement engines from the UK. These eventually arrived during our first visit to San Juan Puerto Rico, which had we but known, was to become a sort of second home for the ship during our time out here.

'The new engine had no sooner been fitted and test flown than we were sent off on a casualty evacuation operation; this time it was to the assistance of the Panamanian tanker M/T Adoration, some hundred miles north-east of Antigua. The rendezvous was made at midnight on 21 August, and after Gurkha's medical officer and a stretcher had been transferred by helicopter, we winched off a Greek seaman with acute appendicitis, plus two American paramedics who had been parachuted to the ship earlier in the day. We returned the patient to hospital in Antigua, enabling the tanker to continue her passage to the Persian Gulf. The whole transfer, including some ten

winchings and working with a strange and unpractised ship, was interesting and not an exciting time and we are glad to hear that our casualty was later recovering after his operation.

'After further island visits and a replenishment at sea with RFA Resource, Gurkha arrived in Chaguaramas Trinidad on 1 September for a maintenance period during which the Flight disembarked to Piarco international airport for continuation flying. During this time we were also visited by the 829 roving Air Engineer Officer who arrived to carry out vibration tests on the aircraft. It being his fifth visit to the island he was also able to help us with the social side of our visit which proved to be most enjoyable.

'We re-embarked as the ship left Chaguaramas on 25 September, taking part in several anti-submarine exercises on passage to La Guaira, the port of Caracas, with the submarine HMS Odin which was on passage to Australia. It was nice to get in some practice with a submarine, a rare animal in these waters. During our visit to La Guaira we gave a sea day for the benefit of embarked Venezuelan officers and also exercised the Royal Navy's right to march through the streets of Caracas when we mounted a colour guard for a wreath laying ceremony at the Simon Bolivar Monument. This right was granted in recognition of the assistance given by the Royal Navy during the nation's fight for independence from Spain. The fact that the ceremony was carried out in a tropical downpour did not seem to decrease its popularity with the citizens of Caracas.

'The ship sailed for a further visit to San Juan for our FOCAS annual inspection which took place on 31 October and 01 November, but not as we had hoped on passage to New Orleans. Instead we were sailed at short notice and remained on patrol throughout, a disappointment to us all and not least to the FOCAS staff who disembarked at a time and place which bore no relation to their program.

'During our deployment the ship had spent a total of some four weeks in San Juan, so it was a bit like leaving home when we finally sailed from there on 20 November for Santo Domingo. On passage we carried out a replenishment at sea and Vertrep with RFA Reliant. The wasp was hurriedly recalled later in the day on receipt of a signal from the naval aircraft Materials laboratory which recommended rejection of the engine due to excessive iron content in one of our oil samples. The engine was changed and tested in time to enable some flight participation in the Dominica/Britex, the annual joint exercise with forces of the Dominican Republic. A mark eleven Depth Charge went off with a satisfying bang apparently impressed the visiting officers but sadly failed to frighten the local fish.

'The spectrographic oil analysis program has given us warning of imminent failure into engines during the last six months, though in one case the signal unfortunately arrived very shortly after the engine had in fact failed. However, these two cases have

served to highlight the value of the programme and we are grateful for the prompt warning which probably saved a serious accident.

'*Gurkha is now on her way back to the UK where we hope to arrive on completion of our Captains (F) inspection on 15 December in good time for Christmas leave.*'

As time passed WASP operations matured but were always challenging. Below is a diary of a year of operations in HMS *Naiad* by Paul Green, who was a Naval Air Engineering Mechanic on the Flight at the time. The aircraft was known as 'Scrumpy', something to do with the name of the Flight Commander – Steve Bramley.

1981 August

'We returned from leave with a new team of junior ratings and went back to work at sleepy Portland and a week of glorious sunshine was spent on maintenance and ground training. We received a great shock to the system when the ship required the aircraft on board for Fleet Contingency Ship 1 (FCS1) duties due to HMS *Plymouth* developing engine problems. We departed Portland at 1540 and arrived on board an expectant mother at 1630.

'After a quiet weekend and the repair of HMS *Plymouth* we disembarked back to Portland Monday afternoon where we carried out static weapon loads in the morning, but the planned afternoon flying was cancelled due to a fault on the aircraft's flotation gear. This was rectified by the end of the day; there were then more static weapon loads and some winching and load lifting sorties carried out. Unfortunately, the aircraft vibration check was out of limits and required a late-night Thursday cleaning the dampers, plus a track test flight on Friday morning to get it smooth again. Serviceable just in time for the weekend we were on standby to rejoin the ship on a shadowing mission which never materialised. On 24 August we re-embarked for real FCS 1 duties. We steam clean the flight deck and repainted the white lines. The First Lieutenant was happy, for a while! We then spent a glorious week ground training on "part of ship" duties. At the end of the month there were "Navy Days" with no active flight participation. We were now looking forward to flying again.'

September

'The month started slowly with the ship alongside in Devonport but the pace increased to a crescendo of warfare training by the end of the month.

'Ground training, static loads, and part of ship with divisions thrown in for good measure at the start of the month. The opportunity was also taken to have ship and divisional photographs taken; the Flight Commander and leading aircrewman carried out annual QHI checks and engine off landings together with wet and dry dinghy drills prior to going to Gibraltar on 9 September. We sailed and the weather was clamped, 1400 flying had to be cancelled. Next day there was flying with AS12 missile loads and the leading regulator as a practice casualty, plus the more usual deck landing and ship controlled approaches. During the passage through the Straits of Dover we carried out night AS12 load drills.

'On 11 September we visited Amsterdam and this was marked by the Leading Aircrewman breaking his collarbone during a rugby match immediately after arrival. He was flown to the naval hospital at Haslar on Sunday. After leaving Amsterdam we had a 1 ½ hour flying exercise with a stand in crewman from the engineering team. The last week was another week of warfare training. With unhelpful weather we disembarked Scrumpy to Portland for his vibration checks on Wednesday, joining without radio as both PTR 177's had failed.'

October

'This was a busy month; commencing with Portland syllabus training and ending with the flight disembarked at RAF Gibraltar.

'It was a Thursday and the weekly war was underway, but there was no flying for Scrumpy until afterwards, when the warfare officer CASEX (anti-submarine exercise) provided plenty of action. The day ended with an impromptu and quick reaction senior officers trip of three submariners from the submarine *Olympus*. On Monday we went straight into helicopter controller training and a good 4hours and 50 minutes day and night flying. We flew members of the ship's company during the morning and afternoon submarine exercises. Murphy's Law said that, "when flying in instrument conditions thou shall have a radio failure" and the Flight Commander with Sub Lieutenant Rees on his first aquaint had one! Luckily, accurate mental dead reckoning found the ship, which was joined using negative radio procedures. The planned night flying was cancelled whilst the snag was investigated.

'With the radio problem unsolved an afternoon flying exercise was flown on the standby radio to qualify Leading Seaman Roy Bland to be helicopter controller. We then disembarked to Portland at 1430 to throw the might of the HQ squadron team behind the radio snag investigation. During the evening, a further snag was discovered with the radio changeover switch and the control box. Eventually Scrumpy was able to re-embark. And after the Thursday war sailed for a visit to Hull which, despite very cold wet and windy weather, proved most enjoyable. We sailed from Hull without our Senior Maintenance Rating, who had to attend Stonehouse for a check on his deaf right ear.

'We then went on passage to Gibraltar with lots of flying and weapon loads, clearing icy England, the stormy Biscay, into the warm blue southern skies as we approached the Mediterranean. For the last week of the month we disembarked at RAF Gibraltar where we soon settled in. At the end of the month Scrumpy suffered a generator failure which necessitated robbing the spare engine.'

November

'November proved to be a very good month for the Flight. The weather was excellent, the flying good and after two and half weeks of husbandry, Scrumpy appeared as new. The first week had a busy flying programme without an aircrewman. The Flight Commander progressing in his general flying, night flying, navigation and instrument flying, he also managed many aviation aquaints with members of the ships company including the Commanding Officer.

'The Flight Commander's wife arrived with news that a baby Bramley was on the way; whilst he recover from the shock ample opportunity was given to carry out a first-class husbandry job on the aircraft. Hangar paintwork was also progressed to good advantage. On 19 November our aircrewman returned with a freshly repaired collarbone. After tackling publication amendments he was given a back in the saddle programme by the Flight Commander before recommencing flying.

'At the end of the month there were two days excellent flying with wet winching of twelve squadron aircrew (Buccaneers) from a single man life raft, to an RAF launch which provided excellent training value and no one was lost! Load lifting and a photograph exercise were also carried out together with the search for a Russian Foxtrot submarine. On the night of the twenty-sixth we commenced three hours planned night flying, starting with a one hour twenty minutes sea navigation exercise. After one hour we were recalled mysteriously, but why, something drastic? Unfortunately, the Buccaneers night flying for the first time from Gibraltar had made too much noise at the Governor's dinner party been held at St George's Hall in the north face of the rock. The RAF, with typical dramatic overkill, immediately cancelled all night flying. Apart from this, we received first-class assistance from our light blue friends and the detachment proved to be a great success.'

December

'Our time in Gibraltar sunshine was rapidly coming to an end and we were all looking forward to going home. The last session of general flying, load lifting, and aviation acquaints Gibraltar, before the Flight Commander briefed the new officer of the watches before pre-embarkation on 7 December. We had an eventful first day on board doing sea trials with Scrumpy embarking early to join the ship 50 miles west of Gibraltar en route to assist a Moroccan fishing vessel. After landing, our task was altered to medical evacuation (medevac) to rescue a British couple injured in a car crash in the north of Morocco.

'The Flight Commander flew back 75 miles to pick up a surgeon Commander from Gibraltar whilst the aircrewman prepared details for the Flight into the little airstrip of Al Hociema.

'Meanwhile, the ship was suffering many and various mechanical breakdowns and for some time it wallowed helplessly in the Mediterranean. Our gallant crew, launching from the stricken ship, arrived at the Moroccan coast just before sunset to discover a distraught Clare Riley with a broken arm, very pleased to see them. However, the Moroccan gentleman gathered there, some with sidearms, were far from helpful and it took one hour's diplomatic smiling before the aircraft was allowed to leave.

'The initial plan was to make two trips, but they were abandoned, and Scrumpy did a "cushion creep" take-off on its way back to English deck plates in darkness with a stretcher case, the man suffering a spinal injury, plus four others!

'*Naiad* flight maintainers took over to get our patient safely out of the aircraft, an aircraft which due to their efforts remained flying without problems throughout.

'The ship, with its port engine inoperative, arrived in Gibraltar at 0400 to hospitalise our two patients and itself. Claire Riley and her fiancé were on their way to recovery by the end of the week. Unfortunately the ship's port engine was not.

'On Sunday, 13 December, *Naiad* cut its losses and sailed home taking charge of Diomede and Euryalus for exercises en route.

'The Flight soon established itself back into day and night flying working up a new helicopter controller. Monday also provided a full days flying, but Tuesday saw the ship meeting gale force eight and nine winds and high seas as we neared Biscay.

'All further flying was cancelled until disembarkation on the very cold overcast morning of 17 December. Despite the poor conditions the homeward flight went smoothly and Scrumpy arrived at Portland at nine in the morning. It was good to be home, it was even better to go on leave.'

1982

January

'After a good leave we return to Portland to discover that *Naiad* flight were close runners-up in the Sopwith Pup trophy. (An FAA award for the best operational effectiveness.)

'That bit of good news astern, the Flight settled down to prepare the aircraft for a routine survey which only required twenty hours rectification work. On the Wednesday evening, 7 January, news arrived that the ship was being sent to Rosyth for ten weeks for repairs on the port engine. The Flight would stay disembarked at Portland. With Dorset under snow the Flight Commander was initially trapped in Martinstown. In the end he and the SMR battled by car through snow drifts to Plymouth in order to collect as much gear as they could to put in the poor overworked mini. The rest of the month saw more flying and the commencement of weapon loads, as well as helping other ships conduct sea acceptance trials.'

February

'The Flight continued at Portland whilst the ship was being repaired at Rosyth. The Flight Commander was confined to bed with a nasty attack of flu. The SMR and another Petty Officer also suffered. On the sixteenth the Flight Commander took off for Edinburgh and arrived in Turnhouse by midday Wednesday after an overnight stop at Finningley due to freezing fog to the north. An interesting snag-free trip that took five hours twenty minutes flying time with an adverse wind.

'After a hectic day on board the daring duo departed Edinburgh at 1345 in low cloud and poor visibility, which got decidedly worse further south. They arrived at Bulmer at 150 feet and had to stay the night in the hospitality of 202 Squadron and Border Radar.

'By Friday the weather was much better and it was with a low-flying clearance that Finningley was found by midday for another overnight stop. Anxious phone calls to Portland got the airfield open on Saturday and the weather cleared sufficiently for a safe arrival at 1345.

'At the end of the month the Flight worked hard on the aircraft to repair it for its annual maintenance check test flight, which was very successful, which meant we could then commence an early Easter leave.'

March

'This month we rejoined the ship and were supposed to go to sea. We came back from our early leave on 9 March prepared for re-embarkation at Rosyth. The aircraft took off at 1020 on 16 March from Portland and flew to Finningley via Brize Norton for an overnight stop courtesy of the boss's parents. The flight equipment and baggage was loaded into a chacon and picked up by low loader. The rest of the flight arrived at Edinburgh by Heron at 1330 on the seventeenth, Scrumpy arrived at 1430 after a good flight via Leeming and Bulmer. Total flight time with an adverse wind was five and half hours.

'We moved back into the ship and got ourselves sorted out, but then most of the Flight moved over to Prestwick to carry out night DIDTACS and flare drops with 819 Squadron. Due to communications and transponder problems the exercise turned into a flare launching and dropping event, but a valuable one hour fifty minutes night flying was achieved. The opportunity for some magnificent mountain flying on the Isle of Aran was not missed and provided excellent training value. On return to Edinburgh, Scrumpy formated on an 819 Sea King carrying the Flight back to Turnhouse, which also gave our aircrewman insight into Sea Kings.

'Due to further engineering problems the ship did not sail, so the Flight took the opportunity to go on weekend in two hire cars. At the end of the month, Flight Commander and aircrewman travelled to Portland to carry out site training AS12 S twelve firings. Good results were obtained with two missiles fired from 400 feet and two from 200 feet. A one-hour twenty minute radar exercise was also accomplished that night to complete the required hours. The ship was further delayed sailing until third of April by steam leaks. Efforts were concentrated on cleanliness both inside and outside the hangar. We were not sure whether April would see *Naiad* at sea. With the Falklands crisis looming large we wondered what it is like in the South Atlantic at this time of year.'

April
'This was the month that was to cause a dramatic change in the course of the navy that had been hit by cutbacks. The Argentines invaded the Falkland Islands and the navy prepared for war despatching a task force 8000 miles south. Meanwhile, *Naiad* was only to get as far as Portland for Basic Operational Sea Training (BOST)!

'The ship made passage to Portland on 5 April and some flying was conducted en route, it was alongside by Wednesday night. After the Easter weekend we prepared for BOST by carrying out some doubled lifts, winching, load lifting and decontamination exercises. The first week was a shakedown week with the staff sea check on Wednesday. Poor visibility and a ships communications failure tended to make a "satisfactory" showing more interesting! On Thursday we had a very successful flying exercise covering dummy drill torpedo drops and continuing with a practice ditching exercise. A single seat life raft was dropped and a Petty Officer demonstrated day/night distress and mini flares from the crash boat whilst the supply officer gave a commentary over the main broadcast. The first harbour week slipped by very easily - enjoyably in fact - with no trouble over deck drills.'

May
'With ships being sunk and lives lost in the Falklands, anything BOST could throw at us seemed tame, but with modest beginnings we went on to achieve good results.

'The first sea week was very low-key for the Flight, particularly as the Flight Commander contracted flue again. Sub Lieutenant Knowles ably stood in during Wednesday but the Flight Commander was recovered enough for the Thursday war. There was no staff monitored flying that week.

'The next week began with a deployment exercise on Monday morning and an opportunity evening Flyex which nearly developed into a search and rescue sortie when a Townsend Thorson ferry suffered an engine room explosion south of Bournemouth. Both the Flight and the ships company reacted very quickly, but our assistance was not needed in the end. Flying continued throughout the week with staff covering submarine exercises, torpedo drops and the Thursday war. An age old saying was relearned, "never question the staff's judgement!"

'The second harbour week produced a very enjoyable Disaster Exercise in which the Flight performed well and with great spirit.

'The third sea week, the ship began and ended it with engineering problems, sailing late on Monday having to spend the weekend in Devonport from Thursday. Otherwise things went well and the ship really started to click. Tactical serials, a weapon load and deployment to HMS Birmingham went very smoothly and the assessment coming from the staff showed "good"!

'Only the last week and a final inspection to go, will *Naiad* make it? Will the Flight hold good? Carry on reading for more sizzling adventures.'

June
'June glorious June! A busy and productive month with changes, excitement and new arrivals. The weather remained typically British and most variable.

'We nearly made the final week of BOST, which was to include the final inspection. We arrived in thick fog after repairs in Plymouth with a boiler defect. We remained alongside all day Wednesday repairing the port engine and finally sailing at 2200. The Flight Commander turned in early ready for his 0500 shake and fought many a Thursday war in his slumbers.

'Rolling over at 0620 the following morning he entered auto, convinced he was late for the inspection. Half-dressed and flying out of his cabin door he almost attacked the steward for not shaking him, only to be answered, "but we are just outside Plymouth Sir, the wars been cancelled!"

'So *Naiad* spent the next week carrying out repairs on the totally unserviceable engine. Scrumpy squeezed itself out from between south of the jetty and HMS *Fox*, with the Flight Commander aircrewman and sadly our departing helicopter controller, Leading Seaman Bland on board, and returned to Portland.

'On 8 June the aircraft and six of the flight detached to RAF Brawdy to become 'flagship Scrumpy' for Vice Admiral Cassells, Flag Officer Plymouth's visit to South Wales. This proved to be an excellent little visit with some very enjoyable flying over the Welsh countryside, landing on football, rugby, cow and sheep dung pitches. We also cut the grass at Haverford West and help to deplete the beer stocks in the local area.

'The planned VIP trip on Thursday had to be cancelled due to severe thunder and lightning which managed to take out Brawdy's transmitters. However, it did not prevent Scrumpy from getting home to Portland by 1330 watching out for the white jagged bits falling out of the clouds.

'There then followed two weeks of warfare and helicopter controller training with the aircraft never missing a sortie and clearing twenty-six hours of flying, mainly anti-submarine exercises, but with the occasional senior officers taxi service for Rear Admiral Gerken to relieve the monotony.

'A weekend in Le Havre in company with HMS *Torquay* also perked up the spirits and stopped the wine cellars.

'On Friday night we took on the mantle of FCS1, but we managed to get a weekend in from Portsmouth. Although originally bound for Scotland on Tuesday, a programme change meant that we did not sail until Wednesday, to Portland, just for a change!'

July

'Throughout July, *Naiad* held the esteemed position of FCS1, split between training submarines in the Clyde and syllabus training back at sunny Portland. It was to be a long hard month for the Flight in which we achieved over forty hours airborne with the only chink of light, the end of the tunnel, being eleven days summer leave.

'The first week of the month, during a pleasant voyage to Faslane, we achieved a very useful flying exercise which included a commanding officers familiarisation, ship controlled approaches, load lifting and winching, and an ad hoc photographic exercise of a passing French force.

'We then carried out a scenic tour of the west coast of Scotland, commencing with a very enjoyable load lifting sortie to the top of Aron to land an expedition party in truly beautiful weather and excellent surroundings. The next day produced some cloudy weather, cancelling a planned low-level navigation exercise around Ben Nevis. However, we managed to explore Skye with four aquaints flown later in the day. That night we carried out a navigation exercise and some more ship controlled approaches.

'After a brief visit to Faslane, *Naiad* sailed at 1745 back into the exercise areas for "cockfight", launching the aircraft at 2130 to locate an Alpinen class Russian intelligence gathering ship in the Rathlyn/Islay gap. This was done with the aid of a beautiful clear night and we returned to carry out some night winching and ship's controlled approaches. A busy week of flying including an AGI Photex, many weapon loads, and the occasional visit to Prestwick. We also dropped sixteen 4.5 inch flares during DIDTACS with 819 Squadron.

'On 19 July we disembarked at Portland after an Ikara* type D firing to allow the Fleet Target Group to embark for HMS *Illustrious'* Sea Dart firings.

'With half the Flight remaining at Portland working on the aircraft, the other half of the Flight, with the Flight Commander, stood watches, remaining on board for the successful *Illustrious* firings. The hangar was full to capacity with the flight of eight target drone aircraft, reduced to six by Sea Dart missiles.

'We ended the month in a typical *Naiad* manner, syllabus training of helicopter controllers and two nights of deck landing practices, plus a continual flow of anti-submarine exercises. All this and Scrumpy seeming to be the only serviceable airborne asset. Still, our disembarkation on Thursday did mean a small spot of summer leave and a much welcomed break.'

August

'We returned from a brief but much-needed summer leave to carry out an engine change on the aircraft and thoroughly prepare from forthcoming Mediterranean deployment.

---

* IKARA was the missile system fitted to the front of some Leander class frigates. The weapon was actually a weapon carrier in its own right in that it carried a Mark 46 ASW torpedo which it dropped as programmed by the ship. Although this was also a primary role of the Wasp its reaction time was much faster.

'On the thirteenth, Scrumpy's new power plant was installed, wet and dry dinghy drills complete and being Friday the thirteenth we set off on weekend. The next week, a long day on Monday saw the boss duty and the Flight working hard to prepare the aircraft for its ground run. The next day the Flight Commander took to the air in a headquarters aircraft to take part in a four ship formation exercise commanded by the Squadron Senior Pilot. On return, the Flight was still working hard to complete maintenance on Scrumpy. On 18 August, after days of glorious weather, the ground run on the aircraft took place in pouring rain and low cloud, only to reveal a defect on the free power turbine governor, causing low rotor speed. The afternoon was spent searching for the correct replacement. However, the Flight Commander did manage to fly under instruments to Yeovilton for his annual handling check. The weather cleared in time for a successful sortie, i.e. he still a Wasp pilot. The next day, with time running out from our planned extended long weekend, the rotary transducer for the torque meter on the intermediate driveshaft decided to wrap its hand in, causing another delay until 1430 for the ground run. Luckily this went smoothly, although the heavens opened again. At 1640 the Flight Commander embarked and pushed through the clouds to complete a successful engine change check test flight, finally finishing at 1900 having also tracked and vibration analysed Scrumpy, which was now finally ready for the Mediterranean. We were ready for *our* weekend! We re-embarked to *Naiad* at 2045 in Weymouth Bay on 23 August. By 29 August we had arrived at Gibraltar having conducted very successful day and night flying exercises including some excellent weapon loads. After arriving we had a memorable flight run ashore to *Bianca's Pizzeria* on the Flight Commander's American Express card.

'We then conducted a passage to Naples with no planned flying. The Flight worked hard to completely repaint the flight deck so that it was pristine ready for Naples and the twenty-fifth activation of the Naval On Call Force Mediterranean (NAVOCFORMED). This is a temporary force of ships that regularly comes together to exercise and practice NATO operating procedures. Ships from the US, UK, Italy, Greece and Turkey are the usual players.'

September

'On Wednesday, 1 September, the NAVOCFORMED Flight Commanders met on board USS *Estocin*, an Oliver Hazard Perry (OHP) class frigate, having had fifteen minutes notice that it was planned. This lack of organisation was to be a continuing theme throughout the activation of NAVOCFORMED. The *Estocin* had a Sea Sprite helicopter and four pilots. The Italian ship *Alpino* operated an Agusta 212 with three pilots and the Greek ship, *Themistocles*, operated an Alouette 3 with two, and then there was just the one of us. The meeting was friendly and different concepts of operations, aircraft limitations and cross deck operations were discussed using the wonderful American publication which is so restrictive and occasionally ludicrous, called HOSTACS. (A NATO publication – Helicopter Operating from Ships Other Than Aircraft Carriers.)

'Thereafter our five day stay in Naples consisted of getting to know each other, the Flight took a look around the other flight decks and aircraft to prepare ourselves for cross deck operations and we ensured that Scrumpy was in good fighting form. In excellent weather that was generally to be the norm we all started to get much browner, except for the SMR whose feet and ankles swelled up after flight deck painting, causing him to check the springs on his bunk.

'The 6 September saw the force sail for week one and Scrumpy launched for a photographic exercise with the Italian Agusta 212. Any thought of encrypted call signs disappeared when over the airwaves came, "hey Steve let's go up front now and take the pictures!" We then began the first cross deck operations to *Alpino* which proved no problem. Meanwhile, after a thorough briefing the Alouette 3 landed safely on our deck. This was found to be a safe operation with the Alouette landing in its normal 1 o'clock or 11 o'clock position (day visual flying only up to sea state three). The following morning at 0200, Scrumpy launched for a surface search which proved to be a good one hour twenty-five minutes sea Navex for the aircrewman. The "enemy" were not found because the *Alpino* had decided to cheat! At 1045 that day, while slumbering gently to regain his eight hours, the Flight Commander heard the pipe, "HELICOPTER DITCHED, HELICOPTER DITCHED".

'His first reaction was, "can't be, I'm still in bed!" Twelve minutes later Scrumpy was airborne dodging the lightning and ignoring the high sea state heading towards the position of the American ships ditched Sea Sprite. Luckily, all the crew were recovered by the American ships sea boat, having escaped safely from the aircraft which took only 5 to 7 seconds to sink. They do not carry flotation gear! Scrumpy spent the next two hours searching for wreckage but there was very little. It subsequently transpired that the Sea Sprite had suffered a tail rotor failure. Now there were three helicopters left.

'The week continued with Scrumpy performing; conducting anti-submarine exercises, passenger transfers and cross deck operations with the other ships. Smooth winch transfers were carried out to the Turkish ship who we found to be precise with the flight deck drill and always gave us an excellent wind. However, the standards of personal flight safety with regard to clothing and ear defenders was poor. This was generally the case with the Greeks and Italians also.

'At the weekend, in Livorno, the Flight Commander tried unsuccessfully to cheer up the American aviators but he had more success cheering himself up on Ouzo with the Greeks. The visit gave us all an opportunity to see the merits, or otherwise, of Italian architecture in Florence and Pisa. On Sunday the Italian *Agusta 212* returned to *Alpino* having flown ashore the previous Thursday with hydraulic problems. Week two continued with Scrumpy flying in the wee hours for surface searches and carrying out some successful flare drops on "surprised enemies"! We also carried out a photographic exercise and marking for *Naiad's* Ikara firing and recovered the missile debris very quickly using a ships diver in a double lift harness. The weekend was spent in Genoa.

'The last two weeks of NAVOCFORMED were involved with exercise "Display Determination", a frustrating period with little planned activity, although Scrumpy did manage some reconnaissance and probe missions. Palermo provided the weekend break and afterwards *Naiad* had two days running the show. For the first time a comprehensive flying programme was produced and on time. This was obviously too much of a shock because the Greeks went unserviceable and the Italians claimed they could only carry out winch transfers to *Naiad*!

'*Thus, in the final week, as in the preceding three, Scrumpy carried the aviation load with surface searches and cross deck operations. We landed safely on the Greek ship's deck but had to hover over the Americans immense deck due to their strict adherence to limits. The ludicrous thing is they are cleared to land an RN Sea King!*

'On the penultimate night after superb service, even the mighty Scrumpy wavered when the fore and aft cyclic actuator went unserviceable causing a slightly unnerving porpoising through the goldfish bowl night sky. Unfortunately, during its replacement it was found that the rod eye end bearing connecting the actuator to the control run was badly worn. So, as NAVOCFORMED ended, we waited a replacement bearing to put Scrumpy back into the sky for our forthcoming Dartmouth training squadron deployment with HMS *Fearless*.

'Time to paint the flight deck guardrails grey!'

Chapter 6

The Cod Wars

The so called Cod Wars were a series of disputes between the UK and Iceland over fishing in the waters around the island. In the end, Iceland had the upper hand as it threatened to pull out of NATO which, during the Cold War, would have been a disaster, as the island had a significantly strategic position. That didn't stop there being a series of clashes at sea between the tiny Icelandic Navy with small gunboats and the Royal Navy. The first major confrontation was between 1958 and 1961 and ended when the UK agreed to a 12 mile limit, albeit with some provision for British trawlers to fish inside in certain areas and at certain times of the year. However, in September 1972 the Iceland government unilaterally increased the limit to 50 miles. The government, which had just been elected, decided that they were not bound by previous agreements made by the preceding administration.

Almost immediately they deployed patrol ships which streamed net cutters behind them which they would attempt to drag across a trawlers wires to cut them. At first it was very successful, for example, on 18 January 1973 eighteen trawlers had their nets cut.

On 17 May all British trawlers withdrew, two days later they returned, but this time they were escorted by Royal Navy frigates. All that summer the two sides confronted each other and ramming incidents between the Icelandic gunboats and RN frigates were common. However, with mediation through NATO, on 8 November an agreement was signed which allowed the British to fish within certain areas of the 50 mile limit as well as limiting catch sizes.

It didn't end there. In November 1975 the Icelandic government increased its territorial waters to 200 miles. The British government refused to recognise the change and the third and most serious Cod War began. In the end the Royal Navy deployed a total of twenty-two frigates. Several older ships (HMS *Jaguar* and HMS *Lincoln*) were taken out of reserve and fitted with wooden plated bows to protect them in ramming incidents. The navy was prepared to accept damage; HMS *Yarmouth* had its bow torn off, HMS *Diomede* had a forty foot gash ripped in one side, HMS *Eastbourne's* structure was so badly damaged it was reduced to a moored training ship. Even after agreement had been reached, HMS *Falmouth* rammed the Icelandic ship *Vis Tyr* which was in the process of cutting a British trawler's nets. Despite being rammed twice the *Tyr* still managed to cut the trawlers wires, but was severely damaged in the process.

Once again the threat to pull out of NATO and shut the base at Keflavik, which would have had serious consequences for the protection of the north Atlantic, was successful. On 1 June a final agreement was reached whereby up to twenty-four British trawlers were allowed to operate within 200 miles, but were limited to a tiny total of 30,000 tons of fish. The effect on the UK fishing industry was marked and in 2012 some compensation was eventually paid to the fishermen who had lost their livelihoods. The cost to the Royal Navy was over a million pounds.

Many of the ships deployed carried Wasps. There follows three accounts of how the aircraft fared in what was a very unusual situation for the Royal Navy.

HMS *Andromeda*

Tony Hogg was the second pilot of the Wasp Flight in HMS *Andromeda* for the third Cod War. The following is his account:

'Having done well on flying training I was selected for the single engine Wasp helicopter. Similar to the army Scout helicopter, but with castoring wheels not skids; the Wasp was essentially the "eyes and ears" of a frigate and an ASW weapon carrier. Precisely designed for operation from those frigates, with short blades and high rotor RPM, the Wasp seemed on first encounter to be a most unlikely looking flying machine. Allowing for many foibles such as self-destructing windscreen wipers and a relatively low thrust wooden tail rotor, together with other traits, it was built of strong stuff to handle frigate deck work in severe weathers. Experienced Wasp pilots loved the machine but in my first tour it was a significant challenge. In water (should the engine stop) the Wasp was known to sink like a stone and it also dropped like a stone in "engine offs". With no wheel brakes, but wheels that castored to enable swivelling into the relative wind on deck before take-off, shore based landings were arrested simply by having the rear wheels castored inwards. One day at Merryfield (with instructor Tony Horton) the shock of ground contact at the conclusion of an engine off, caused this novice to sever the tail rotor drive shaft with the main rotor blades. We didn't realise this had happened until conducting an all-round lookout; before taking off again we were confronted with an organised display of tail rotor components laid out over a large area on the runway.

'There were fifty-five ramming incidents between the Royal Navy frigates and Icelandic patrol vessels during the third Cod War – Nov 75-Jun 76. The dispute was over fishing rights. The aggressive Icelanders used up to eight patrol ships to attempt to cut the trawls of the UK fishing fleet fishing in their waters. The Royal Navy fielded several frigates, RFAs, MAF vessels and Defence tugs. Some frigates from the Royal Navy's reserve fleet were fitted with railway sleepers around the bow to prepare them better to survive ramming incidents. RN steam frigates found close manoeuvring with the Icelanders' capable, robust and highly responsive diesel patrol craft hugely challenging. In the light of Dennis Healey's defence cuts, there was, of course, more at stake for the Royal Navy than simply fish. The dispute ended in 1976 after Iceland threatened to close access to the NATO base at Keflavik.

'Married in August 1975, it was sod's law that I deployed immediately to the Mediterranean in HMS *Andromeda*. But Christmas for the newlyweds lay ahead. Wrong! HMS *Andromeda* deployed in December and over Christmas to do battle with the Icelanders in those huge and freezing seas off Iceland. *Andromeda* was involved in two major ramming incidents on 28 December and 7 January, having to return to base after the second incident for repairs.

'So what did it mean for a "green" second pilot?

'Certainly the most significant impression was of the close manoeuvring of ships, the dangers concerned and the major collisions themselves which generally occurred on the sides of the flight deck. It was not uncommon to find the bows of an Icelander breaking through the flight deck safety nets and overhanging the flight deck itself. The Christmas "Sods opera" was an all-time great with me having constructed a frigate out of cardboard and attached around my waist as the fair *Andromeda* who, during the performance, was regularly interfered with by the irritating "Janner with his spanner" in the form of a very large ship's gunnery officer. One day, a routine lecture on the hazard of alcohol given by the doctor in the wardroom finished abruptly as the bar was destroyed, either by the impact to the ship's side behind the bar of an Icelander, or a freak wave.'

It was not uncommon to find the bows of an Icelander breaking through the flight deck safety nets and overhanging the flight deck itself. *(Tony Hogg)*

'But seriously… the Wasp was extremely rugged but also unforgiving. The threat of icing was a constant concern. The weather seemed to be binary: it either consisted of giant columns of snow–laden cloud or crystal clear days with extreme visibility. On reflection, and with the benefit of many years' experience since, at times in very poor weather conditions, we probably flew the Wasp rather too far from the ship. The only way of finding ones way back was by real discipline and skill with the "circular plotting board", or by courtesy of a simple radio direction finding.

'Flying consisted mainly of locating and plotting the position of the UK fishing feet and Icelandic patrol craft. I flew many sorties with "Tom", a giant trawler skipper liaison officer from Grimsby, in conditions that taxed the aircrew. Tom was open about his fear of flying and would only join me aloft if I held his hand throughout the flight! Two huge men in a small cockpit holding hands!'

Bundled up against the cold. *(Tony Hogg)*

'The rugged little Wasp shrugged off tremendous punishment in deck landings with the Leander class frigate decks seeming impossibly small. Windscreen wipers were to be used sparingly when absolutely needed, as they were prone to disintegration in snow. A "heads" (toilet) visit before the flight was particularly advisable as the effects of involuntary release later in the cold conditions risked electrocution from the electric socks that we wore.

'Again, with the benefits of many years of flying and ship command experience, this was a silly war that should have been avoided by the politicians. The conditions were extreme and it was surprising that only one life was lost in that fishing dispute. It always seemed to me, on reflection, an anathema for good seamen to intentionally collide with others in those often frightening sea conditions.

'I certainly "learnt about flying from that", in my time off Iceland. Rescues later in 1978, in very wintry conditions off Cornwall, where a number of medals were won (I was awarded an Air Forces Cross), were definitely facilitated for me by experience from conditions off Iceland in 1976.

'The Wasp was a remarkable aircraft. The tail rotor of today's 15 tonne Merlin helicopter is about the same size and thrust as the Wasp main rotor of 1976. Such is life…'

HMS *Naiad*

Another account comes from Bob Turner who was the Flight Commander of HMS *Naiad* during the third Cod War:

'Whilst the embarked Wasp helicopters were primarily tasked with reconnaissance, or stores and passenger transfer missions, they began to develop harassing tactics against the Icelandic gunboats. This arose to some extent through frustration with the Rules of Engagement by which the ships were constrained in their riding off manoeuvres and by the fact that the ships were sometimes too far away from an incident when the gunboat began to close in to cut the nets. From mid-April onwards, *Naiad* Flight had started to get very close to the gunboats' bridges as they started their approach to the final circular track around the victim fishing vessel. The aim was simply to disrupt the Icelanders' ship handling and buy sufficient time to enable the fishing vessel to recover its nets before the gunboat could cut them. The Wasp was extremely manoeuvrable and could be positioned very close to the bridge wing of the gunboat. This created a very heavy and disruptive downwash, often enhanced by whipped off wave tops and deafening noise. This cumulative effect made ship handling, bridge communication and the passing of conning orders virtually impossible and on several occasions caused the gunboats to break off from their cutting manoeuvre. Most importantly, it gave a degree of confidence and comfort to fishing vessel skippers that, even though the nearest Royal Naval escort was possibly 30 miles away, there was still some mutual support and limited protection provided by the helicopter.

'The Captain of HMS *Naiad*, was himself a very experienced helicopter pilot and was aware of the risks. He satisfied himself that the aircrew, pilot, Lieutenant Bob Turner and aircrewman, Leading Aircrewman 'Titus' Oates, were driving to the edge of the operational limits but not beyond.

'However, on 26 April, an opportunity arose which moved the stakes a little higher. Turner and Oates had been tasked on a search mission to find the un-located gunboat *Aegir*. Sometime after take-off they received a radio message that *Aegir* was closing the fishing fleet at speed, and that apart from the ocean-going tug *Euroman* there was no protection. *Euroman* was very strong, but much slower than any gunboat.

'Arriving at the scene, Turner and Oates got stuck into their harassment role. In Turner's words, "we had the starboard front undercarriage wheel nestling in the bridge wing". The bridge team in *Aegir* were really unhappy and there was lots of spray, noise and confusion.'

Turner and Oates in intimidation mode. *(Bob Turner)*

'A heaving line and wheel spanner were produced as a deterrent to the helo, but the attempt to lob them up into the rotor was blasted away by the downwash, much to Titus Oate's amusement. Meanwhile, looking across the cockpit, I could see that *Euroman* was approaching from the port side and, despite her speed disadvantage, lining up for a possible ramming attempt. I told Titus to keep the *Aegir* bridge team's attention and from the faces on the bridge wing I could see that he certainly was achieving that. I found out later that he was gesticulating and performing forms of obscenity probably well outside the Geneva Convention. By this stage, *Euroman* was disappearing from my view below the helicopter, but I could see that she was under heavy helm to port. I called to Titus to give me the "up up" call at the right moment and he did just that. As Wasp 324 disappeared vertically from the scene, with Titus still energetically performing his lewd routine, *Euroman* passed under us and struck *Aegir* fair and square on her port side. As we flew past moments later we could see that *Aegir* had hauled off and that there was some damage to her hull. It was a great feeling which helped to overcome the frustrations felt by all the Naval, RMAS and fishermen in previous months. We called this tactic the "Rammex". There was plenty of chatter between the fishing fleet on the radio after this incident and Mike Osborne, our MAFF liaison Officer, was particularly happy. We had to admit that we had been lucky with the relative wind over the *Aegir's* deck at the time and the small fuel load then in 324. These factors had given us the scope to fly the Wasp right to the limits and get in really close.'

There was also considerable press interest at this time and Bob recalls another incident where the Royal Navy once again managed to impress:

'There had been considerable media interest in the action in the Designated Fishing Area, both by television crews and journalists. To participate, they were normally committed to at least ten days away from the UK and each unit returning home often carried at least one journalist for the transit.

'Peregrine Worsthorne of the Sunday Telegraph was transferred from RFA *Tidepool* to HMS *Naiad* by Wasp Helicopter on 29 April, a trip which he did not enjoy. However, he was soon finely accommodated as a personal guest of the Captain's and settled in quickly to the routine transit south.

'At this stage, the First Lieutenant, thought it would be a good idea to hold a Ship's Variety Concert, commonly known in the Fleet as a "Sods' Opera". This was soon adjusted to be named "The Euro Naiad Song Contest" and each department onboard was expected to contribute. The contest was to be compered by the Captain's Steward, Leading Steward Jimmy Green, who was a particularly garrulous and likeable rogue, whether afloat or on a run ashore. Jimmy Green had already eyed Peregrine's fine dark green velvet smoking jacket and persuaded him to loan it for the duration of the contest.

'The contest commenced after supper in the junior ratings' dining hall on the evening of 2 May. HMS *Naiad* was by then on track down the Irish Sea in deteriorating weather. Peregrine was seated next to the Captain who had thanked him for lending the smoking jacket to the compere and explained the form for the evening, including how he should vote. Peregrine was amused by the concept, humour and quality of the earlier acts. The ship's company was in a relaxed "up channel night" mode and the tins of beer were flowing freely and perhaps not totally in accordance with the Queen's Regulations. As the show went on, the weather deteriorated further, as did the quality of the acts. By now, *Naiad* was rolling heavily; the Captain calmly explained some of the lyrics to Peregrine, the rows of steel chairs slid from side to side in unison and empty beer cans rattled across the deck. Peregrine was becoming increasingly worried by the state of his velvet jacket as Jimmy Green wound up the tempo at the same rate as he was spilling beer. Although "Nil Points" was a common score (and the Supply Department even scored minus as supper had included Arctic Roll for pudding yet again), the stokers were in the lead after an epic performance from some of their more robust leading hands. A serious looking signalman then appeared, barged to the front, and spoke to the Captain. He quickly withdrew from the dining hall along with the Operations Officer and a number of key players. Clearly something was afoot.

'Shortly afterwards the pipe was made and we were off on a search and rescue mission to assist the French trawler fleet caught in storm force winds to the south of Ireland. This happened quickly and effectively and Peregrine was heard to remark how amazed he had been by the Royal Navy's ability to switch from the exacting and arduous task in the fishing grounds, to a humour enriched and relaxed party mode, then immediately and seamlessly switch back again to the serious business of search and rescue in storm conditions. He had also lost track of his smoking jacket, but this was returned later the next day. It had received considerable attention from the Chinese laundry man, but was still not looking quite as sharp as when it had first arrived on-board.

'Peregrine was later to write favorably of his experiences.'

HMS Tartar

This account is from Gordon Douglas, who was a member of the ship's flight and who later went on to become an AS12 missile aimer and finally a fully qualified aircrewman. *Tartar* was a Tribal class frigate:

'During the time spent on *Tartar* we were sent to the North Atlantic, above 70 degrees north, the Arctic Circle. This was to provide a naval presence and to ensure the safety of the trawlermen and their boats during what was called The

Cod War. Fishing rights and territorial waters were being disputed between Britain and Iceland and it was up to the Royal Navy to police the water around the UK and the protection of the UK's fishermen in the extreme north. Before departure a modest training period was conducted, mainly in attempting to avoid collision with large naval tugs.

'It was immediately apparent upon arrival above the Arctic Circle that the weather was to be the main factor to get used to. It was bitterly cold as well as rough. Much time was spent below decks due to the weather. (Apart from the helicopter crews.) A standard announcement on the ships Tannoy system was, "the upper deck is now out of bounds; hands to flying stations". The helicopter was always needed to fly in all weathers, either carrying out routine searches or transferring personnel between vessels.

'After the initial few weeks we came to accept the fact we were going to get colder than most. Our foul weather clothing was good enough for weather encountered in the UK, but inside the Arctic Circle the weather was extreme and the standard issue foul weather clothing was simply not enough. We did manage to wangle the best foul weather gear from the supply officer, who also happened to be one of the F.D.O.'s. Eight arctic Parkas arrived on the ship; every member of the flight was issued with one. They were to prove to be invaluable in keeping the harsh icy winds from eating through to the bone.

'The ships cooks also did a grand job of looking after our welfare, piping hot food would be brought up to us in the middle of the night, and was well received by all of us. We had to contend with a lot outside, but the cooks must have suffered having to supply hot food round the clock in the very rough seas we were in.

'I imagine for the aircrew, the flying must have been bitterly cold as most of the sorties were flown with the front doors off, ensuring that escape from the aircraft could be easier. The aircrew did have the benefit of flying suits fitted with an electrical harness that provided them with heated gloves and socks, so that at least their extremities would be warm. For us, the maintenance crews, we hid in the warmth of the hanger or electrical maintenance room (EMR), until the helicopter returned. Then we got cold stowing the "cab" (helicopter). On a Tribal class frigate, putting the helicopter to bed was not the easiest of jobs to do on a normal deployment; in these colder climes it was even more hazardous. We didn't have the luxury of safety lines so a member of the team used to hang onto your clothing when leaning over the side to pull up the safety nets and then again when placing the heavy covers over the top of the hanger to keep the helicopter covered up.

'On a Tribal Class, the hanger was below the flight deck, the flight deck then became the hanger deck. The Wasp would be positioned over the deck in a precise location to be lowered down into the void below. Then, the deck dropped to swallow up most of the helicopter, leaving ten to twelve inches sticking up above the flight deck level. Some eight to ten curved covers were manually positioned and then locked into place over the top of the helicopter to ensure the sea and wind didn't get in. It was hard, and at times dangerous, manoeuvring these huge covers, especially at night in stormy seas when the flight deck would be pitching and heaving.

'Life really got interesting when HMS *Tartar* met with an Icelandic gunboat with hostile intent. We used to play games like "dodgems" with Her Majesties war canoes. Tannoy announcements such as; "Stand by for collision port side" would be immediately followed by "Stand by for collision starboard side". At one stage we were all at our emergency station in the junior rates dining hall when the usual message came over the tannoy, we all braced for the impending bump and scrapping of hull against hull, which came seconds later. To our shock the blue sea beyond the ships bulkhead, or outside, depending on your perspective, was now very visible. Gone was the ships library. Replacing the library was a long gapping thirty foot gash down the port side of the ship. Most of us bolted to the other side of the dining room, which was our shelter station, a Royal Marine tried to keep everyone calm, but was trampled over in the rush to get away from the new ventilation hole that had appeared.'

'These comings together were quite common, not so that gaping gashes resulted, but the grinding of metal on metal sound was unnerving and potentially lethal. The Icelandic gunboat skippers would manoeuvre there vessels very close to the Royal Navy boats to provoke the naval Captains into some form of retaliation. A major coming together occurred when a gunboat met HMS *Falmouth* and the *Falmouth* rammed the gunboat head on, not once but twice. All this whilst a camera team were filming the whole thing for national news. Photographs distinctly show the two impact points.

HMS *Falmouth* after her coming together with a gunboat. *(Gordon Douglas)*

'Such was the damage to *Falmouth* that the bows had been removed up to the damage control bulkhead, any further aft and the ship would have been in immediate danger of taking in water or worse! *Tartar* was tasked to escort the *Falmouth* back to the UK, or until a rendezvous was made with a pair of ocean going tugs which had been despatched to escort HMS *Falmouth* to dock for repair. The *Tartar* was then to return to her patrol area above seventy degrees north. For a war where no bullets as such were fired, there was a great deal of damage to Her Majesty's warships.

'Tribal Class frigates had a unique and sneaky feature which became very useful in deterring Icelandic gunboats from venturing too close to us. Tribals were fitted with stabilisers - fitted below the waterline - and were retractable inside the hull when sea conditions allowed. They normally protruded about 1.5 metres from the side of the ship beneath the waterline. A technique we would use to deter the Icelandic gunboats from wanting to get too close was to turn the *Tartar* port or starboard, which would mean the stabilisers would then protrude at right angles. If a gunboat came too close to us it would impale itself on the stabilisers. This happened during one meeting with the Icelandic gunboat *Tyr*! So bad was her damage, *Tyr* transmitted a distress call (Mayday). Our Captain elected to escort the now sinking gunboat into Reykjavik harbour. Upon leaving the harbour we were unceremoniously pelted by the locals with rotten vegetables and rocks from the breakwater. After our hasty retreat from the Icelandic coast we again returned to our patrolling of the sea to ensure our fishermen had us handy in case of more harassment from the gunboats.

'Every morning whilst operating above 70 degrees north we would start by freeing our part of ship of ice which had accumulated overnight. Too much ice would possibly topple the ship due to the excess weight, so we would remove the ice with rubber hammers. You had to avoid touching anything metal with your bare flesh as you would end up leaving your skin on the frozen metal.

'Life on the flight deck was good; we had the best kit for the weather out of everyone on board. Eight arctic weather Parkas had been procured before we left the UK and the helicopter ground crews had them all barring one which was given to the Captain. It was probably "Merry" England's, the SMR, as he never left the confines of the flight office. It was bitterly cold and we were very exposed on the back end of the ship. Whatever the weather we would be outside in the elements. On one occasion it was so cold the helicopter winch froze. No matter how much tapping and hammering it wouldn't budge, it had been frozen solid. There was many an occasion when the rest of the ships company wasn't allowed on the upper deck due to the appalling weather, we would be out in the elements getting the helicopter ready for flight or putting it away after a flight.

'During one routine winch transfer, John Pugh, the flight aircrewman, was pulled from the Wasp when winching to an RFA or Royal Fleet Auxiliary, a tanker. It was Sunday morning and we had been tasked to collect the Padre for the Sunday church service. It was only a short flight as the RFA was only a matter of yards away as the transfer was to be conducted whilst we were refuelling at sea, or RASing! The helicopter hovered over the flight deck of the RFA and John lowered the winch hook with the rescue harness attached. The ground crew then walked into the hanger with the winch wire to place the attached harness around the Padre who was waiting in the hanger. John pulled the wire and gesticulated with his hand to move the Padre under the helicopter, the Padre needed to be directly under the helicopter to be winched up. Without looking to see why the winch wire was being tugged the crew member on deck pulled the wire again in an attempt to get closer to the Padre, this resulted in John pulling the wire even harder, followed by another tug from the deck crew member, which then pulled John out of the helicopter. Fortunately, John was wearing his dispatcher harness so was now dangling on the end of his harness a few feet below the helicopter and thirty or forty feet above the deck of the RFA. As the two ships were only a few yards from each other it was observed by all the upper deck crews. Our aircrewman did manage to clamber back into the helicopter and successfully winch the Padre into the Wasp, you can only imagine what he must have been feeling. We laughed about the incident for ages, but it took John a long time to see the humorous side.

'The seas in these parts were lethal. It wasn't uncommon to see some of the fishing vessels disappearing under huge mountains of water. One night, about three in the morning, most of the ships company were in their beds due to the heavy seas outside, the ship was bouncing around a great deal when we went to bed that night. Many guys, including myself, had a habit of hooking their beds up to make a "V" shape in which we placed our mattress. This helped keep us in our beds when the ship was moving around, this was one such night. The tannoy burst into life with "Brace", nothing more, from the Captain. Followed immediately by one heck of a bump then by a loud slap as the flat underside at the back end of the ship struck the water! The subsequent ripple had several people thrown out of their beds! A few limbs were broken throughout the ship as a result of that impact. For several days, as a result of the continuous bad weather, no one was allowed on the upper decks to check for damage. Not even the flight, which was unusual, even in the worst condition we normally had to get the Wasp ready for flight, but not this time. The ship was now without radar, so maintenance crews needed to check that as a matter of urgency. Several other systems had failed and they too needed investigating. A leak had been found in one of the forward sonar compartments and this was being bailed out by hand into the forward head or toilets. The bailing out continued for many days to keep the water level down in the forward sonar space.

'After 3-4 days, when the seas had calmed down to a level that was deemed safe enough to get personnel out onto the top decks, the ships company ventured out to check what damage we had. As it transpired it was extensive! Our main 909 Radar had gone, literally. All external ladders and emergency life rafts had gone, as had emergency suits and radios. Also the ships boats. The breakwater, the huge "V" shaped metal barrier immediately before "A" turret, was now parallel with the main deck. "A" turret itself had been rotated round and the barrel had struck the superstructure and put a dent in the ships side. Several days later, when the alignment on the barrel was checked, it was found the barrel had been damaged too and rendered unusable. Bridge windows had been smashed in and required temporary repairs to keep the elements out.

'The extensive damage was reported back to the Admiralty in the UK and as a result of having no emergency boats or emergency equipment, we were to return to the UK for essential repairs. The *Tartar* was ordered to Newcastle to carry out the repairs and was to depart immediately, one of the ocean going tugs was ordered to escort the *Tartar* back to UK waters and safety. At the entrance to the River Tyne our First Lieutenant asked the Captain if he could send a party of men over the side to paint part of the ship so that we would look presentable for the transit up the River Tyne to our berth. The Captain replied, "no, let the public see what we have gone through for their fish".

'The ship repairers soon had us ready for sea again and with our short visit over we were back to sea and back to the Icelandic gunboats and their ramming tactics. On the *Tartar*, we had enough problems with fuel pumps catching fire - as well as cracks in the hull caused by the collisions. Compartments were being pumped out continuously to keep the water down.

'Back on the flight deck during a routine maintenance check of the rotor head I noticed a potential problem with a couple of the rotor blades. There were gaps where the end laminates - layers – were. I was able to slide feeler gauge blades under several of the laminates, or doubler plates. On checking the good book for the tolerances for this type of thing, I read there was no such tolerance. It should not have been possible to slide anything under. I informed "Bunny" Warren, my Petty Officer, who duly informed "Merry" England, the SMR. It was decided that a full set of new rotor blades were required. The boss was informed, he in turn told the Captain - chain of command in action.

'The rotor blades were changed and I flew a test flight to check them out and track the blades. Track the blades means to get the rotors to fly in such a way that they fly a similar profile with minimal vibration. Getting as little vibration as possible was critical to the helicopters flight characteristics. This was down to me. My job was to sit in the left seat next to the pilot and direct a strobe light at reflectors fitted to the tips of each rotor blade. Each reflector was a different colour to identify which rotor needed adjustment. If a rotor flew out of true it wasn't a big deal as long as it didn't cause any vibration. If a blade flew out of true then small adjustments to the control rods were made and another test flight to confirm if the vibration was reduced. I would do the adjusting of the control rods. My Petty Officer, Bunny Warren, would check my work and someone else would oversee the whole operation. It was beholden on me to get it right as I was the one who had to go up with the pilot and do the in-flight checks. The Wasp was unique in that the rotors were tracked for a smooth flight and not, as for other helicopters, when the blades had to fly in nigh on the same flight path. For my occasional flying duties they gave me a whole sixty-six pence a day.

'As a result of my finding the defective rotors I had been recommended and received a commendation for my vigilance. I also appeared in the Fleet Air Arm's

Cockpit magazine. That was the second time, first on 848 for a bob weight, now this one.

'A unique feature of the Tribal class is, instead of the hanger being at the same level as the flight deck, the helicopter had to be lowered into its hanger. The Wasp would be rotated on the deck, then once in position lowered into the hanger, the flight deck now becoming the hanger deck. This lift became very useful on one occasion.

'During another routine inspection one of the front oleos (shock absorber) was found unserviceable, to repair it would mean leaving our operational area and finding calm waters so that the helicopter could be raised on jacks to allow us to change the unserviceable items. This meant being off station for nearly two days, whilst essential it was obvious the Captain of the Tartar was not too happy. I had an idea, and put it to my chief thinking I would be ignored. He informed the boss, Lieutenant John Skinner, who then suggested to the Captain there may be a way to change the defective item without much time delay. It would require the ship to maintain a steady course but not leave the operating area.

'My idea was, instead of using jacks to raise the helicopter, we utilise the lift and lower the lift under the defective oleo. The helicopter was positioned then lashed to the deck. A single jack was placed under the Wasp closest to the defective oleo, simply to take the weight and not lift the helicopter, and then the flight deck was lowered until the wheel was free of the deck. The wheel and oleo were then removed, the new item replaced and everything retightened. The lift was now raised and the jack taking the weight removed. The work was complete in less than an hour. The Captain was happy and we had a working helicopter. My boss wrote to the squadron and informed them of what we had done and the practice became standard operating procedure for similar problems on Tribal class ships. Having the lift on this occasion became as asset and not inconvenience!

'As I was the flights flying maintainer I had a full set of flying kit which I made up myself in the survival centre back at Portland. The kit was frequently used as I used to go flying with the boss and John every opportunity I could. On one occasion, the Tartar was working off Murmansk, Russia, getting intelligence information and generally maintaining a presence. During one night flight, we came upon a Soviet Riga class frigate; we illuminated it with the Wasps landing light and flew past it several times. We then came across a Russian November class submarine on the surface and repeated our game of directing our landing lamp at it. The Russians must have reported our presence because it wasn't long before our ships Helicopter Controller (HC), reported two bogeys closing us. Bogeys are the code words used for unidentified aircraft.

'Within minutes we were passed close enough to make the Wasp bounce around the night sky in the slipstream of two very fast jets. We suspected they were MiGs, but at night we could only guess. It was very frightening. To make matters worse the Riga now managed to get a radar lock on us with one of her gun systems and the pilot, John, had to fight really hard to break the lock and flee back to *Tartar*. I found the cat and mouse element quite exiting and was unaware at the time of the danger of being caught in a ships gunnery radar.'

Chapter 7

The Falklands

The Falklands War would at last allow the Wasp to Bare its teeth. *(Steve George)*

In 1982 Argentina invaded the Falklands and the Wasp was one of the aircraft that deployed to meet the threat. In fact two Wasps were already there, embarked in the Ice Patrol Ship HMS *Endurance*. Other aircraft soon followed in; the Type 12 Frigates, HMS *Rothesay*, *Yarmouth* and *Plymouth*, the Type 21, HMS *Active*, the survey ships, *Hecla*, *Herald* and *Hydra*. Aircraft were also embarked on the Merchant ships *Contender Bezant* (two aircraft) and *St Helena*, although this last ship didn't arrive until after the war was over.

Below is the amazing account of the Flight embarked in HMS *Endurance*, the only RN warship in the area when hostilities broke out. Tony Ellerbeck was the Flight Commander and his story shows just how flexible the Wasp was when called on for the first time, to go to war for real:

'Our final work period in Antarctica over and our penultimate visit to Stanley before return to the UK to be scrapped, we called in at South Georgia on route to investigate claims that the Argentine Navy (ARA) had breached diplomatic etiquette to drop off scrap metal dealers at the old whaling stations. Although their intentions were known through SIGINT (Signal Intelligence) no sign of the Argentineans was found. However, after we had headed off to the Falklands an intercept from Buenos Aires to ARA *Buen Successo*, congratulating them, was intercepted.

'We had just disembarked both Wasps and all personnel to a shearing shed at Green Patch. This would allow HMS *Endurance* to use the hangar as accommodation for the replacement Royal Marine detachment they were about to collect from Montevideo, Uruguay. The Flight were going, carry out some high level vertical photography of Berkley Sound and also help eradicate infected sheep from the Tumbledown area during our time ashore. CPO Kingshot and I were also planning to catch a few sea trout in the interim!

'Sunday morning was designated as the time for the final football match for the Stanley Shield. As two of the Flight were in the ship's team I flew them over and waited to watch the match. Halfway through the first half, Captain Nick Barker came over and told me there was to be an urgent meeting at Government House regarding the South Georgia situation. At the meeting it was decided that *Endurance* would sail the next day to South Georgia and the Flight were to re-embark. We were told we could leave kit behind as the plan was we would return after a week or so and allow the roulement of troops to take place, albeit somewhat delayed! As the FI detachment of Royals had not been to South Georgia they came with us and our Droggies (hydrographers) were over the moon because they could stay in Stanley to draw up all their charts and soundings in the comfort of Government House billiard room. It would save them time in Taunton Hydrographic Office upon the return to UK. Little did we know then what was to happen; especially, because at this time we were the ONLY RN ship south of the equator anywhere in the world!

'On arrival in South Georgia we went straight to Grytviken for two reasons; the Foreign Office didn't want to upset Argentina and we wanted to have urgent discussions with the British Antarctic Survey (BAS) Base Commander and personnel. During the passage the shuttle diplomacy carried out by Al Haig between Argentina and Britain was fully underway trying to find a compromise to the impasse. The British wanted the scrap men to complete an immigration process and Argentina refused to allow this to happen. We stood by to remove them when instructed.

'Two days later a French yacht (!) reported that an Argentine naval Antarctic patrol ship - a modern *Endurance* equivalent - the *Ara Bahia Paraiso* was in the vicinity. This was surprising as there hadn't been any SIGINT of her passage. We were delighted because we thought that now they were removing the scrap men we could all go home and finish our seven month deployment.

'David Wells and I took Captain Barker on a recce. The orders from the Foreign Office were that we were not to be seen, so a nap-of-the-earth flight to a small bowl on a peninsula overlooking Leith was undertaken. There at anchor was the BAH P and in the silence of the bay, two boats could be heard and seen ferrying back and forth between ship and shore. You can imagine our shock when we saw the boats going in full and returning empty and we realised that this could only go one way now. Whilst we took in the scene and David used the Hasselblad camera to record the action, we were very surprised to hear the sound of a jet engine start and to see an Alouette helicopter get airborne from the BAH P. They did one circuit of Leith and then unerringly flew straight towards our concealed position. When almost overhead they obviously spotted the dayglo and red paint of the Wasp - they could hardly miss it! They circled us waving and headed off to Stromness whaling station. We started up and returned to Mother and a long satellite phone call to the UK. The Flight set about painting the Wasps with a camouflage scheme because we knew that we would be doing more reconnaissance flights.

'Now it was known that the Argentine armed forces had arrived we were tasked with keeping them under observation. We flew daily to insert and recover RM observers on Grass Island. There was concern that the Argentines may have landed at other places, so recce flights were flown along the coast. The BAH P had stayed in the area and when *Endurance* put to sea to allow the recces to cover the northern end of the island, she followed about a mile astern. A plan was hatched on the bridge of *Endurance* to indulge in some spoofing. The *Endurance* Wasps were fitted with maritime VHF radios to enable contact with shore stations and other merchant ships. The plan was that we would get airborne with a rattan fender under the rear seat and a bright red immersion suit and head 20 miles north and go into a hover. On the way we would call HMS *Superb* (SUP) using her international call sign on Channel 16 before changing to another channel saying we were on the way with our doctor and asking for instructions as to where to transfer him.

'It worked like a dream; BAH P turned and followed our track and when LACM Bob Nadin wasn't replying as "Superb"over the air to my transmissions he was busily putting the fender into the immersion suit! We verbally pretended to winch up a "survivor" and headed back to Mother, passing close to BAH P. The survivor was by now was sitting upright on the back seat. It was no surprise that the Argentine broadcast out a warning of a British nuclear submarine in the area - good spoof!

'Next day SIGINT showed that the Argentine Special forces had been landed on York Island at the entrance to Stanley by the submarine ARA *Santa Fe* and the invasion was to take place the next morning.

'That evening *Endurance* was ordered to "Proceed with all Despatch" to defend the Falklands. Rather than leave South Georgia defenceless, it was decided to leave the enhanced Royal Marine detachment behind to defend Grytviken, which was officially the port of entry. This was met with objections by the BAS people, and by the Base Commander in particular, who was the official representative of the British Government. However, Nick Barker pointed out that the situation had changed and he was the senior officer. Captain Keith Mills and his men took loads of ammunition and explosives in order to prepare a warm welcome for any invaders. He was later honoured for his outstanding bravery with the award of the Distinguished Service Cross.

'It was decided to wait until dark in order to evade detection by BAH P. She was a mile off the entrance of Cumberland Bay like a cork in a bottle. A total "darken ship" was checked using the Flight's hand-held Low Light TV (LLTV) device and at 2200 we drifted at 3 knots down the western coast, appearing on any radar in all respects like an iceberg. The Navigator took us inside Elephant Rock, and with shelving depths of 15 feet, we were eventually clear to the south. He was awarded a Mention in Despatches for his skill and professionalism. Instead of going directly to the Falklands we went south about South Georgia and into the teeth of a Force 9.

'That night we briefed to get airborne at first light. SIGINT showed four Argentinian warships stationed between South Georgia and the Falklands with the specific task of stopping us and our brief was to get airborne as a pair, armed with two AS12s each, and engage the enemy by flying down the line between Mother and their last known positions. There was no real plan of what to do after an attack, especially if the point of no return had been passed. We stripped the Wasps of the flotation gear and I decided that if we could get a good 15 knots over the deck we would overload the aircraft by 10%, giving us a better range. I went to bed in my immersion flying suit and awaited a call. About 0430 I heard the quartermaster coming down the stairs from the bridge and a knock on the door; "Captain wants you on the Bridge Sir". Up the flight of stairs and I could hear the speaker hooked up to the radio. They had tuned to the Falkland HF Farmyard natter net and everyone was giving blow-by-blow accounts of the invasion as it happened. Nick Barker said; "Well there's nothing we can do there so we will go back to Grytviken".

'We scuttled round the south of the island again and next morning found us steaming up the coast. The Sparkies (radio staff) had tuned to another HF set that had been left behind with the RM party. The Marines were telling the BAH P and the frigate ARA *Geurrico* (GUR) not to land personnel and the Argentines were telling Keith Mills to lay down his arms. I was scrambled with David Wells to conduct a recce.

'We landed in Reindeer Valley of the Barff Peninsula overlooking Cumberland Bay and Grytviken. We could hear explosions from Grytviken and lying not quarter of a mile below us spewing oil was the frigate GUR. We could see what we thought were the dead and wounded being cared for. The BAH P was in the middle of the bay and the Alouette helicopter was ferrying back and forth. On the area known as the Hesstesletten, immediately opposite Grytviken, was a Puma that the Marines had shot down. This information was being relayed to *Endurance*, who in turn was in direct contact with Captain Fox in Northwood. I found out afterwards that he was in direct touch with the Prime Minister. Although not unusual at all now, in 1982 this was possibly the first time action from the front was being relayed directly to the top of government.

'At this stage I asked permission to carry out an attack on the GUR that was lying motionless below. With AS12s we could have had fun, but this was denied because *Endurance* was of more value due to our SIGINT capability in the area. Perhaps a Nelsonian ear with a bit of "static" could have been used, but instead we returned to Mother after a couple of hours.

'*Endurance* stayed in the area using large tabular icebergs to lie against in order to give no radar echo. We were running very low on fuel at below 15% and food was a problem. Our hurried departure from Stanley had prevented refuelling and "storing ship" with the anticipation that we would return within ten days. We flew some recce missions and listened to the BBC Overseas Service as the nation girded its loins for the departure of the Task Force.

'Once the Task Force was on its way we prepared for the arrival of a fleet in what we considered to be our "patch" of the earth. Eventually we headed north to rendezvous with the advanced guard of the Task Force. Having now been on rationed food for a week or more the sight of an underslung load of beef being dropped in the sea was almost too much for some. It was imperative that *Endurance* refuelled, so the tanker trailed a half-mile hose over her stern and this was grappled and hauled aboard. No quick release RAS gear on *Endurance*, it was bolted to the deck and thirstily stuffed into tanks. (Note: Normal warships refuelled alongside the tanker but *Endurance* was of an older design.)

'Two months earlier, we had embarked a film crew with us making a film about *Endurance's* final deployment and they were not exactly happy about now being in a war zone. They left us to return to the UK and we welcomed the SAS in their place. More briefings about the terrain, the beaches, and specifically about the weather. We might have saved our breath because within forty-eight hours they were being lifted off glaciers with the resulting loss of two Wessex 5s.

'The night that the SAS were inserted I was tasked to put in SBS personnel. We had left behind two civilian wildlife film makers, Cindy Buxton and Annie Price, who also had a radio. The last thing the military wanted was someone saying that the Task Force has arrived, so I took an SBS person and the Chief Caterer to tell them we were back and to stay quiet. Tommy stayed with them to offer some protection.

'So after dark we launched with three blackened SBS folk to land them at the head of Hound Bay, a fiord about 5 miles long and tapering from a mile to 1/4 mile at its head, 2,500 foot mountains either side and a 9,500 foot mountain range 5 miles upwind. The wind was blowing directly down the fiord at 25-30 knots and the cloud base was 250 feet. We were not allowed lights, radio or transponder, but could use the radio altimeter. Off we set with David Wells lying on the floor with his head round the wind deflector holding the LLTV. I was on instruments at 200feet. Calls of "dark, dark, dark" from David meant we were over the sea as we crawled up the fiord at 60 knots. Cries of "light, light, light" meant we had strayed over the land with the prospect of disaster in the surrounding mountains. We had experience of the radar altimeter misreading over snow in Antarctica so treated the readings with caution. After ten minutes it started to snow heavily and this built up on the windscreen, occasionally going over the top of the cabin in lumps towards the engine intake. As we moved up the fiord, the rotor cloud from the wind over the mountains became quite violent, and suddenly, with full opposite stick, we rolled left to 90 degrees and the airspeed went below 20 knots. Having no roll control I ruddered it over and lowered the nose to get airspeed and pulled as much power as I could. Negative G caused David to grab the back of my seat, treading on a white-faced

SBS soldier and his first call was "50 feet and climbing" before returning to his Low Light TV. We were very lucky. We decided to call it a day.

'Now to find Mother! Whistling downwind with moderate turbulence we headed for the R/V position, which was 5 miles seaward of an island. Still at 200ft we found the island but no sign of Mother, who was completely blacked out except for the Glide Path Indicator (GPI). The weather was worsening and a diversion to the island was being considered to sit out the night when David, using the LLTV, spotted a glimmer and we turned towards it. Ten minutes later we were having a debrief on the bridge and the SBS decided to go in by Gemini dinghy. They beached and flooded their engines but at least they got ashore. Next morning we flew in their Gemini – underslung - which was a slow process because the first time we did it, it spun round and shot upwards when the airflow got under the bow! Certainly not a cleared load for a Wasp. Once again we were flying very low in what was enemy territory. That evening our SIGINT intercepted the surfacing signal from the submarine *Santa Fe* just a few miles north of Grytviken, and we understood she would be off-loading specialists and missiles before putting to sea, where she would try to attack the ships. Our small task force retreated some 20 miles from the coast, but because *Endurance* was a converted merchant ship and sounded like Big Ben underwater, we became a banished pariah and sheltered in a shallow cove near Hound Bay.

'From dawn the next morning we were at Alert 5 with two AS12s. The Rules of Engagement were that only ships or submarines on the surface could be attacked because by now there was a real nuclear submarine close-by. We had restocked the previously empty food stores and I was just enjoying a breakfast when, as the bacon and eggs were put in front of me, "Action Wasp" came over the tannoy. HMS *Antrim* (ANT) had launched their Wessex 3 to carry out a surface search for the submarine and had spotted it on the surface leaving Cumberland Bay. They attacked with Mk11 depth charges and straddled her.

'We were airborne in three minutes thanks to excellent work by the Greenies completing the arming circuits. As we transited north towards the place where the attack had taken place we climbed to about 750ft and it was not long before I spotted her still heading out to sea. David was using the gyro stabilised sight and sweeping side to side, but with no success. It took a good nudge for him to revert to a Mark1 eyeball, but after that he was on it. We of course had no distance measuring, so guesswork came into play and David decided to hold the missile on the target rather than try to drop it in the last few hundred yards as per the text book. We went through the pre-firing checks, selecting the starboard missile and with me saying, "your target is the submarine ahead, 3-2-1, Fire". It all started to happen. I actually called "Bruiser loose", which caused great excitement back on Mother.

'The missile stayed on the rail for what seemed an age and then away it went, appearing to climb until David gathered it. I had actually hit the stopwatch, but to be honest, was far more interested in watching the missile. The flare was easy to follow and David made an excellent job of guiding it home. It struck the submarine fin and passed through the fibre glass skin but hit a ladder and exploded a couple of feet beyond that. On its way through the fin it took the leg off the man who was machine-gunning us. "Bruiser hit" went out on the radio and we prepared for another shot. We later had it confirmed by the MoD that this was the first guided missile ever fired in anger by the Royal Navy. There had been rockets and unguided missiles of sorts, but this was the first guided one! Who would have thought it would come from a Wasp, with a plethora of Sea Cat, Sea Wolf, Sea Slug and Sea Skua deployed worldwide.

'We did a small circle and selected the port missile. Our discussed intention was now to put the armour-piercing missile through the pressure hull where the fin joined the hull. Once again we went through the ritual and away went the second missile. It ran perfectly until it started to move despite David's inputs. It hit the water some 10-15 yards short of the target. As we started to cut the wires from the second missile, we saw the submarine start a turn back to Grytviken. We headed back to Mother to rearm.

'Perhaps at this stage I should explain that in Endurance we did not have the frequency "chips" that allowed us to retune the radios to comply with specific complans (communication plans) dreamt up by senior officers in grey warships. Consequently, we ended up with five helicopters airborne on three different frequencies and we couldn't talk to each other!

'Having rearmed, we nipped over the Barff Peninsula to carry out another attack. As soon as we had launched, the second Wasp was ranged and launched to come and join the party. The *Santa Fe* was now back inside Cumberland Bay and turning for Grytviken. A check showed the target was clear and we fired a third missile. This was aimed at the hull astern of the fin and once again David Well's excellent guiding put the missile into the after ballast tank. As we continued to attack, the port missile was selected and fired, but this time it was a "rogue" and after initially running true it veered left and climbed in a spiral out of sight.

'We later learned that HMS *Plymouth's* Wasp had flogged in some 40 miles with just one missile due to all up weight and had seen our second missile too close for comfort before firing his missile and flogging all the way back to his ship. (See separate account.) If only we had been able to talk to each other, he could have refuelled and rearmed on *Endurance* five miles away! Tim Finding and Bob Nadin in Wasp 435 passed us as we went back for another rearm. They scored another hit on the fin before coming home.

'David and I launched again and returned to Cumberland Bay, which was now devoid of helicopters and more importantly submarines. We searched but couldn't see the *Santa Fe* anywhere, so knowing that the Argentines were using the old BAS radio station for their communications to Argentina, we agreed that we would attack that building to isolate the troops even more. We ran in from the Hesterslettern and intended to use the port missile so that we could break right after the attack away from the high ground and also the enemy positions. "3-2-1, Fire" resulted in nothing! The missile didn't even fire its gyro. We tried again with exactly the same result. As we were still trundling in at 60 knots we were about one to one and a half miles away and closing, so we quickly selected the starboard missile, which went away perfectly. David gathered it and put it exactly on the wooden building. However, at this stage the Argentinians were getting upset and I could see tracer coming up as well as at least three missiles. David suddenly cried, "I can see it, I can see it" and I thought he meant the tracer. The missile suddenly started a climb and then dived. I thought David might have been hit, but the next thing to happen was the steel plates from the submarine erupting into the sky as the missile struck the snort system at the rear of the fin where it joined the hull. A perfect shot! He had spotted the submarine alongside the jetty at the last minute.

'We were now attached to 5000 metres of copper wire leading to a smoking submarine! David fired the wire cutter and I rolled the aircraft over the wires and dropped to the surface of the sea. We were about 400-500 yards off the beach by this time, but making a fast crossing target for those firing the tracer. On the way back to *Endurance* we were told that a recall of all aircraft had been made and so our morning's fun was over. Coffee and biscuits over a debrief and with the Wasp at Alert 5 once more, it was back to the Uckers board. (Uckers is a naval variant of Ludo and hotly contested.)

'Lunch promised to be a more sedate buffet at action stations, but as soon as I touched a plate it was "Action Wasp" once more. This time we were to collect a Naval Gunfire Spotter, Lieutenant Brown R.E., from *Antrim* and conduct Naval Gunfire Support (NGS) as the small task force softened the Argentine defences prior to an assault using the SAS and the embarked RM detachment from the ships. Sadly, there was a whole Company of Royal Marines spoiling for a fight on an RFA sent 100 miles away beyond reach of the *Santa Fe*, but they were unable to join in. As we loitered in Cumberland Bay, waiting for the ships to get ready and establish communications, we were using our fuel and it became evident that unless I landed the whole event would have to be postponed. I talked this over with David and the army officer and we landed on a peninsular with a good view of the area, including Grytviken. An amusing aside was when Lieutenant Brown gave me a cracking salute after running a circle of 200 metres radius with the words, "Ground Secured Sir". He then got on with the business of NGS. Having done it as a Junglie and then again in Cumbria on the Lynx IFTU, it was soon apparent that he was going by the book with just "2 guns 2 rounds fire". Despite *Antrim* having a steady drift to her guns which allowed the fall of shot to walk impressively towards the enemy, it still wasn't as impressive as it could be - so I whispered, "How about 2 guns 25 rounds fire for effect?" An impish grin crossed his face as he repeated it over the radio and the earth bounced to the fall of shells.

'Slowly, he adjusted them towards the emplacements on the beach at Grytviken, but within minutes David spotted the first white flag to appear on Shackleton House and I rushed to the Wasp to tell *Endurance* on Channel 16 that the Argentineans were surrendering.

'We asked what we should do with Lt Brown and he was ordered to join the troops on the ground. As we dropped him off with the troops in front of us, Major Guy Sheridan RM came over and asked me to take him into Grytviken to accept the surrender, which I did. I nipped back to collect an SAS friend, John Hamilton, and bring him over as well. Guy Sheridan reappeared and asked me to CASEVAC the injured submariner to have his leg amputated properly. Whilst I waited for the sailor to be brought I shut down and got out to stretch my legs.

'The Argentineans were sitting with their hands on their heads covered by the SAS. One of them got up and started to walk over to me despite shouts and guns being cocked. He said, "Hello Tony and how is Janie?" It was Argentine Lieutenant Commander Horatio Bicain, a friend from Mar-del-Plata who I had met in 1981 at the *Endurance* cocktail party. I had told him I was so impressed with the beautiful country I would be bringing my wife when we returned in 1982 and he promised to take us home for dinner. When we met again in February 1982, I introduced him to Janie, and although we didn't go for dinner due to other commitments we did have drinks with him.

'Now he looked behind me at my armed Wasp and said, "Oh no Tony - not you!" I asked him what he was doing there and he just said, "Captain *Santa Fe*".

'We took the injured man to *Antrim* and then thankfully returned to *Endurance* thinking it had been an epic day. *Endurance* was ordered to sail with HMS *Plymouth* to Leith, where the original Argentine Special Forces had not surrendered and there were still the original scrap men to remove. On arrival in the bay, *Plymouth* called on the Argentines to surrender, or at least let the scrap men leave, which they agreed to. The SAS had gone ashore and were preparing for an assault the next morning. A council of war was held in *Plymouth*, resulting in a plan to go out to sea overnight and return at dawn to soften the enemy with gunfire from *Plymouth*. By this time, as we were about to leave *Plymouth*, a straggly line of lights could be seen leaving Leith and making their way to safety. Comedy returned to the scene, because as we desperately tried to find a very darkened *Endurance* in the pitch black, we eventually saw her and as we came alongside the Officer of the Watch, Doctor Neil Munro, left the bridge and called down to us that we were not to worry as he had just that minute accepted the Argentineans' surrender over the radio! Captain Barker didn't need a pilot ladder to get on board – he was not amused! The next day I flew in and noticed an 'H' where there had never been one before. It was a huge booby trap with nails and scrap metal waiting for the first helicopter to land.

'The next day was a quiet one with moving the submarine away from the only main alongside berth in Grytviken. During the move under her own power, with a prize crew on board, an Argentine, CPO Artuzo, was killed through a mistake. That night I had to carry out tactical questioning of my Argentine friend who was very upset at the loss of his engineer. I gave him the option of either being silly or discussing quietly his movements and actions since we had drinks in Mar-del-Plata over a couple of pints of Courage Sparkling Bitter. Thankfully he chose the beer and despite having read the Argentine movements it was revealing to hear how he had hidden in the area of the Falklands and put the Premiero Tactical Buzios (SBS) ashore prior to the invasion. The next night I had to do the same with Alfredo Astiz, who commanded those SF, and who was a very different man in every way.

'The recapture of South Georgia was complete. *Endurance* stayed as the Harbour Master and organised the Ships Taken Up From Trade (STUFT). We deployed the Wasps, with AS12s loaded, to key points near the ships, covering any approach paths that an attacking aircraft might take; it should be borne in mind that the Argentine Air Force C130s were bombing ships and they were the threat due to the range involved. It had been established that a missile fired at one of these had caused it to abort an attack.

'After being deployed away from the UK for six weeks short of a year we finally made it to Chatham. We stayed with *Endurance* to carry out a fly-past with two additional Wasps sent from 829 as she entered the lock. We then left and flew home to Portland with a dubiously legal formation of four wasps along the Thames at 250 feet!

'Horatio Bicain and I still chat and text each other with, "Come on you English" and "Vamos Pumas" whenever there is an international game of rugger. We met again in London and this time he insisted that he would buy the beer and ask the questions – but that is another story!'

HMS *Plymouth*

Flight Commander Lieutenant Commander John Dransfield
Aircrewman LACMN J. Harper
Aircraft XT 429

The Flight took part in the attack on the submarine *Santa Fe* during the liberation of South Georgia and fired one AS missile at the submarine, although no damage was seen. Subsequently the ship sailed to join the main Battle Group. The aircraft was employed on various general duties including Naval Gunfire Support (NGS). On 2 June whilst in San Carlos, the ship was strafed and hit by two large bombs. The aircraft survived with minor damage, only requiring a tail rotor change due to shrapnel damage.

HMS *Plymouth* with XT 429 ranged on deck at Gibraltar prior to sailing south in 1982. *(J. Dransfield)*

John Dransfield describes one particular Special Forces Operation that took place on the night of the 22 May:

'From taking part in the reoccupation of South Georgia, to the landings at San Carlos in the Falklands, we had been busy in Wasp XT429 carrying out the multiple tasks required from a small ship's flight.

'"Mother" was HMS *Plymouth*, a Rothesay class frigate under the command of Captain David Pentreath. After covering the landings the days were spent in San Carlos on anti-aircraft duties and the nights out on various missions.

'On the 22 May, *Plymouth* was tasked to support Special Boat Service (SBS) operations in King George Bay on the west coast of West Falkland, a challenging distance to complete under the cover of darkness.

'It was to be a night off for me as the landings were to be carried out by our ship's boat. The first was to put a reconnaissance patrol of four SBS Marines ashore on the south coast of the bay. The second to land a patrol together with a large quantity of high explosive to join a patrol already ashore to sabotage the Roy Cove Settlement airstrip on the north shore.

'I was called to the bridge to be given a general brief on the mission. This did not go well, as I expressed some surprise that blowing up a grass airfield could be effective, which was not considered to be a positive attitude; it was clear my presence was no longer required so I left and hunkered down in the wardroom. This was now the doctor's operating theatre and very quiet as he was thankfully short of patients and lurked there ready to operate on anyone with the slightest sign of sickness.

'There had been great excitement amongst the seamen led by the First Lieutenant as they prepared for the landings, and as I felt the ship slow ready to launch the boat I decided to go up on deck to watch, however at that point the tannoy burst into life:

'"Flight Commander to the Bridge, Flight Commander to the Bridge."

'I was met by a grumpy Captain who marched me to the bridge wing, pointed to the dark shore and pounding surf, while telling me that as the conditions were unsuitable for the boat I would have to land the SBS Patrol.

'I did feel that I was somehow considered responsible for the surf, not an unknown occurrence in the Falklands in winter, but I knew my place. "Yes Sir," I said.'

XT 429 stripped down for action. *(J. Dansfield)*

'There followed a very rapid briefing. There was no moon, no detailed maps, no local knowledge, and the insertion had to be carried out without any lights. It was decided to make two trips to keep the wasp at a sensible weight and enable my crewman and guardian angel, Joe Harper, to come with me.

'A landing zone was selected close to a small inlet opposite Shallow Harbour House. We launched and assisted by the ship's radar headed in. It was very dark, but the coastline and inlets were clearly visible and I could see the outline of the 500ft hills further inland.

'We identified our inlet, slowed to 40kts, and commenced a gentle descent from 200ft into the blackness. While I concentrated on the instruments Joe was leaning out of the door watching for sight of the ground. The heather was dark and featureless, but Joe was able to see enough from about 50ft to con me, and at 10ft I had enough visual reference to establish a hover and place the wheels lightly on the ground. Like any Special Service personnel, our two passengers needed no encouragement to leave us, and we were off and away in seconds.

'*Plymouth* was of course blacked out; our procedure was to carry out a radar assisted approach using minimum radio, then on finals the discreet deck lights were switched on, which could only be seen from above in the stern arc and were most effective. Initially, the effect was spoilt by our Flight Deck Officer who used his illuminated wands to guide us in and could be seen for miles. I seem to remember an application of gaffer tape reduced their illumination to an acceptable level.

'We quickly launched with our second two passengers. This landing was expected to be more straightforward as a red torch would mark the landing site; however, this led to my first big mistake of the night. We soon saw the torch, and commenced a descent. The radio altimeter had just passed 100ft and I was slowing through about 55kts when Joe shouted, "UP! UP!" As I pulled in power the 10ft altimeter warning light came on and I glimpsed the ground flashing past under the wheels. We shot skywards like a startled pheasant and flew a very rapid and embarrassing circuit to a rather steeper and successful descent to the landing zone.

'*Plymouth* was already setting off at full speed to the next rendezvous, and having caught up we landed on and settled down to see what else the night had in store for us. I watched as a couple of decks below the sea boat was very slowly and carefully loaded with the large amount of explosive required.

'The previous buzz of excitement had now evaporated, probably partly due to the abandonment of the boat landing. However, I suspect the reality of taking a small boat laden with explosive up a small creek in enemy territory was also beginning to sink in; I must admit to having an unfair but satisfying vision of my First Lieutenant seated on enough explosive to blow up an airfield with bullets whistling past his ears.

'"Flight Commander to the bridge, Flight Commander to the bridge."

'My Captain greeted me warmly, "John, how much explosive could you carry in your helicopter?"

'We had run out of time. Carrying explosives in a helicopter was usually subject to endless briefings and authorisations due to the static electricity generated by the mass of moving parts. Not tonight!

'The plan was very simple. There was no need to take Joe, as all I had to do was load up with the maximum load of explosive, fly up the inlet, turn left and land on the 'T' thoughtfully provided by the torches of the shore patrol. I would then shut down, the patrol would unload and blow up the airstrip, and I would then take them back to *Plymouth*. What could possibly go wrong?

'I informed my hardworking Flight of the new task so they could prepare the Wasp, and remained on the bridge for a short while to glean what I could from the poor maps available.

'Returning to the flight deck ready to go I found not a lot was happening. Unloading the sea boat and getting the explosive up to the flight deck was a very slow process, and only one small packet had arrived on deck. I decided he who was in charge of the transfer should be the lucky person to inform the command of the delay, and was just setting out to find him when:

'"Flight Commander to the bridge, Flight Commander to the bridge."

'First the good news, contact could not be established with the shore patrol and the mission was cancelled. The bad news was that I was now tasked to go and find them.

'Joe and I were joined by the SBS officer on board as liaison, and we set off for the airstrip. Even the stars were now obscured and it was pitch dark. I could see the water and just make out the silhouette of Cooke Hill rising to 850ft south-east of the settlement. However, everything else seemed enveloped in a strange black, grey and purple haze, the most disorientating conditions I have ever flown in.

'We circled over the airstrip watching for the Morse recognition code "A" from a torch, but saw nothing. On the plus side no one seemed to be shooting at us. A rapidly moving flashing white torch was briefly seen, but was clearly someone running for cover. Our liaison officer decided we should land, as the ground party would not know who we were, so we set up an approach.

'Joe could just make out the airstrip looking straight down but I had no visual reference. I started a descent at minimum speed; the rate of descent was slower than Joe wanted, but I was reluctant to increase it at slow speed so close to the ground. Eventually a grey shape appeared out of the gloom. It was a house beside the strip and I was able to establish a visual hover over its garden. I offered to air taxi back over the strip, but was told the position was fine, so having seen a pole and asking Joe to check for washing lines, we settled on the ground.

'Despite the racket from the Wasp the impression was of an eerie silence. We were only a few yards from the house and I could see the curtained windows, but there was no sign of life. Joe was armed with a sub machine gun and leaning out of the door ready for action, my pistol remained in its holster as I had my hands on the controls ready for a quick getaway, while our liaison officer peered hopefully into the darkness.

'I then had my biggest fright of the night. I felt something crawling up the back of my neck and my bonedome lifted and pushed forward. I instinctively reacted by slapping the back of my neck, and discovered it was my hair as stiff as a porcupines bristles! I was obviously a bit tense, but being scared by my own hair, ridiculous!

'Our liaison officer decided that the patrol were still not sure we were friendly so we needed to signal. In discussions with the SAS during our South Georgia exploits they had mentioned how difficult it was to locate or understand what a helicopter was doing at night due to the echoing clatter from the blades, a light provided instant clarification. However, as there was no sign of enemy activity we decided to go ahead.

'This gave me a chance to do two things for the one and only time in my naval career. I had always wondered why the wasp had a small signal light under the fuselage, now I was going to use it. I was also going to make use of the time and effort put into teaching me to send and receive Morse code at BRNC Dartmouth by flashing "A" into the darkness.

'Small as the signal light was, on that night it seemed to give off enough light to be seen from the moon. ._ ._ ._ ._ ._ ._ ._ ._

'Nothing.

'"They must be at the emergency rendezvous." The What! This was news to Joe and me. Our liaison officer produced a scruffy piece of paper purporting to be a map which, huddled together, we examined by the dim light of a vibrating torch, and from which we established that the rendezvous was at the head of a small inlet a short distance up the coast.

'By now our fuel was already below our normal peacetime minimum, and I estimated we had just enough to do a fly-past of the location before returning to Mother within our war time limits.

'With relief I got airborne, and on arriving off the inlet we were rewarded with the sight of the correct identification signal, then back to Mother for a quick suck of fuel and disembark our liaison officer.

'It was a four man patrol so we needed two sorties to recover them. The SBS carry a large quantity of equipment in their "Bergens", enormous rucksacks from which they will not be separated. They are also carrying their weapons and ready use ammunition, so space and weight are at a premium. To minimise weight and maximise space the Wasp's flotation gear had been removed, all doors were off, seats out, and a cargo net secured to the floor for our passengers to hang on to.

'On arrival back at the inlet I could see little in the inky blackness, but it was obviously rocky and undulating. I decided on speed over stealth, switched on the landing light and made a fast transit the short distance to the patrol's position and a swift landing. Shadowy figures appeared from below the lip of the gully, from which Joe selected two and we were soon ready to go.

'I now made my second big mistake of the night. I estimated I had plenty of room for a normal take-off before turning down the inlet out to sea, however, in the gloom I had forgotten just how small my visible world was. No sooner had I lowered the nose to accelerate, it became very black ahead and I realised I was already halfway across the inlet and heading for the rocks on the far shore. I think I can probably claim the fastest ninety degree turn ever achieved in a wasp, a manoeuvre which left me pointing out to sea down the inlet in a high hover with no airspeed.

'I think I then probably lost the plot for a minute! Diving down to just above the water to pick up speed I flew down the inlet, which was only just wider than the wasp, at low level with the vague shapes of rocks flashing past the rotor blades, before pulling up over the sea and heading for Mother. Pure exhilaration; although Joe did not seem to share my enjoyment.

'Another fast turn round and a repeat performance back to the landing site for our remaining two passengers. However, to our surprise, three hulking shapes detached from the shadows and headed towards us. "Oh, there are three of them," I said to Joe, "looks like we will have to make another trip". Joe was unusually forthright in indicating that this was not his preferred option and that he would get all three gentlemen on board.

'Surprisingly quickly Joe called ready to lift, and with the help of a favourable breeze which had sprung up I was able to carry out a conventional towering take-off and accelerate out to sea without further drama. However, Joe suddenly came on the intercom sounding very urgent but almost unreadable; I was just able to make out, "Slow down, Slow down", and then became aware of a presence to my right. It was a dishevelled looking Joe peering at me from outside the cockpit a few inches away. Having loaded our passengers there was no room left for him, so he was standing on the undercarriage, hanging grimly on to the centre strut of the cockpit. I slowed to a sedate pace for our transit back for the last landing of the night, which thankfully did not take long as *Plymouth* had been closing our position since locating the patrol.

'The debrief was very short. How did it go? Asked our liaison officer. I told him we had used the landing light to speed things up. A look of horror appeared on his face. "You were very lucky, when illuminated they should have shot you down!"'

HMS *Yarmouth*

Flight Commander Lieutenant P. Miller
Aicrewman LACMN J. Da Souza
Aircraft XT 429

The following is an article taken from *Flight Deck* magazine that tells her story:

'After sailing on 8 April from Gibraltar, en route to the Falkland Islands, the Flight commenced an intensive all role training programme, including weapon loads, role changes and general Flyexes. Where possible loads and role changes were included in the task force tactical training serials. By the time of arrival off Ascension Island on 16 April the Wasp that been reverted to its war paint scheme.

'By 27 April, all training to been completed and the Wasp was tasked at alert 8 dawn to dusk as the Task Force approached the TEZ.

'After entering the TEZ the ship detached with HMS Brilliant and was later joined by two Sea Kings to conduct ASW operations in an area to the north-east of the Falkland Islands on 1 May. Most of the day and night was spent at action stations and several sonar contacts were gained and prosecuted by the ships and helicopters. The Wasp dropped three depth charges which all detonated and flew a 4 hour 40 minute sortie with only two refuels. The Sea Kings were kept on task by HIFR and airborne crew changes. On rejoining the task force to the east of the Falkland Islands next day the Wasp resumed its dawn to dusk alert 8 task.

'When HMS Sheffield was hit by an Exocet missile on 4 May, Yarmouth was in the vicinity and went to her aid. The Wasp was role changed to vertrep/casevac and launched to ferry extra firefighting equipment to, and casualties and survivors from, the stricken destroyer.

'The Wasp was able to land on the burning ship several times. Whilst Yarmouth was alongside the Sheffield taking off survivors, it was assessed that we came under torpedo attack. She broke away to use mortars. The Wasp was recalled to role change to ASW and launched with two torpedoes to assist the ship and joined Sea Kings in the submarine prosecution. One torpedo was dropped by the Wasp.

'On 8 May, Yarmouth was detached from the main group to locate and tow Sheffield clear of the TEZ. The Wasp was used to search for the abandoned ship, which was eventually located. During the final stages of connecting the two, the Wasp was actioned to investigate a contact held by the ship, but after a fruitless search the helicopter returned to winch off the towing party from Sheffield's *forecastle. As we were unescorted and still in the TEZ, the Wasp remained at alert 8 for a further thirty hours during the slow eastern transit. On the morning of 10 May,* Sheffield *sank.*

'Yarmouth *was detached from the Carrier Battle Group on 19 May to rendezvous with the Amphibious Group and to escort them into Falkland Sound for the landings. The ship entered Falkland Sound early on the 21 May and shortly after daybreak the group came under frequent air attacks. During one of the raids HMS* Antrim *was hit by a bomb, which did not explode, and during a lull the Wasp was launched to supply her with equipment to remove the bomb. During the raid at 1730 the crew observed* Argonaut *being attacked and damaged just outside San Carlos and rendered immediate assistance by air lifting three casualties to SS* Canberra*. Throughout the airlift the group were under continual attack and the Wasp was able to land on* Argonaut's *flight deck to embark casualties.*

'During these air attacks HMS* Ardent *was also damaged and* Yarmouth *was sent to her aid. The Wasp was recalled to assist in airlifting the casualties and survivors from the ship and these were taken to* Canberra*. The air attacks ceased after nightfall and* Yarmouth *remained in the sound on anti-submarine patrol.*

'The ship sailed into San Carlos water to take up its anti-air warfare station on 22 May and remained in the area until 1 June. Generally, the Wasp was tasked to operate in support of the Amphibious Group conducting surface search in Grantham Sound; coastal patrols to Cape Dolphin; load lifting and HDS. Throughout this period the ship was at action stations one hour either side of sunset and sunrise.*

'We sailed out of San Carlos waters on 1 June to transit 300 miles east to rendezvous with MV* Stenna Sea; *spread for a 48-hour maintenance period. After rendezvousing on 3 June we departed to rejoin the CVBG on 5 June.*

'On re-joining,* Yarmouth *was tasked for Naval Gunfire Support (NGS) - using shore spotters - on the Tumbledown, Woody Brook, Mount William and Sapper Hill areas, firing initially from the southern gun line (Choiseul Sound area) and latterly the northern gun line (Berkley Sound area), between the 6 and 15 of June. For these night NGS operations the Wasp was at alert 8 in the surface search role, and ship at action stations. During gunfire support on the 10 June the Wasp was launched at 0540 to identify an unknown surface contact close inshore. The contact was identified as MV* Monsunnen*. After NGS early on 12 June, HMS* Glamorgan *was hit by an Exocet missile and the Wasp was launched to transfer extra firefighting equipment and a medical officer, even though the ship was listing and on fire. The helicopter was able to land on the flight deck to assist.*

'*After the ceasefire on 14 June and standing by for NGS on 15 June,* Yarmouth *was detached to the South Sandwich Islands via South Georgia to rendezvous with* HMS Endurance *in order to assist her in the call for a surrender on Southern Thule. We arrived at Southern Thule on 20 June and the Wasp landed an NGS team on nearby Cook Island (the first recorded landing on this island). In the event the small Argentinian garrison surrendered without the use of force and the Wasp was used to transfer the senior prisoner of war and the ship's commanding officer to* HMS Endurance *for the surrender ceremony.*

'Yarmouth *departed with ten Argentinian prisoners of war on board on 21 June for Port Stanley and arrived off the port on 25 June.* Yarmouth *rejoined the battle group and participated in the "Falktrain" serialised program from 27 June to 6 July. On 7 July,* Yarmouth, *in company with* Exeter *and* Cardiff, *detached from the battle group for UK via Ascension Island. The ship's Flight disembarked to RNAS Portland on 27 July and proceeded on leave.*'

HMS *Hydra, Herald* and *Hecla*

One of the most important roles for the aircraft was casualty evacuation. *(Steve George)*

Hydra:
Flight Commander Lieutenant Commander R. Bryant
Aicrewman CPOACMN S. Huxley
Aircraft XT 432

Herald:
Flight Commander Lieutenant S. Eddings
Aicrewman LACMN S. Spear
Aircraft XT 794

Hecla:
Flight Commander Lieutenant C. deV Hunt
Aicrewman LACMN T. Monks
Aircraft XT 420

HMS *Hydra* in her hospital ship paint scheme, all three ships were similar. *(R. Bryant)*

All three survey ships were converted to act as hospital ships and their aircraft painted accordingly. Roger Bryant gives his account of his time in Hydra which also covers the deployment of the other survey ships:

'*Hydra* Flight continued to ready itself to embark for survey operations in the Outer Hebrides – forecast for March/April 1982. But at the very beginning of

April, the Argentine presidency made a practical statement about sovereignty of the Falkland Islands and occupying troops landed. Flight members were mostly saddened that we would miss out on the recovery action, and I personally reminded the appointer that I had been First Lieutenant of HMS *Fearless* just three years ago and they must be thinking of bringing the reserve LPD forward. The Flight continued preparations for embarking for survey duties until I received a somewhat guarded open line call saying that we were not going north, but rather south, and that I needed to dig out my white uniform. We were to go south with *Hecla* and *Herald* as mini-hospital ships – the precise role was unclear.

'So, XT 432 was decorated with red crosses on a white background (which the flight enlarged considerably as soon as we were clear of Portland) and we practiced low flying Navexes and winching bodies in Robinson stretchers.'

XT 423 in her 'War Paint'. *(R. Bryant)*

'We embarked in HMS *Hydra* alongside in Portsmouth on 23 April and sailed south the following day with the good wishes of most of the nation behind us as expressed by crowds of the public at various vantage points as we sailed.

'On the way south we practiced medical emergencies and introduced the medical staff to helicopters. Frequency of NBCD exercises increased in the ship's daily training programmes. Mess decks were modified to serve as wards. Tinned food stores had been embarked and stowed on office decks and covered with plywood. At Ascension Island, more stores were brought on board and then we continued south in company with *Herald*. We understood that no significant military move would be made by the British Forces to retake the islands until the Red Cross ships - SS *Uganda*, with *Hecla*, *Hydra* and *Herald* were assembled. We still didn't know what our role was to be, but I did practice duskers on a few occasions. The "H" boats were not equipped for night flying. The deteriorating weather as we went further south introduced conditions which, in the ordinary course, and as per wind diagrams and ship movement limitations, would have stopped flying operations. Sometimes up to 70 knots of wind over the deck, with associated ship movement, causing the screw to beat at air.

'The hospital ships sailed under the Geneva Convention. All crypto had to be landed, and, of course, we had no offensive or even defensive armament. Our main defence was to advertise ourselves, but some viewed that the red crosses on the ships and helicopters made for easy targeting. The ship was fully and excessively illuminated at night. And, of course, an Exocet fired from 25 miles was not interested in red crosses painted onto ships. We were as good a radar target as any other vessel. Best information on the situation was gained from the BBC World Service at 2300 each evening. Overhead, at times, both British and Argentinian aircraft could be seen.

'With a bridge watch keeping qualification, I stood my watch whenever I could while being well aware of my primary role. Having been First Lieutenant and NBCDO of an LPD and having held minor warship command, I was able to contribute quite a lot when RAS-ing evolutions were carried out and when serious NBCD matters were discussed. Recognising the vulnerability of the ship, most evenings, before tuning in, I rehearsed the blind exit from my cabin to the upper deck. When not in my goon-suit, I ensured I was not too distanced from my survival suit and lifejacket.

'We dealt with our first casualties on 20 May and thereafter were frequently cross decking with *Herald* and *Hecla*, transferring casualties from *Uganda* or, on one occasion, *Canberra* (the flight deck for'd of the bridge). Invariable when taking fuel and water from an RFA, the Flight would be used to transfer mail and stores. The day before the 14 June surrender, I twice flew to the deck of one of two of our Argentinian counterparts, *Almirante Irizar* to collect medical stores brought out from the mainland. *Bahia Paraiso* was the second Argentinian. On the second trip to *Irizar*, we had established two-way VHF radio contact. But the military writing was clearly on the wall, and body language and a few hand gestures suggested that they were less than delighted to see me.

'The task of the three H Boats had evolved into transporting stabilised casualties - up to eighty per trip - from *Uganda* up to Montevideo. From the H Boat, they would be moved directly to an RAF VC10 already at the airport and waiting for a flight to UK, and then onwards to RAF Hospital Wroughton. No immigration paperwork exchanged hands in Uruguay and the episodes were kept as downbeat as possible. Ships would sail soon after the last casualty was in the ambulance and on the way to the airport. On one occasion, *Hydra* had sailed and the VC10 found a defect on start-up. We were recalled, and the casualties re-embarked to repeat the operation as soon as possible.

'On the two/three day passage from the Islands to Uruguay, we started the casualties' rehabilitation process and accommodated men in appropriate spaces – senior rates with senior rates, officers in the wardroom. Junior rates of the ship's company slept in offices or wherever, while casualties occupied their bunk spaces, which had been partially modified to cope with injured. On *Uganda*, casualties were treated equally - a company commander may have been bunked alongside a private from another unit. In *Hydra's* wardroom, we had a mess dinner on the night before entering Montevideo. I took on the task of gathering together enough tropical shirts and shoulder boards from my colleagues, for the casualties, and then, from old chart paper and with coloured pens, drawing casualties' ranks in regimental style to cover the RN shoulder boards. Some of our guests were reluctant to surrender their outfits rather than step back into UK wearing the RN AWDs in which they had arrived - and we let it go.

'Each of the three H boats did three or four trips up to Montevideo – often in pretty poor weather. *Hydra* carried 251 casualties in four trips. The H boats had been augmented by one doctor and one MA before leaving UK. Certain of the ships companies were given basic training in casualty care on the way south, but it was up to the entire ships company to help out where needed, irrespective of rank/rate - and they did so. I recall helping Welsh Guardsmen, whose hands were in polythene bags and smeared in "flavine", to "ease springs". Casualties and senior commanders alike expressed great gratitude for the way we treated our guests.

'Although I flew Argentinian casualties, *Hydra* never took them in - I transferred them to *Uganda* or to *Almirante Irizar*. This was not a policy decision, rather one of sensibility.

'After the ceasefire, with mines littering the islands and no air bridge established, since the runway in Stanley was still cratered, *Hydra* remained around the islands until the end of August 1982 in case of a need to repeat a run to Montevideo. We visited homesteads and villages out in "the camp", offering diesel, sugar and flour. Often, we carried a civilian doctor on his rounds or flew islanders to the doctor in Port Stanley. The Kelpers had not been resupplied since the end of March and were most grateful, not only for the stores, but for the trouble that had been taken to eject the Argentinians. When opportunity arose, they were most generous with their hospitality, and I had one particularly memorable mutton lunch at Darwin settlement. When offering the three basics to the two inhabitants of the single house at the place known as Rincon Grande, they showed disappointment at the limited sustenance on offer - they asked for tonic water as they were fed up with drinking neat gin!

'Goose Green, of course, was known to everyone who had any interest in the goings-on. It was marked as a major centre on the map. I missed it on the first recce - it consisted of very few buildings, far fewer than I'd expected.

'When the Civil Commissioner (aka Governor Rex Hunt) returned, I had the privilege of flying him on some of his rounds of settlements. In our general flying over the islands, I'd take as many of the ship's company with me to show them what it was all fought over and to meet some islanders. I clocked up my 2,000 hours during one daily roundabout. We also did some professional surveying work with transponders and photography before sailing finally from Port Stanley in the first days of September.

'HMS *Hydra* arrived back in UK waters on 23 September 1982. Rather than disembark to Portland on the way up channel, as would be usual, the Flight remained on board to go up harbour at Portsmouth as part of the ships company. And I'm glad we did. Tugs spraying coloured water, the hydrographer embarked and his flag flew from a lashed up mast on top of the hangar - we were damned if we were going to have our large Red Cross flag displaced from the masthead before we had got alongside. Throngs of the public cheering from the east side of the narrows as they had on our departure exactly five months before. As the last ship home of those that had been in the task force at the time of the San Carlos landings, we were the last ship to receive this public salute. The Flight's families had been bussed from Portland to Portsmouth to see all this and that is where initial reunions took place - among the rest of the ships company of which we had been proud to be members. In the mail we brought on board on 23 Sept, we received a blue glass shade to replace the red of the Wasp's rotating tail obstruction light. This in accordance with the international regulations for Red Cross aircraft. This was duly fitted and was flashing during the procedure Alpha move up harbour on the twenty-fourth.

'The wardroom Trafalgar Night dinner was a splendid affair. We invited back all the officers that we had carried up to Montevideo - this time in their proper mess kit rather than Action Working Dress. Also invited was the Air Commodore-in-charge of the RAF Hospital at Wroughton and the delegate of the ICRC who had visited all hospital ships periodically and who I had flown to and from our two Argentinian counterparts.'

Roger also added the following observations about some of the demands of flying in such cold conditions:

'It was policy, when flying over the sea that the two front doors of the Wasp were removed and wind deflectors fitted in lieu. This to allow easier escape in case of a ditching.

'In the Falklands winter, it became pretty cold and even when wearing a bunny suit inside the one-piece goon-suit, and activating the electrically heated gloves and socks, the cold did get though.

'On one occasion, when trying to land on *Hydra* with considerable movement on the deck and a strong wind blowing, I had difficulty assessing when everything was going to come together to allow a reasonable landing. I had one or two goes and aborted.

'I realised then, that my physical reactions were milliseconds astern of the brain messages. So I completed a circuit, shook myself up and happily landed at the next attempt.

'On shut down, although I could manage the switchery, my hands were too cold to pull the circuit breakers and I had to call in a flight member to do that for me. I learned the lesson and the associated dangers and was prepared thereafter.

'Perhaps we should have had gentle warming of the bonedomes!'

MV *St Helena*

Flight Commander Lieutenant Commander D. Heelas
Aicrewman POACMN J. Taylor
Aircraft XT 795

The ship went south to act as 'mother ship' to the minesweepers which were needed to clear the area. They arrived on 10 July, almost a month after the surrender, but with plenty of work to do.

David Heelas recalls what it was like:

> 'I was on my first shore job running the BRNC Dartmouth Flight, when I received the call to deploy down south on RMS *St Helena*, one of many STUFT (Ships Taken up from Trade) ships. She was fitted with hangar, flight deck and full night flying capabilities in six days in Portsmouth dockyard, but we then had to delay our departure for two days because of engine problems, before setting off for the south Atlantic not long before the end of hostilities.
>
> 'Our role was to provide support and maintenance facilities for two minehunters, HMS *Brecon* and *Ledbury*, who were deployed to counter-mine unexploded ordnance in the waters around Port Stanley and San Carlos. Our principal task was to deploy and maintain portable navigation beacons on hilltops for the minehunters. This presented a number of problems! One site was located in an uncleared minefield, so I was unable to land, but placed a wheel on a rocky outcrop whilst a crewman jumped down and manoeuvred the equipment, including heavy batteries, out of the cab. This was in the middle of the South Atlantic winter, and it was not always easy to maintain a stable hover. On one occasion, I recorded a gust of 90 knots (the normal operating speed of the Wasp) whilst in a low hover.
>
> 'Another problem was the low cloud. We had to re-supply the beacons with fresh batteries every twenty-four hours, so that the minehunters could continue their operations. However, the tops of the hills were more often than not in thick cloud. I therefore developed a technique for "walking" up the hill in the Wasp. I would fly in the clear to the base of the cloud, and hover into wind. I would then taxi up the hill whilst maintaining visual contact with the ground. It seemed simple and safe, and I congratulated myself on my inventiveness!!

'However, on another occasion I was collecting equipment for relocation. The site was atop a fairly sheer cliff jutting out of the sea, and I had to hover virtually downwind. I was well loaded before we started, and with some difficulty I got to the top and picked up the extra gear. On the way down, I found myself unable to keep the aircraft steady as we tried to descend through the cloud, and eventually decided on a descending turn away from the cliff to gain airspeed as the only way of regaining full control. I therefore did a sideways diving manoeuvre designed to ensure that the tail didn't hit the cliff edge. I went straight into thick cloud, and onto instruments, and more by luck than judgement ended up in a controlled descent, breaking cloud at about 150 feet above the sea.

'With her work completed, the ship returned to the UK on 13 August, arriving home on 16 September.'

Gordon Douglas recounts his deployment to the Falklands four years after the war finished – it was still a busy place.

HMS *Euryalus*: Falklands Patrol, 8 July 1986 to 18 December 1986, Wasp Mk1 XT791.
Aircrew:
1st Pilot: Lieutenant Commander Pete Lankester
2nd Pilot: Lieutenant Rob Dowdell
Aircrewman: Petty Officer Acmn Gordon Douglas

Ships: HMS *Euryalus*, HMS *Arrow* and RFA *Orange Leaf* (tanker for the trip down).

'We embarked first week of July for our journey to the South Atlantic from Plymouth. Stopping at Gibraltar, Ascension and the Falkland Islands. Spirits were unusually high considering the time we were looking at being away from home. For many of us it was the first long detachment in a while.

'One of our first tasks was to pick up our last mail and top up of fresh bread before leaving the shores of the UK for five and a half months. The Wasp was used to transit to HMS *Drake* and collect the goods, no real problem! Until it came to packing the load into the back and onto my lap. The only place we didn't have stores was on the boss's lap. There would be no way of explaining why we couldn't bring all the mail with us on our last flight from mainland UK.

'We started our engine, engaged rotors and attempted to get into the hover. Bells started ringing, which instantly dragged our eyes to the torque meter, it was well over the max tolerance of 103.5% Power was reduced and plan 2 went into operation. It was decided that a cushion creep take-off was the next best option and possibly only option. The only problem was 80 to 100 yards in front of us, in the shape of HMS *Drakes* twelve foot security fence.

'The collective lever was raised and a low power setting applied, we were now sitting on the cushion of air beneath the helicopter. Slowly we crept forward, building up speed, but little in the way of height. It was not looking good as we rapidly approached the security fence, "well here we go," said the boss and pulled in power on the collective and we scrapped over the fence and dropped over the other side, tail rotor clearing the fence by inches. We were still only feet above the water of the Tamar. Slowly we gathered height, until at last, close to Drakes Island, we were at a height that almost seemed like flying altitude. We made it to the ship which was just of Plymouth Breakwater. I have never been so glad to get over a fence in my life; I was very impressed by the cushion creep take-off.

'(Almost as much as the crew probably was with the mail!)

'The next few weeks were spent with the usual deck operations and flying practices to enable us to operate in the South Atlantic. Darkened operations were the scariest. I used to bribe the life buoy spook to cup a cigarette in his hand so that I could use the night vision monocular sight to locate the ship. Never be without a night vision aid when night flying. Absolutely invaluable.

'We conducted sorties to all the ships we were in company with. Several winching sorties were carried out without hitch, however, when it came to load lifting it became evident that the rear flagstaff on the *Orange Leaf* would have to go. To deliver loads to the small deck at the stern of the RFA, a 30 foot wire strop had to be used due to the obstructions around the transfer area. The flagstaff presented a real snagging hazard, it was gone the same day. The crew of *Orangeleaf* very kindly cut the staff down, greatly increasing the minuscule area we had to operate to and reducing significantly the risk of an accident. Gibraltar was a good blow off steam session. Crew cuts were the order of the day, weather would surely get hotter as we approached the equator and continued further south. It was pointless getting the rabbits, (presents to the uninitiated). HMS *Invincible* had just sailed when we arrived at Gibraltar so we (the deployed ships) were the only ones alongside. I used the time to go to RAF North Front and a top up of our FLIPs (Flight Information Publication) that I thought we may need on the journey south, taking into account we would be passing some of the more dodgy

African states. Pinner, in Middlesex, were sending up to date NOTAMS, etc. HMS *Arrows* Observer didn't altogether inspire my Captain, (Captain Jeffries) or myself with any confidence, when asked if they had bothered with up-to-date maps, etc, they didn't really seem to want to bother. Just as well I did. Confirmed a few weeks later when HMS *Arrow* planned a Flyex in an African active danger area.

'After sailing from Gibraltar the gunnery exercises continued, as well as our flying serials. The newly installed BMark's (anti-aircraft guns) were fired for the first time. At night they illuminated the sky with their threads of reddish trails crisscrossing in an attempt to hit the parachute flares used as targets.

'The Captain and First Lieutenant decided that the crossing the line celebration would wait until the return from the Falklands.

'Next stop Ascension!

'To pass away the boring days at sea, much entertainment was laid on, enthralling kite flying competitions that even the second pilot didn't win, his kite was quite rubbish if truth be known. His kite had the flying characteristics of a house brick attached to a length of string. Some people took the whole kite thing quite seriously, poor sods. It did, however, lighten the mood and was another excuse for a few beers.

'The transit down the west coast of Africa was fairly uneventful, although a nosey P3 Orion maritime reconnaissance aircraft (French origin), came to see what we were about. He did a swift fly-by, photos taken by both sides no doubt, both official and unofficial, then it flew on. We continued flying exercises that were carried out to eradicate boredom and to ensure we were all ready for operations when we arrived. The emphasis was now on darkened operations and reduced EMCON, or reduced radio/radar transmissions. This is where the ship switches off all external lighting, radars are switched to standby and not transmitting. With all the navigation lights, radars and radios switched off, we play let's find each other. Certainly improved my navigational skills! (That and bribing the lifeboat spook to cup a cigarette so I could see the heat source through the night vision aid.)

'One of the hardest things to coordinate was to get the HC's (helicopter controllers) to pass accurate wind information immediately before the launching of the helicopter. The Wasp is connected to the ship by an umbilical we called a telebrief. This allowed us to talk to the ship without using our radios and thereby giving away our position. When the helicopter lifted off the deck, the telebrief, which was tied to the deck, was pulled from the bottom of the Wasp and communications ceased. At sea the wind is the hardest thing to calculate, as the wind is a variable, as is the ships course and speed. To return to a moving position such as a ship at sea, it is imperative that both wind and ships data are accurate and precise immediately prior to getting airborne. Two lives depended on it. If push comes to shove the ship could switch on her radars and give her position away in an attempt to locate us and getting us back on board safely. I must say that we were fortunate in that we did not require using the facility.

'Another problem that was peculiar to me, was disorientation when sight training at night.

'This was to simulate the night firing of the Wasp's AS12 missiles against hard targets. Using the M260 sight in daytime is no problem as there is always the horizon as a visible datum and your brain can handle the disruption to the senses. At night! With no visible datum and with the motion of the helo, the brain, (well my brain), did one swift hard over. When I left the sight, removed my eyes from the protected eye pieces and focused on the horizon, my whole body would instantly lean over. A common complaint called the leans! It played havoc with my senses, to the extent I really felt bad after a night sight training exercise. On more than one occasion I reacted that violently my helmet struck the pilot; simply because my brain couldn't handle what it was seeing rather that what it felt I should be seeing! Fortunately I never had to put up with it for too long and not at all when we finally arrived in the Falklands.

'The opportunity was taken to swot up on our bird recognition, to that end one of the ships brighter ornithologists among the ship's crew printed the *'Idiots Guide to Birds in the South Atlantic'*. This composed of, the Black Bastard, the Lesser Black Bastard, Spotted Black Bastard, Yellow Billed Black Bastard and so on. You get the general idea. All produced in booklet form as silhouettes.

'On arrival at Ascension Island it was all bustle and go, crews were transferred ashore to sort loads out before load lifting essential stores in readiness for the last leg of the journey, it was now 6 August. *Arrows* Lynx, and ourselves, spent over an hour lifting stores to the three ships in company. The Ascension Island personnel had done a superb job in getting all our stores sorted into some sense of order and priority, it made the ground crew and our job that much easier. Loads were marked with load weight and destination so we knew at a glance what we could lift and to where it was destined. After retrieving the ground party we sailed for our final destination. There was to be no loitering around Ascension Island. Next stop Falkland Sound, Falkland Island. We had little time to take in the sights of Ascension, we were informed of a strange black fish that swam the waters around the island, but before we knew it the small fleet of three vessels were under way again. Before arriving in the Falklands, things started taking a serious turn. Live weapons were being prepared and loaded into the ready use lockers, mortars were loaded and test firings made. We never even hung around to collect the fish that were killed in the subsequent detonation. No fish suppers on this operation.

'On 16 August 1986 we sailed into Falkland Sound and flew to RFA *Fort Austin*, landing on her upper landing deck. Sea Kings were occupying the lower landing area. In Falkland Sound were the ships RFA *Fort Austin*, HMS *Brilliant*, HMS *Rothesay*, HMS *Arrow* and ourselves, quite a little armada. Not exactly as it must have been in 1982 when the task force would have arrived. I met Lieutenant Woods, ex of 819 NAS on *Fort Austin*; he was with the detachment from 826 Squadron. They were quite delighted to see us. They would be departing for home when the handover was completed.

'The main thing I hoisted in was, you'll be learning the area for the first month, enjoying it for the second month and totally fed up the third month. This was indeed the way it turned out.

'The operations at Stanley were very good; satellite communications were also on offer. Quite a few days were spent making up our Jog Airs (quarter mill maps), minefields had to be plotted, as well as all the many landing zones and refuel sites across the islands. Most of our tasking would consist of surface searches and personnel transfers for R & R (Rest and Recreation).

'Whilst the ship was in Mere Harbour undergoing minor maintenance, we the Flight tended to disembark and operate from Mount Pleasant Airfield for weeks at a throw. (MPA, known to most of the aviators as "Death Star", mainly because the place always looked half finished.) It had a load of new features that many UK airfields didn't have yet. The one that springs to mind is a landing aid for fixed wing, affectionately called "rabbit". This was a light that strobes along the approach centre line, appearing to disappear down a hole, then reappear and repeats the process. I suppose the F4 pilots must have thought it was good.

'It really got on the nerves of us slower helicopter crews.

'The accommodation in MPA was good; as well it should be, having recently been completed. The Flight had to share rooms with RAF personnel stationed there, and they did their best to make you feel like intruders. The guy I had to share with was a smelly sergeant storeman, who drank brandy like there was no tomorrow, never left his cabin, not even to use the shower. Tommy Hodge, the Flight "greeny" (electrical specialist), dipped in as usual and made a good contact in his room-mate. He could speak and had a sense of humour not like the chap

I shared with. He would enter the cabin, pour a glass of brandy and lay out on his bed. There was to be no conversation with him at all. I felt I had seriously intruded into his personal world.

'Tommy in his usual entrepreneurial style had the chef at "Death Star" make some fresh bread. He had them bake some 'stotty' loaves, 'Geordie' flat bread, very tasty. Tommy checked to see if we were flying near the ship, we were, although not tasked to land as most/all the ground crew were at MPA. Tommy liaised with the ship and had a deck party made ready to receive a load of stores. Tommy came along as he had requested he be winched down to the ship with a package for the Captain. On arrival at the ship, the underslung load of bread was deposited on the flight deck. Tommy was then winched down clutching a hat box. On deck he duly disappeared up the starboard waist towards the Captain's cabin. A few minutes later he appeared and gestured for us to come in and winch him back to the helicopter. Back at MPA Tommy informed us the Captain was most impressed with the Flights ingenuity and had been concerned that we had gone to all the trouble for him. When Tommy explained we had deposited a crate full, for the ships company, he was over the moon.

'The refreshment arrangements at MPA were outstanding for us also. In the morning before getting airborne, I collected the day's supply of bagged meals, enough for the crew and passengers of a Tri-Star. (A Wasp can take two crew and up to three passengers!) The inflight rations would be sorted; the boss and I would take a considerable portion and leave the rest for the ground crews. There was always enough to take some back to the ship in the evening if we needed kit from *Euryalus*.

'Upon getting airborne from MPA, we would call up for employment on the radio and off we disappeared for the day. It was usually, "can you go to Red 03 then drop one passenger to Kent". (Red 03 being the designation for a helicopter landing site and Kent being one of the radar stations set up on the island for early warning of any hostile intent from the air.) So the day would continue, go to, collect, go to, drop off. It was excellent flying as it was all done tactically, very low-level. It was normally the case of having to climb to get over a fence, or sheep, of which there were many. The sort of flying was quite exhilarating, Rob Dowdell had a habit of flying low towards the top of cliffs or vertical drops and diving the helicopter over them. Normally he managed to get me gripping the sight mount if it was fitted; if not, then I just clenched my teeth and smiled blandly. It all added to the fun of having a flying area that we could go and do what we wished. On one occasion, when transiting between MPA and Stanley (the capital of the

Falkland Isles), we came upon a large military lorry going our way. We reduced speed and descended till we were immediately behind and above the lorry. Very slowly the pilot placed the four wheels of the helicopters undercarriage over the canopy of the lorry, still with about 30-40 knots showing on the ASI (Air Speed Indicator). We broke away from the lorry after a few moments, as it wasn't the most sensible place to be and the hand gestures from the cab where telling us we weren't welcome.

'It was not uncommon for the pilots to hand over flying control of the helicopter to me. Most of the time spent down south we were in a dual control flying mode. I managed to get my hands on the controls often and sometimes with dire consequences. Flying from Murrey Heights to MPA on one occasion, I was given the aircraft; I somehow managed to get it into a power dive. Try as I might I could not get out of the situation. Pete Lankester told me, instead of pulling out of the dive with the collective, to push the collective down, and push the cyclic forward (the opposite of my reactions). The collective was dumped and the cyclic pushed forward, the helicopter started to respond, very shortly we were back at a normal flying attitude. Straight and level with a suitable airspeed indicated. Now I could wipe the perspiration from my brow.

'The first couple of weeks my maps were always in my hand, but then, as the terrain became more familiar, the maps would remain in my navigation bag ready and always at hand. We took in all the local crash sites, Pucara's and Chinooks from the war, all very interesting. Regular landing sites became readily identifiable by their various attributes. Some by the yellow gorse bushes, others by rock outcrops. The landscape was varied, sometimes flat and dull, other times jagged and rocky.

'Flying with two pilots, at differing times, made flying very interesting. Pete was laid back and there for the total flying experience, taking in the variety of the tasks. Rob, he tended towards the geography/geology. To that end he carried geological charts, and his camera. I ended up photographing various rock strata and rock formations. It was very educational and thoroughly enjoyable. Rob did vary his flying; he was the one responsible for scaring the pants off me whenever we came upon cliffs.

'Our joining procedure for MPA was slightly non-standard, in that, we found a nice gully approaching the airfield that would allow the tiny Wasp to fly in without being seen by air traffic control. We would pop up just short of the airfield. The only snag with our approach was the rotor blades were above the gully and the airframe was in the gully. We simply had to watch out for the Falkland Island sheep.

'During our stay the RAF Sea King SAR flight found the crash site of a previously unmarked Pucara; which resulted in the extraction of the bodies for return to Argentina for burial. A fact the Argentineans were grateful about. Full military honours were bestowed on the deceased crew.

'The geography was very similar to that I had met in the western isles of Scotland when on 819, flat, barren, and totally inhospitable. From the air it was all water and hills, I was glad I never had to walk over the place. I can see why the loss of the *Atlantic Conveyor* during the war was such a blow to the ground troops. Peat bogs were everywhere. We would regularly fly into the settlements where the hospitality of the locals could not be faulted. There was always an offer of a meal and a hot drink. We had no problems at all, with the exception of one of the collie's that for some reason liked to bite the tyres of visiting aircraft. I met one of the PO mechanicians, (Bunny Warren) from *Tartar* whilst at Death Star; he was now a fitter working on the S61 of Bristows (otherwise called 'Eric's, after Eric Bristow, a darts player).

'During one of the disembarkations ashore to MPA, we elected to conduct live AS12 missile firings so that I could qualify for my annual firings and helped along due to Pete Lankester being a qualified HWI, or Helicopter Warfare Instructor, so was qualified to supervise the live firings as well as assessing the results. As MPA was not set up for live weapons we moved to Murrey Heights so that we could load and unload the missiles (Murrey Heights was the HQ of the Army Air Corps in the Falkland Islands, AAC, or Teeny Weenie Airways as we nicknamed them). Onion Range was the inland range on East Falkland we had chosen to launch our weapons. So a few days before, Pete and I had taken a load of 45 gallon oil drums to the site that had been chosen as the target area. The cans had been painted a bright orange so that they would be visible in the harsh landscape. They were also positioned on hard targets, old Argie armour or distinctive outcrops of rock. The day of the firings turned out to be a nightmare. A snow storm had gone through and was forecast to remain for the duration of the firings and beyond. We recce'd the area in which we thought we had positioned the oil drums. The snow storm had obscured all the target markers placed previously. I disembarked from the helicopter on several occasions to check possible targets. We did eventually locate the drums and cleared them of snow as best we could.

'On our return down through Onion Range the weather turned against us. On more than one occasion we had to land in the heather to let the snow storm pass over us. To have flown on through such weather could have been fatal. Navigation was difficult, no references due to the snow covering the ground. The constant stopping to let the snow pass was not helping with our bearings. On our eventual return to Murrey Heights we had a very welcome mug of hot tea. It was decided to attempt a firing the next day, based on the latest weather update.

'The following day (13 September 1986), the weather was indeed better, marginally, so we loaded two AS12 missiles and got airborne. Both "Warshot", as we had no training rounds with us down south. We flew north-west and sighted our first target. A circuit was flown and weapon switches made to arm the weapon of choice - 3-2-1-FIRE. The missile flew off the launcher and immediately dived down and right, a "rogue" missile. I conducted immediate action procedures for a rogue missile. I cut the wires and ordered the pilot to turn in the opposite direction of the missile to avoid collecting the miles of copper wire trailing from the rear of the AS12 missile. As the missile malfunctioned immediately after launch, the warhead did not have time to arm itself and was still considered dangerous. Ninety-six pounds of high explosive buried somewhere in Onion Range! The engineers would be needed to make the warhead safe, or, explode it in situ.

'The position of the warhead was plotted for future reference and then we continued to prepare to fire the second missile. All switches were checked, Armament Master set to "SAFE". Another recce circuit was flown, target identified, and continued for an approach to release the second missile. M260 sight was lowered, target acquired, my hand was poised over the T10K release lever. Pilot ordered 3-2-1-FIRE. T10K release lever was operated, the squib operating the gyro on the missile was heard to initiate, nano-seconds later the missile motors kicked in and the missile left the launcher with a loud bang and much smoke. The AS12 raced across my field of vision, having anticipated this I swiftly moved the control stick to gather the missile and control its trajectory and guide it to the waiting target.

'Another rogue, no control over the missile at all, after a few seconds it was obvious I would not get the missile under control. My left hand moved to the "cut wires" switch and operated it. This had the effect similar to the first missile, a down right signal was sent to the control nozzles and the missile dived towards the earth. This time the weapon exploding on impact.

'We returned to Murrey Heights debriefing the ground crew of the past events on the range.

'Then, as we were chatting, we received news the Captain wanted the helicopter back on board, NOW! The weather was not in our favour. The cloud base was below 100 feet; the visibility was not much better. Pete, however, elected to attempt to return to the ship. He decided that Rob, the second pilot, would stay and Pete and myself would fly back. I expressed my concerns regards the weather and the freezing, potential icing conditions. I was ignored.

'So Pete and I climbed into the helicopter as the ground crew removed the weapon pylons and refuelled us. I briefly looked at my map, shouldn't be too difficult as the ship was less than a mile away in Stanley Sound. How wrong I was. We lifted and almost immediately entered cloud whilst still in a low hover. The cloud base was now near the deck. As we crept forward I had a feeling this was not going to be a straight forward transit flight. Pete talked to the HC on the UHF radio and requested the weather and ships location. Weather poor, visibility poor, ships position, Stanley Sound. Great!

'During our transit over the top of Stanley township, we managed to collect a few of the locals television aerials in our undercarriage. The weather was appalling, I will openly admit to being a little scared. We were over the sea in Stanley Sound and the visibility couldn't have been more than 50 yards at best, scary. The ship had us on radar but not visual. It was decided that the best way to get us back on board was to conduct a PVA (Poor Visibility Approach). This involved the ship dropping flares over the back of the stern to guide us in to the flight deck and get to a position where we could see the ship. The HC guided us to where he thought we would pick up the flares, the trouble being the flares only burnt for a short period, about six minutes. Our ground speed was almost walking pace, so by the time we were where the flares should be we were missing them as they had burnt out. So round again. Another problem being that the Sound was not that long and the ship would have to manoeuver to get enough sea room to receive us.

'The PVA was attempted again, this time with some success; we started picking up the flares, albeit we were almost on top of them before we could locate them. We eventually spotted the ships wake and approached the flight deck cautiously. Pete was sweating with the effort he was putting into flying the Wasp at very low altitude and with no visibility. I was concentrating on visual cues and monitoring dials and gauges in the cockpit. We eventually landed on the *Euryalus* to the great relief of all. The Captain was there to greet us, as was the HC who had raced up from the Operations Room.

'We unstrapped and climbed out of the aircraft, nearly six hours we had spent in the cockpit this day in some of the worst weather I had ever encountered. As I turned to look back at the Wasp I noticed the front was covered in a layer of ice.

'I pointed this out to Pete; he looked at it in shock. I was quite angry, that was dangerous. It could have killed us. I took my helmet off and threw it across the hanger, cracking the visor when it struck the hanger wall. The Captain who had observed this did a hasty retreat. I walked to my foot locker where I kept my camera and started taking pictures of the front of the helicopter, all covered in ice. Just as I was taking a second picture the layer of ice fell away and broke over the flight deck. I dread to think what would have happened if the ice had got thicker or had fallen away and been ingested by the engine (singular). If ice had built up on the rotor blades it would have changed the lift properties and we would have crashed. So incredibly stupid and dangerous!

'About half an hour later Pete and I were summoned to the Captain's cabin. We duly entered and sat when instructed. The Captain, (Jeffries), then continued to tell us he had made a bad decision and then said Pete should, as the senior aviator, had the balls to tell the Captain that it was not allowed (the flying of a Wasp in actual icing conditions is simply not allowed). The Captain apologised for his actions, explaining he had received intelligence that the Argies were probing the Falklands and the *Euryalus* was to position itself to be able to react. Therefore it would be prudent to have the helicopter on board. However, we could have found the ship later after she had left Stanley. Hindsight! A marvellous tool!

'One thing the Captain did have a bee in his bonnet over, was the two rogue missiles. One he could understand, not two. No! Someone must be to blame. We explained about the solid motors and the fact they were unstable. The fact the missile bodies were very old and a defect in the solid propellant could have happened years ago. It took a long time to convince him that apportioning blame would be a pointless exercise and that in our experience with this weapon it was simply a bad coincidence. It wasn't the first time, nor would it be the last AS12 rogue missile firing. He was shown my missile log, and lo! A rogue missile appeared. Albeit that number had now increased by two.

'Over the next few days, after the Flight had caught us up on the ship. We carried out a few routine-flying sorties. Nothing regarding the reason we had been recalled back on board for, it turned out to be a false alarm.

'So, on the seventeenth we were back at Murrey Heights ready for another bout of AS12 firings.

'Same targets. Same range. The weapons were prepared with the same attention to detail. Tommy Hodge the flight armourer pouring over them looking for any flaw or anomaly. The helicopter again had the two weapon pylons attached, two AS12 bodies were assembled, minus the lower wings, these would be one of the last items fitted before Tommy carried out his electrical test. Finally, I was sat in the cockpit, engine running, rotors turning, looking at a sign telling me to make switches safe and have my hands placed on my helmet. The board was lowered, which meant that the weapons were on and ready to fire, all safety pins had been removed, all that was left was to take off and not bring them back. Rob was to fly the first attack profile. Pete was sat in the back, monitoring the firing. Back to Onion Range, target identified and an attacking run started. Wind was not in my favour as a 10 knot crosswind was blowing.

'Again we got to the 3-2-1-FIRE, weapon initiated and released at 6,000 yards, 700 feet altitude and a speed of 60 knots. The missile flew right into the M260 sight, I immediately collected it when it appeared in my field of vision, then controlled its flight path using the joystick in my right hand. No problems just yet I'm thinking, ready to lean forward and cut the wires with my left hand. Thirty seconds passed, nicely counted down by Rob, and "Ka-Boom", Impact! Ninety-six pounds of high explosive devastating a great chunk of Falkland rock.

'A change of pilots, now Pete was flying the Wasp. Ready for round two. Same conditions. Similar flight characteristics. Another release and another firing classed as a target. That is to say, had it been a valid target it would have been hit by both missiles. Looks good in the logbook (this would appease the Captain after the last set of failed firings). Once back at sea, we resumed the normal routine of a ship in war patrol status.

'Depending on which sector we were in dictated what degree of alert we would be at. In the West Falklands we would be at almost instant readiness. For the aircrew we would be dressed in flying kit all the time, we had two minutes to get to a state where we could launch. That meant sleeping in our kit too, not too bad for the two pilots, but it meant I was always on alert in the western sector. At Alert 2 the aircrew would be dressed, full flying kit, sat in the Wasp, strapped in, all switched made ready for an immediate start-up of the Nimbus engine. The Wasp would be sat on its launch spot, lashed down. The ground crew would be all closed up in the hanger ready to react to the cry of, "Action Wasp", over the ships tannoy system. The pilot and I would be talking to the helicopter controller via the telebrief umbilical, getting the latest updates, and for me the weather. I had an arrangement with the HC that the last information he passed before launch was an updated wind vector. In the east it was more relaxed, fifteen to thirty minutes notice normally. Time to get dressed and report in a more orderly manner to our action station. Life wasn't all work and no play though! When we were away from any danger, usually to the south, we could relax a little and messes would put on a variety of entertainment.

'During our visits ashore to MPA, we would spend many flights visiting the outlying Falkland Island villages, or settlements as they were known, meeting the locals. We would inevitably be invited for dinner, which would normally consist of boiled potatoes and great slices of beef or lamb with tasty thick gravy. Really welcoming after the food on the ship. Most farmsteads in the Falklands had a landing site, not that it was too much of a worry as we could land in most places. One of the villages in West Falkland had a collie that would meet us and attack the wheels when we were landing and taking off. He was quite a character and always met the helicopters, be it ours or the bigger S61's of Bristows which ran a taxi service around the islands.

(October 1986)
'Once, during the patrol of the duty ships on a patrol, we would be tasked to visit the islands of South Georgia to the south of the Falklands. These islands are the abode of a huge population of wildlife and scientists, to monitor not just the wildlife, but the environment in the South Atlantic.

'Even the transit to South Georgia was something to remember. With the earth being slightly flatter at the South Pole, the distances you can see appear longer, judging distances became that much harder. One iceberg we observed was over twenty-eight miles away, we thought it was ten miles and were amazed to discover it was so much farther. The air was that much less polluted and so the visibility was greater too. Even the colour of the sea was somehow different, clearer.

'We anchored in Stromness Bay and boats were sent ashore, the helicopter was launched to carry out a recce of the area. It was stunning, to hover next to the where a glacier fell into the sea. The noise and the sheer size, I was surprised to see that the colour of the glacier was blue; this was due to the air being squeezed out of the ice by the immense pressures it was subjected to.

'Once the area had been checked, parties of crew members were allowed ashore to explore the town. In the past, Stromness had been a whaling community, now it was a deserted ghost town with broken down shanty houses in a state of disrepair.

'It was great exploring, the local church was where the explorer Shackleton had been buried. We paid our respects at his graveside. Here too was where one of my old pilots, 'Ian Georgeson', and 'Tug' Wilson, had crashed their Wessex 5 during the actual Falklands conflict. He had been part of a three helicopter flight that was to insert Special Forces - then recover them - when they realised the weather was worse than anticipated. It was a real disaster with two of the three helicopters crashing; Ian and fellow Wessex 5 pilot Mike Tidd.

'As well as a walking tour I had the opportunity to fly a couple of sorties around the mountainous area. One dedicated mountain flying flight, the other a photo session for Rob Dowdell. He was fascinated by the terrain, being a geologist before joining the navy.

'After South Georgia we returned to the routine surface searches and weapon drills. October drifted into November and very soon we were looking at the real time of our departure from the Falkland Islands. The relief ships (HMS *Leeds Castle* and another Type 21 Frigate) where already in contact with us regards handover and briefings. With the handover completed we departed past our replacements. Water cannons and rotten vegetables were pelted at the new Falkland Patrol vessels as we made a fast exit to the north and warmer waters.

'Our next stop would be St. Croix in the Virgin Islands.

'We arrived back in UK waters in mid-December 1986. First landfall was RNAS Culdrose and a mail drop and the all-important pick up. The following day we were off Plymouth Sound ready to depart to Portland. All was going swimmingly until the Naval Provost SIB came on board on the pretext that someone had reported a member of the crew was trying to bring drugs into the country.

'The Naval Provost tried to delay the Wasp departing to Portland, but were firmly told by me that they could not search the aircraft with a dog now but they were welcome once we arrived at Portland, but they were not delaying our take-off from the ship as we had clearances by various aviation agencies. The Captain backed me up, ordering the search team off the flight deck when he put the ship to Flying Stations.

'The flight to Portland was most uneventful after the debacle at Plymouth. We arrived at Portland and landed on the south side of the runway as was the procedure when clearing customs. We were met by no-one, SIB or any member of the Provost staff; they were nowhere to be seen. So we reported to the customs office in the main admin building, which was empty too, so we left our customs declaration forms and duly went home for a more private reunion and a well-deserved Christmas break.'

Chapter 8

Personal Accounts

In researching this book many personal accounts were received. This chapter contains many of them and gives an impression of what it was like from a variety of personal points of view.

WASP Tales – Terry Loughran 1973 - 1975

'After a first tour flying the Wessex 1, during the tense period in which the free power turbine in the large single Napier gazelle gas turbine engine had been shedding its blades with catastrophic consequences, it was a pleasure to move on to the first of the (then new) twin engine ASW Sea King Mk1 Squadrons - 824. Graduating from this, through QHI Course, to a "beefer" (instructor) on 706 Squadron, I finally reached the pinnacle as TOSK, Training Officer Sea Kings. I was somewhat surprised therefore, in a terse interview with the pilot appointer (in the COs office, which was, in the fullness of time, to become my own), to be told I had been selected to be a Wasp Flight Commander.

'As a "two ringer" with seven and a half years seniority (no one carries their seniority more publicly than in that short step from Lieutenant Commander) I at least expected to be one of the new breed of SQAVOs - Squadron Aviation Officers. But NO, I was to be the Flight Commander of an elderly, single screw, private, Tribal Class Frigate - HMS *Ashanti*.

'Stripped of all external responsibilities, I immediately fell in love with the Wasp and set about enjoying this spirited helicopter which the Queen had apparently bequeathed me, for my personal use and enjoyment! And while it meant leaving behind a young family, jetting off to Bermuda and taking charge of my own Flight was a joy. Unaware of the tribulation which was to befall the ship, I set to work mastering this unique aviation challenge. The Tribal frigates were the first ship class of the Royal Navy to be designed from the start to operate a helicopter, but you would not have thought so. The hangar was a cube shaped box squeezed in between the after 4.5 inch gun and immediately forward of that, the 10 inch Limbo anti-submarine weapon. The hangar roof was an arrangement of heavy curved panels (removed by hand), while the aircraft came up on the hangar floor, which doubled as the lift and the flight deck. Sitting somewhat precariously on the top of this cube, the flight deck was exceedingly small and subject greatly to the eddies from the crowded superstructure.

'One thing I discovered early on was not to refuel the aircraft automatically on recovery (standard practise in the fleet). It is far easier to put fuel in than to take it out, when, for example, you are tasked at short notice to collect the rather large Governor of Bermuda (and his even heavier bodyguard), entailing a vertical descent through tall trees to Government House, and an even more challenging ascent to the tune of the maximum torque bells! However, all good experience, and by the time we sailed for home I felt the Wasp, the small deck and myself were one.

'Our passage back, ominously, coincided with a strong gale up our stern and an Old Moore's Almanac prediction that a grey ship would be lost in the Bermuda Triangle that year! Day after day the gale (up to Force 10) persisted, as did the advice from the Fleet Headquarters Ocean Weather Centre to maintain our course. One afternoon, in mid-Atlantic, with the upper deck out of bounds, the ship broached, rolling badly; not surprising given the single screw and the powerful following sea. Unfortunately, a part of ship Petty Officer, seduced by the warm sunshine and a following wind, had taken a group of young sailors outside in the sheltered waist. Left swimming for their lives, he died immediately, impaled on a guardrail, and one sailor was lost overboard. Turning the ship around in those conditions was difficult, but retracing our steps was simple, the string of life rafts we had lost provided a clear marker and the man overboard was soon spotted. His lifejacket was inflated, but he appeared dead. Nevertheless, with the ship's company all on lookout, the Captain's priority was to recover the body and he proposed to put a ships diver into the water. I couldn't help but feel that in the conditions he too would become a casualty under the bilge keels and I persuaded the Captain that we should launch the Wasp and I would take the diver.

That was easier said than done in the prevailing conditions, but the Petty Officer mess mates of the deceased PO mustered to help move the hangar hatch covers. However, such had been the extent of the ship roll, salt water had contaminated the fuel lines and a delay occurred while it was cleared. Once airborne, the reality of the wind became apparent, any turn downwind resulting in an alarming ground speed. Equally I estimated the height of the waves from crest to trough at sixty feet with considerable spume and disturbance and I rapidly reached the conclusion that putting the diver down was out of the question. At this stage the ship had lost sight of the man and was unable to conn me onto his position; mercifully the decision was taken out of my hands. I was sufficiently confident, or was it conceit, that there was no deck I could not land on, but on this recovery, the Deputy Weapons Engineer Officer, who doubled as Flight Deck Officer and oft complained he was wasting his time as I ignored him (not true!), certainly earned his spurs. I could not have landed safely without his excellent batsmanship.

'That was not the end of the saga however, as on our return to UK a Board of Inquiry was convened; no green endorsement, no pat on the back, only a censure (by the Gunnery Officer presiding over the Board of Inquiry) for not refuelling the aircraft on completion of the previous sortie!

'In true appointing fashion, suddenly I was to be a SQAVO (Squadron Aviation Officer and a Lieutenant Commander) and joined HMS *Leander* on the staff of Captain F3. We sailed shortly afterwards on a group deployment, a time when the frigate squadron could operate together. It was a mixed bag of frigate types, the only common element being the ships' main armament, the Wasp!

'A couple of months into the deployment three of the squadron ships arrived together in Mombasa and I disembarked our aircraft to the airport for a concentrated period of Engine Off Landings (EOLs) for the three available pilots and my own P2. Given the conditions, warm if not hot, and somewhat sticky if not humid, this could have been considered a high risk strategy, as one heavy landing could have seriously disrupted our part in the deployment. However, after two and half hours of successful EOLs, somewhat relieved I returned to the tower to settle the admin, only for the kindly controller to say, "One thing I've always wanted to know, is what do you do when the engine stops!"

'Several months later *Leander* pulled into Pusan, in South Korea, where we were scheduled to do some defences sales. The new Lynx helicopter had flown, but was not yet operational and Sea Skua was still on the drawing board, but we were to promote them both. The ROK Navy were in need of such a capability, as during the course of our visit, their Chief of Navy had his game of golf with Captain F3 disrupted to take a report on their sinking a North Korean patrol boat! Bizarrely, we were also to offer the predominantly surface-to-air Sea Cat missile in its surface-to-surface mode. Come the day of the live demonstrations, first off was to be the Sea Cat and then the AS12; the early February day was bitterly cold. Owing to my relatively challenged size I could get ten minutes more endurance out of the Wasp than most pilots, but we still needed the doors off to accommodate me, the aimer, his sight and the AS12 missile.

'The Sea Cat was a line of sight missile, reliant upon the seaman aimer to gather it and strike the target. The flight profile gave him a fighting chance, whereas in the surface mode it was a far greater challenge. The one authorised missile for the firing ploughed in not far from the ship and the Captain immediately ordered another prepared. While this suffered the same ignominious fate, we circled, eating into both endurance and body heat. Come our turn, I called, "Crosswind and Downwind Dummy", only for my valiant aimer, Leading Seaman Smith, to tell me his hands were so cold he needed to fire on this run. To the consternation of the ship's controller, I duly called, "Base Leg Live" and when challenged, "Negative - Dummy", I was emphatic that we were "Finals Live" and if the spectators weren't watching they would miss it! Fortunately, they were watching and "dead eyed Smith" not only hit the target, but sank the barge upon which it was mounted! Shortly after recovery I was in the Captain's cabin extolling the virtues of Lynx and Sea Skua to our South Korean guests, but seeing was believing and they wanted the Wasp and AS12!

'Another career enhancing opportunity gone by the board.

'It was many years later that I had my final encounter with the Wasp, when as Flag Officer Naval Aviation (FONA), I visited the RNZN Fleet Air Arm which boasted, at that time, four Wasps. Needless to say I was taken on an aerial tour in one flown by the Flight Commander who, somewhat ambitiously, suggested we finish off with an Engine Off Landing - "for old times sake"! Having moved on some twenty years from Mombasa, I could see the impact of FONA reducing the Orbat of the RNZN FAA by 25% in one afternoon and generously declined.'

Ted Oliver, then a Chief Petty Officer on HMS *Hydra's* Flight recounts an interesting deployment to Iran in the days before the revolution:

'In 1968 the navy was tasked to undertake survey work on behalf of the Iranian government, which at that time meant the Shar. The contract was to provide two ships operating in pairs over three years. The survey season running for the six winter months of each year. The work would be two periods of intense activity with a break for Christmas and a rendezvous with a supply ship approximately halfway through each deployment. Hydra Flight, which is the one I was on, was scheduled for the 1969 deployment, along with HMS *Herald*.

'We left Portsmouth in September 1969, stopping at Gibraltar and Malta on route to the Suez Canal and then on to Bandar-e Abbas at the northern part of the Strait of Hormuz. This was to be the port we would visit for a couple of days every three weeks or so to resupply food etc.

'Even though it was the start of the cooler period temperatures were well up towards the 40 degree Celsius mark. This led to problems when carrying out routine engine power performance checks, the temperature being too high for the relevant graphs to be read accurately. The Wasp being designed for a temperate climate.'

Hydra's Wasp. The Arabic writing has some sort of meaning along the lines of 'Peace to you' painted on by the Captain who was an Arab speaker. *(Ted Oliver)*

'The operating environment was also one for which the Wasp was not suited. It was required to fly in sand laden air without the benefit of any filtration for the air intake. In fact any such filtration would not have been practical in an aircraft with a low power margin. The result was a very high rate of erosion on the engine compressor blades and both main and tail rotor leading edges. This led us to having to change the engine after only 10% of its reconditioning life; such was the loss of power because of the erosion.'

The transmission deck covered in sand with totally exposed engine intake. *(Ted Oliver)*

'A normal day would start at first light and the aircraft would fly well in excess of the norm for a small ships flight, some days ten hours would be a normal days flying. This meant that some servicing operations would be carried out every second day rather than weekly. The flying itself would be in support of the survey parties ashore, both ferrying them off in the morning and returning them back in the evening. Then throughout the day they would be supplied with any equipment they needed, as well as food and plenty of water. The aircraft was also required to carry underslung loads and not having a great lifting capacity meant more flights than would be required of a more suitable helicopter like the Wessex.

'Often the aircraft would return to the ship in the dark, even though the flight deck was not properly equipped for night operations. This was driven by the commercial pressure to fulfil the contract. Not something sailors are subjected to normally.

'At the end of each day the aircraft had to be serviced, which meant that because of the high number of flying hours being accumulated servicing operations were being carried out more frequently and even some of the bigger tasks which could be carried out when disembarked back at Portland had to be done on board.

'But before any work could start the aircraft had to be cleared of the sand that had built up in all the nooks and crannies peculiar to the Wasp. Unlike most other helicopters, much of its working parts such as engine, gearbox and rotor transmission are exposed and make great sand traps. In particular the Z crank bay was especially prone to a large build-up of sand.

'We did get a break from the intense survey flying when the ship spent Christmas in Doha. Wonderful! Not the place for thirsty sailors.

'After Christmas there was the small matter of the Iranian revolution, which meant that the contract was at an end. The ship did evacuate some British expats to Dubai and American ones to an American fleet offshore, after which no country in the region wanted us in their harbours. We ended up being at sea for six weeks, by which time the caterer had run out of cheap food, so we had to eat steak every day, putting his budget well into the red. When we did finally get in to Muscat and took on food, we had to endure eggs every day until the catering budget was in the black again.

'We also had a visit in Bombay (as it then was) from a "help" team from 849 HQ. Not so much a help as an inspection, the result of which was the flight being branded "an accident waiting to happen". This of course by experienced Wasp flight personnel. The problem was they didn't have any experience of the type of operation which we were engaged in. The result of this visit was an FOF3 inspection on the way back to the UK. The strange thing was that once we had left the survey area behind and had the time to undertake the work, we got the aircraft back up to scratch. The inspection team found that far from being an accident statistic we were pretty much just another small ships flight. On our arrival back at Portland the same experts from Bombay were disappointed to find the material state of the aircraft no different to that of the squadrons other Wasps.

'During the training before joining the Flight we had to undergo the weapons training but, of course, once formed for a survey ship we no longer had to bother with it. Some bright spark did say we had to practise loading a drill torpedo one day and this is something that a flight can do in minutes. We on the other hand took so long we managed a stand easy half way through.'

Roger Bryant – Recollections of the Wasp.

'In 1966, I was appointed to relieve Geoff Cavalier as Flight Commander HMS *AURORA* - a "private" frigate - and went through the Wasp conversion and

OFT at Culdrose and Portland. I started to take ownership of XS 540 in July 1967 when the Flight was formed. October and November 1967 were devoted to hopping between the ship and RNAS Portland, and workup – FOST style. Then it was into Casexes and a Joint Maritime exercise in waters off Derry and the Outer Isles. Finally, we embarked at Portsmouth at the beginning of April 1968 and set off to do our spell of Beira Patrol – aimed to blockade unknown shipping entering the port.

'In 1967 those of us forming ships' flights were the second wave of pilots, and, as for the first, the word was circulated that if you do not have an engine failure during the two-year commission, then you are not bearing your fair share of the load!

'*Aurora* sailed south via Gibraltar, practicing both ourselves and the ship in Vectacs, DLPs, radar trials, IF, SCAs, VPHs, vertreps, CTFs and winching until on the night of 17 Apr, I bore my fair share of the load. We were night flying out in the Atlantic rather more than halfway between Gib and Simonstown, when there was a bang from behind me. I was in the middle of a circuit practicing identification of merchant ships to prepare for the task off Beira. The plan, at night, was to find an unsuspecting merchantman, go slowly up its port side from well astern at 200 feet, and illuminate the ship's name and port of registration with the landing light. We had already done a few such manoeuvres successfully in previous night flights.

'On hearing the bang, I radioed *Aurora* that I was returning and briefly explained why, but this call, apparently, did not get through. I was about twelve miles from "mother" and apparently in the radar blind arc – somewhere on the starboard quarter. A second thump made me decide to make a power-on ditching – the ship was still twelve miles away – and I transmitted a mayday which was not acknowledged. I later heard that that call had not been received. Ts & Ps at that stage seemed normal.

'The whole decision making process was abruptly terminated when a third bang was accompanied by apparent partial disintegration of the engine, and the engine platform going up in flames. But from 200 feet there was just time enough to enter autorotation and take the speed off the aircraft before settling on the water without too much drama. This, of course, is from memory forty-nine years on!!

'Only one flotation bag operated – the starboard one. Anyway, wet dinghy drill routine kicked in and both the crewman and I exited the hull without difficulty. We linked up and secured our dinghies together and shortly after, tied ourselves to the floating hull. The crewman was in a state of some shock.

'We activated SARBEs, but no contact could be established with *Aurora*. I knew that the ship only had one boiler connected - max speed 18 knots. I knew, also, that she was about twelve miles away and so calculated that *Aurora* would pick us up in less than one hour's time taking into account ship reaction time and slowing-down time as she approached. By firing a mini-flare every five minutes that would just about exhaust my supply, and if I'd got it wrong, then the crewman's were still available. The error of my ways was later pointed out – we should have alternated firing flares.

'The seas were steep and I feared that the hull might be lifted up and deposited on top of us in the dinghies if we did not create some separation. Or if the hull sank, would it take us down with it? We decided to sever ourselves from the hull and accept the possibility of being unable to detect it once rescue arrived. We deployed shark repellent. And so we then settled down to wait for the rescue, and indeed, after a while we did spot the ships lights heading in our direction.

'Turning the clock back a few minutes, I've mentioned that we were in the ship's radar blind arc, and that mutual voice communications were just not working for us – at last, we were not receiving. On the fight deck, the team were, I expect, having a brew, but the LMA, who in those days, was required to be on the flight deck during "flying stations", was taking the air outside the hangar. He was a brilliant young man with a fine personality, but he wore spectacles with pretty thick lenses. So when he reported seeing a ball of fire in the sky astern of the ship, he was not initially taken very seriously.

'The ship's motor-whaler duly picked us up just less than an hour after ditching, and took us on board. At the time of rescue, we had no sight of the hull. Of course, I reported to the Captain on the bridge and we discussed tactics. The TAS team closed up and started pinging in the hope of detecting the Wasp. A search pattern was established and from the upper deck, the sea was combed with the lights from signal projectors.

'There was no detection of the hull and after several hours searching, we moved on.

'Subsequent thought was that the turbine had shed a blade or two - that was the engine weakness - which had penetrated the engine casing and severed a fuel line, thus fuel was being sprayed onto the hot engine casing causing a mega-conflagration. Certainly, in my brief journey into the Atlantic, I was able to read the instruments without the aid of emergency lighting.

'Fortunately, HMS *Gurkha* was rounding the Cape homeward bound and Keith Simmonds transferred his Wasp to *Aurora* and we were in business again.

I did not fly until Simonstown, where, at SAAF Ysterplaat I underwent a post-accident aircrew medical, checked out our new baby in the air and did a few basic ground drills - including an inconclusive compass-swing. "Ysterplaat" is an Afrikaans word translated as "Iron Place". The swing was later repeated at sea and we think, with more meaningful results.

'XT 434 then served me, the Flight, and our ship well for the remainder of the commission, which took us to Beira Patrol, a four-month spell as Gulf Guardship, Singapore and back home in November 1969. Paddy Syer was my relief.

'On one occasion, I'm not sure where or when, I lost a few crates of beer when transferring stores to a conventional submarine by underslung load. The net load in question was exclusively boxes of beer which seemed to still be snugly packed together when I deposited the net on the after casing. Dismay all round when I released the hook and the sides of the net opened to let some cases into the oggin. Not to let our submariner colleagues go thirsty, I returned to the ship and took replacements internally. There was a bit of movement on the submarine, but a two wheel landing onto the said casing was feasible and gave the sure opportunity to hand the replenishments case by case to the eager recipients with not a drop spilt.

'I then joined HQ 829 Squadron as a staff pilot and soon went on the IRI course. Soon after qualifying I had a crash draft in June 1970, to HMS *Minerva* in Simonstown, to relieve Nigel Dark who had to return to UK. So, it was back to Ysterplaat for air tests again with XT788. Then off on the round to Beira, Gan, Singapore, the Solomons and New Hebrides, Auckland, Dunedin, Sydney, and Bunbury at the beginning of November 1970, where my permanent relief, Peter Royston, took the weight.

'Of note, the ships main gunfire control system went haywire as we traversed the islands on our way from Singapore to New Zealand. The gyro unit of the gun direction system on top of the bridge was established as the culprit. But without an alongside berth with crane within hundreds of miles, the OPDEF, it seemed, would be an ongoing issue for some time, until; "I think I may be able to help you out, sir!" So, once we had sailed from Gizo, with a gentle sea and a favourable wind. On 21 September 1970 I lifted the defective gyro out of its seating and replaced it with new. A single nylon strop was not long enough to allow positioning of the "pony" above the ship's mainmast obstructions, so, with two strops joined together and with one FDO on the bridge top and the other on the mast upper radar platform, the OPDEF was rectified - all except for a bit of electrical connecting - within, according to my flying log, fifteen minutes.

Authorities at home expressed displeasure at my having linked two strops together in contravention of Flight Safety Signals! But the ship's GO was delighted.

'In Dunedin in mid-October 1970, the Wasp was due some deepish maintenance involving some disassembly which was started on the first day in harbour. At the evening cocktail party, the Captain met commercial fishermen, one of whose boats had gone missing at sea. "Not a problem, my helicopter can search." "But, Sir…" The Flight was recalled from shore by any means and the aircraft was put back together, with the Supply Officer/FDO overseeing it all, and with me being shaken periodically during the night for test running. We were airborne at first light, but did not find the missing fishing boat.

'Fast-forward now from February 1971 to November 1981 when I came into serious contact with the Wasp again as nominated Flight Commander, HMS *Hydra*. The re-famil grew, almost, into a full blown conversion, and by the time I had done Survey "OFT" - airborne photography, etc - and was ready to join the ship and move up to the Outer Hebrides to collect chart data, three months had elapsed.

'Part of the Survey Flight "OFT" took place at RAF Cosford - the RAF School of Photography a few miles to the north-west of Wolverhampton. There we were trained in and practiced the art of vertical photography from height - necessary for charting coastlines. My appointment prior to returning to flying had been on the staff of CBF Hong Kong. During my time abroad Diana, Princess of Wales, had been suffering from undue and intrusive attention from the media and an informal no-fly zone had been established around Highgrove House - the country residence of Prince Charles - some five miles to the south-west of RAF Kemble. The zone had not been published as a NOTAM. With the camera fitted and carrying other baggage, it was not possible to make Cosford from Portland in one go and I planned to take on fuel at Kemble - then a practice area for the Red Arrows display team. On 7 December 1981, as I approached Kemble, the Red Arrows were in mid-display routine and I was invited by Kemble ATC to loiter… yes, five miles to the south-west. ATC may have given a height, but it was not high. Eventually, I refuelled and got underway again. On arrival at Cosford I was greeted by a flustered young crab officer who instructed that I was required to report to the Station Commander without delay. "What did I think I was doing deliberately buzzing Highgrove House when there was a no-fly zone established?" I of course was blissfully unaware of the unofficial exclusion zone - until then - but defended myself by saying that I was then under control of RAF ATC and was merely doing what I was told to do. I heard nothing more, but supposed that someone in ATC Kemble was in receipt of a serious re-briefing.'

Note: At this point in Roger's story he gives account of his involvement and that of the other survey ships in the Falklands War. For continuity this has already been placed in Chapter 7 above.

'Following some leave, HMS *Hydra* got on with the work that had been scheduled for earlier in the year - surveying the waters of the outer isles and some deep water data collection. Thereafter, Mombasa and the Musandam Peninsular, with final disembarkation at Portland on 13 April 1984.

'The final entry in my logbook records that in February 1997, I got my hands, as P2, on a Gazelle of the Vojska Republike Srpska Air Force for thirty minutes. I had been placed on the retired list in April 1994 and was then a regional director with the OSCE permanent mission to Bosnia Herzegovina. Keeping track of military developments was part of my mandate and I was formally visiting the air force as an inspector. My questions during the briefing revealed that I knew something of the subject matter. The (one star) commander of the flying wing was the pilot, but spoke no English. I spoke no Serbian. So my military liaison staff officer sat in the back seat and interpreted. He was a Belarussian naval Commander who had been the engineer officer of a "Red October" Soviet nuclear submarine. And, after thirteen years, I could still fly a reasonable circuit and execute a damage-free landing – even with the main rotor going round the wrong way!'

Nigel Cunningham gave his account of some of his experiences as an aircrewman, including a rather unusual internal load. His pilot of the time went on to rather better things (see the foreword to this book).

'I joined the Royal Navy in 1976 as a Junior Assistant Cook, but during a draft to 820 NAS, where I worked in the aircrew refreshment bar (ACRB) in HMS *Invincible*, I was first introduced to the aircrewman's branch. During Operation Corporate in 1982 I submitted a request form to branch change, and in April 1983 I found myself at the flying training school at RNAS Culdrose.

'During the 1981 defence review, six Type 12 Frigates were placed into mothballs, but as a result of the ship losses during the Falklands campaign, those ships were recovered and therefore the Fleet Air Arm had to quickly generate six small ships flights. The result of this was that rather than pursuing a career as an ASW aircrewman flying the Sea King Mk 5, I found myself at RNAS Portland completing a conversion course onto the WASP HAS Mk 1.

'The Wasp HAS Mk1 first flew in 1962 and so was a mature aircraft by the time I came to adorn its left-hand seat. The single engine Wasp was under-powered, had little passenger space and used a slow hydraulic rescue hoist. But it was a pioneer for today's naval aviation. The Lynx and Wildcat flights who operate from the decks of Frigates and Destroyers today, do so in exactly the same manner as we did in the 1980s. The Flight consisted of a Flight Commander, Senior Maintenance rating and seven rating maintainers, along with an aircrewman. The aircrewman had many secondary duties which included a daily wrestle with the MUFAX weather machine. (If it didn't work, then the alternative was to hand-produce a colour drawing fashioned from a complex received signal.) All of the Flight planning publications, NOTAMs and Flight operations were conducted by the aircrewman. But the main role of the Wasp aircrewman was as the airborne missile aimer. The aircraft was credited with the AS12 and SS11 missiles. Both missiles were French designed air-to-surface missiles which were wire guided from a range of about 7-8 Km. Fitted with a Booster motor which subsequently ignited a sustainer motor the missile flew for approximately thirty seconds before it impacted the target. Easy to load and rearm, the missile was also relatively cheap and consequently the RN had plenty of them. Consequently, each aircrewman was afforded three missiles each year in order to hone his missile aiming skills. Missile firings took place in Lyme Bay North range, just to the east of Portland, with an arming point established at a small establishment just to the west of Weymouth. AS12 missile firings really were the sport of kings. With weeks to go the excitement grew as the aircrewman concerned honed his skills on a simulator which could be fitted to the aircraft.

'During the autumn of 1985 I was drafted to HMS *Rothesay* Flight. The Type 12 Frigate had Commander Warren Benbow in command, with Lieutenant George Zambellas as the Flight Commander. Embarkations to Rosyth were challenging in a Wasp and normally took in excess of four hours flying (Portland, to RAF Lyneham, to RAF Cottesmore, to RAF Leeming, to RAF Boulmer, to Rosyth), however, the ultimate sortie and still my world record happened on 26 August 1986 when Lieutenant Zambellas and I flew Wasp Has Mk 1 XT785 for eight hours during a Load lifting/Vertrep sortie at Ascension Island. (Photo attached.) Wasp Sorties were not always routine. In August 1986 we were asked to pick up two reindeer from a remote site at Grytviken on South Georgia. Reindeer had been introduced to the South Sandwich Islands as a means of food for the Whalers, but once whaling in the South Atlantic has ceased the reindeer population flourished and consequently each year there was a cull. Rothesay had been offered two to supplement the chief caterer's budget and we were tasked to recover the beasts. On the face of it a simple task and the attached photograph taken by the Flight Commander shows me dragging the first of our passengers across the frozen glacier towards the aircraft. What neither of us had planned for was the manner in which I was to lift a twenty stone dead weight into the back of the aircraft. The answer? Wrap the rescue strop around the animal and then guide it into the cabin with the pilot having winch control. The result? Reindeer blood and entrails all over me and all over the back of the cabin, BUT more importantly - venison for the entire ships company for two weeks.'

John Beattie is a well-known and respective aviator who flies Wasps and other historic aircraft to this day. However, he supplied this short tale which shows some of the other dangers of operating aircraft from the back of small ships:

HMS *Ashanti*, in the Bay of Biscay, the morning following a stormy night in 1977.

'I was Squadron Aviation Officer for the 8th Frigate Squadron, visiting one of the squadron ships, HMS *Ashanti*, whilst on passage to Gibraltar. During the night in question my cabin mate was thrown, complete with wooden bunk, across the tiny space, damaging him and destroying the bunk. In the morning there was a bit of a commotion at the rear of the superstructure, where four or five men were peering out of the screen door, looking aft. From that vantage point could be seen the mortar well and flight deck and also the door to a very small compartment under the flight deck, that held the Wasp's spare engine. A door that was open and taking in a big wave every now and again! Not so good for the spare engine, even though it was encased in a rubberised storage bag. The Flight Senior Maintenance Rating was there and chose his moment carefully, every seventh wave was supposedly followed by a brief lull. We used that folklore when landing on a small ship and I never found an excuse to doubt it. After just such a wave, he dashed across the short space, slammed the door shut and put on several of the eight clips but couldn't have been counting waves, as a big "goffer" came rolling in over the side and washed him overboard! Luckily, he was wearing a lifejacket partially inflated, as was the custom. The message was quickly passed to the bridge and the Captain executed a "Williamson's turn" to get the ship back alongside and upwind of the somewhat concerned swimmer. Scrambling nets were thrown over the side, but alas the SMR was too tired to climb unaided, despite much vocal encouragement. The ship was rolling heavily, despite it being quite a nice day. Two "swimmers" (ship's divers in wet suits) climbed down the scrambling net and just about carried the SMR to the top. He was none the worse for wear after a tot or two, but probably still has nightmares over the event.'

John Beattie also features in a story by his then second pilot, Simon Thomas and yet another unusual feat conducted by a Wasp - this time the world piano playing height record:

'June 1978. I was a couple of months into my first tour, John Beattie's P2 in Ajax Flight. It was RAF Cosford's inaugural air show, and the whole flight had detached for a few happy days whilst disembarking to Portland from the Liverpool area. I vaguely remember a beer call for the participants the night before, held in some Nissen hut - belonging to the Scouts, I think. Outside, against the wall which was being used temporarily for aircrew relief was a mouldering old upright piano, which John had procured as a "display enhancement", so we could compete with Pitts Specials and fast jets...

'At some stage, we must have found a means of transporting said piano from the hut, to a spot out of sight behind a grass-covered aircraft shelter on the south side of the airfield. From somewhere, came a length of stout cord which would happily have tied a minesweeper alongside. All we needed now was a pilot (Beattie), an aircrewman (Schofield), and an idiot (me). So the display started – the idiot wobbled out on some dodgy old RAF bike across the airfield, crashed and got winched up by a handy Wasp. Back to the shelter, out with the cargo strop and on with the hawser. Rising phoenix-like into the sky, with torque bells protesting, 421 started a spiral climb (yes, pretty sedately) over the centre of the airfield. Over the Tannoy, the commentator announced an attempt at the World Highest Flying Pianist (or something similar-sounding) record. Out came the rescue strop again, with the idiot dangling in it. I tucked my feet into the upright legs, waved my arms up and down like Jerry Lee Lewis on amphetamines, and the Tannoy music started. At around 1,000 feet, I withdrew my feet, clenched my buttocks, said my prayers, and the piano was released, complete with two smoke flares. In retrospect, perhaps I shouldn't have secured the lines to the flares on my wrist with a slip knot, as my hand nearly went with it. Least of my worries, you may say. Anyway, I watched the doomed, fiery piano fall to earth. That was when I noticed a grass runway at right angles to the main... oops. Target neutralised.

'So, a single-engine helicopter, three POB, an underslung load, a sucker in a strop, in a virtual hover at 1,000 feet. What could possibly go wrong with that?

Tell you what, my mum was watching and she was definitely not 'appy. Probably cheered up when she had the film from my camera developed - two or three pics of a line of Flight bottoms included. Thanks, boys.'

Note: In the days of analogue film cameras it was extremely risky to leave said device unattended. If found, certain photos would be taken (as above) and it would be the person (often the wife or mum) who saw them first after collecting them from Boots!

David Issitt was a flying engineer and did a tour on HMS *Endurance* in the Antarctic. During that time he personally replaced his aircrafts engine - almost certainly the only time this had been done by the pilot himself:

'Ah! The Wasp helicopter. An aircraft you either loved or hated. For me it was love - I loved its simplicity (other than trying to explain the workings of the Z crank, which was far from simple) and it was fun to fly, but much of the fun came from where I operated. I was lucky enough to be a pilot in the ship's flight of HMS *Endurance* and accrued most of my Wasp hours in Antarctica.

'Coming to 829 Squadron from a front line Sea King squadron in 1983 was a big change and the simplicity of the Wasp was welcome; no complex systems to learn, no blade fold to go wrong and no four-hour sorties!

'The Wasp was easier to maintain too - so easy that when I snagged an ECU during a hectic Antarctic work period the SMR suggested that I should do the engine change as the rest of the flight was busy on the flight deck conducting an all-day load lifting evolution with the remaining cab. Well, the chance to get amongst it was too good to miss, so, manual to hand and tool box signed out I set about it with occasional visits from the SMR and M1 to make sure it was going well. ECU changed, it was up to me to do the tethered ground run and then test flight. I can't imagine getting away with that with any other aircraft type! The test flight was interesting and involved going somewhat outside the flight envelope for a governor topping check - achieved at 13,500 feet and -26° C. (The authorised maximum was 12000 feet due to reduced oxygen at altitude.)

'Wasp tour over it was off to RNAY Fleetlands as an MTP flying Chinook, Sea King, Lynx and Gazelle and bringing to an end my days in the Wasp. Or so I thought... After Fleetlands came RNAY Wroughton and the chance to fly the Wasp's close relation, the Scout. After an interesting five day conversion at Middle Wallop I found the Scout to be as much fun as the Wasp and I certainly didn't miss the flotation gear! Towards the end of my tour there the Malaysian

Navy bought some Wasps from the UK and they were prepared for export at Wroughton so I took to the skies once more in that angry, buzzing insect of a helicopter - bliss!'

The following slightly tongue in cheek account is by Peter Spens-Black who, unusually, was appointed to fly the Wasp after several years flying the far more sophisticated Sea King Mark 4. This probably illustrates the 'culture shock' many pilots went through in the aircraft's later years when there were more capable and better equipped machines around:

My First Time

Instructor:	'Right, this sortie is purely to give you an introduction to the aircraft, demonstrate the layout of the cockpit and give you a feel for how it handles, OK?'
Me:	'No problem.'
Instructor:	'I will be doing the hands-on flying and you just get used to the cockpit.'
Me:	'Roger that.'
Instructor:	'So that's the pre-start up checks complete…'
Me:	'Where's the Tactical Air Navigation display?'
Instructor:	'There isn't one.'
Me:	'So no Decca navigator?'
Instructor:	'Nope.'
Instructor:	'So now we are burning and turning, pre take-off checks complete, signal to the marshaller and gently pull in the lever and then…'
Me (With slightly higher pitched voice):	'Why is the fire alarm going off?'
Instructor:	'No, no. That's not the fire alarm, that's the over-torque audio signal.'
Me:	'But we are in the hover and there's no load or weapons?'
Instructor:	'Welcome to my world!'
Me:	'Where are the fuel computer controls?'
Instructor:	'There aren't any – it's a fuel control unit.'
Me:	'What, like a carburettor? Analogue not digital?'
Instructor:	'Sort of, but they teach you all that in ground school.'
Instructor:	'Well here we are at 2000 feet with ten miles to run to Bovingdon Range.'

Me:	'How do you know?'
Instructor:	'It is on the map.'
Me:	'So no VOR reading?'
Instructor:	'Nope.'
Me:	'So I'm guessing no DME?'
Instructor:	'Yep.'
Instructor:	'I'll demonstrate some flying manoeuvres around Bovingdon and then we'll head back to Portland and land via a GCA.'
Me:	'Can't we do an ILS approach?'
Instructor:	'Ain't fitted.'
Instructor:	'You got all the flying instruments sorted?'
Me:	'Not yet. Why is the fuel gauge in the middle of the panel and twice the size of all the other instruments?'
Instructor:	'You'll learn.'
Me:	'OK. But the Attitude Indicator seems to be bobbing around a lot and doesn't seem to replicate what's going on outside.'
Instructor:	'Because it's not an AI but an Artificial Horizon.'
Me:	'Hey, we had those as standby instruments in the Wessex 5. Cool, historic.'
Me:	'So the UHF radio sounds OK, but where do you change channels?'
Instructor:	'This selector here.'
Me:	'But it's only marked 1 to 12?'
Instructor:	'Well, that's all you need for 12 channels.'
Me:	'12? What if you are diverted to an airfield that is not on 1 to 12?'
Instructor:	'Oh, they'll hear you on Guard. OK.'
Me:	'So the fall-back option is 243.0 MHz?'
Instructor:	'Yep.'
Me:	'But what happens when we deploy around the globe.'
Instructor:	'Then the skill is getting an R1 on your Flight who is a wheeler-dealer.'
Me:	'What? Why?'
Instructor:	'Because he needs to be a key player on the frequency crystal market and able to swap, borrow or steal from other Flights so that he has all the possible destinations, Area Air Traffic and military options covered.'
Me:	'Wouldn't a multi-frequency ARC 52 radio be a better option?'
Instructor:	'Of course, but we don't have one.'

Me:	'Hang on, most civilian airfields and air traffic don't have UHF radios, just VHF.'
Instructor:	'Yes, but when you deploy they retro fit a VHF radio.'
Me:	'OK that sounds reasonable.'
Instructor:	'Yep, but the downside is that when you switch on the VHF you lose the intercom with your aircrewman – but don't worry you soon develop a workable sign language. But don't try it if you have a stab failure – you tend to explore the flight envelope, which can be disconcerting.'
Me:	'So when we are on a NATO type exercise, we will be working with large ASW forces so we will need to operate on HF.'
Instructor:	'Ideally that's true, but we can't fit in an HF radio and there's probably not enough fuselage to fit an effective aerial. Anyway, if you have anything of import to say, someone will probably relay it for you on Guard, so no problem.'
Me:	OK, so likewise we may be called upon to work with ground forces and having learnt from bitter experience they tend to shoot at you unless you have cleared your approach on VHF Tactical radio – except, of course 2 Para who will shoot at you anyway. So where do they fit the Vtac?'
Instructor:	'Nope – no Vtac. I suppose you could get the crewie to wave a white flag?'
Me:	'At night? On NVG.'
Instructor:	'Good point. What's NVG?'
Me:	'Night Vision Goggles – they give you a 10,000 times magnification of the available background light from the moon and stars. And I've just realised that my next question is pointless.'
Instructor:	'Ok. So the cab is pretty manoeuvrable and engine-offs are not too difficult if you have sufficient height and a fair potential landing site. We only do practice engine-offs at an airfield, but I will now demonstrate an autorotation and we will come to the hover in the clearing you see ahead. I will lower the lever promptly, flare the speed off to 60 knots and settle into a steady descent maintaining the NR (rotor speed) with gentle applications of the lever. OK, we are passing 150 feet, into wind and NR is spot on. I now begin flaring to reduce the forward speed and wipe off the rate of descent. And here we are with the speed almost all washed off and levelling at fifteen feet and…'

BANG BANG BANG BANG BANG CRUNCH.

Me:	'F*** was that?'

The aircraft bounces, sways and eventually settles onto four oleos and the engines settles into ground idle.

Instructor:	'Right, they will go into detail of this in ground school. But now you are ahead of the game because you have just witnessed the "Nimbus Surge" and how well the a/c lands when you don't actually have any torque going to the rotor head.'
Me:	'Ok. Right. Um - Have they invented the mobile phone yet?'
Instructor:	'What? No I don't think so. Why?'
Me:	'Because I urgently need to phone my b*sta*d of an appointer and ask why he has chosen me to be the lead player in his practical joke of appointing someone from the Sea King 4 to this nineteenth century anachronism? Oh and I think I will get a taxi back to Portland, but thanks for the eye-opener.'

And finally - If it wasn't true it would not be believable. Here is tail of the demise of one Wasp - all caused by a bowl of custard! This story was supplied by Pete Prescott the aircrewman on HMS *Zulu* Flight:

NO, COOK SCROTE, I DON'T THINK IT'S GOING TO POLISH OUT!!

It wouldn't be believable if it wasn't true! *(Steve George)*

'Graham Jackson and I had just returned from a sortie, it was during the evening meal – about 1800. The Flight decided to put the cab away in a bit of a hurry, those crewman that remember the Tribal class frigates will know the system of carrying the large heavy covers that fitted over the top of the cab once it had been lowered down on the lift.

'Once this was done we all went for our meal. Halfway through the meal there was the dreaded, "FIRE! FIRE! FIRE! Fire in the hanger, fire and emergency party muster at the hangar, Flight personnel to the hangar at the rush".

'I arrived to see the Wasp trying to squeeze through the hangar covers and the covers breaking free from the clips, there were large amounts of smoke pouring out of the hangar as the lift motors were burning out while trying to raise the Wasp with the covers still in place.

'Once the power was isolated and the fire extinguished the panic was over and we were left with a Wasp helicopter a little shorter than it was thirty minutes earlier.

'So what happened?

'For safety reasons there were two push button switches that had to be pressed at the same time to allow the lift to go up or down, warning bells sounded during this process, there is also a main isolation switch that was off and locked when the cab was stowed.

'During the rush to go for dinner the main isolation switch was left live, no problem, as it takes two people to press the buttons to rise and lower the lift.

'Meanwhile, a chef in the galley tipped a big pot of custard down the back of the range causing a power surge that melted the contacts in the two switches in the hangar activating the lift motors; this would not have happened if the main switch had been in the off position.

'So Zulu Flight became known as Pigmy Flight, we had to go without an aircraft for three weeks. Wasp helicopter 442 was written off.'

Pete Prescott looking at his squashed helicopter. *(Pete Prescott)*

Classic comment from the young sailor carrying out his watch while patrolling the quarter deck.

He rang the bridge saying to the Officer of the Watch, 'The bells are ringing, the budgie is trying to escape and the hangars on fire'.

This is a true story as the subsequent inquiry proved. As you can see from the photos it made a right mess of the cab.

A right mess. *(Pete Prescott)*

And then then a postscript: from Stephen Williams:

'Yes it is all true and I was the man who rang the bridge with the comments as stated.

'I was an REM at the time and Pete had his bunk below mine, small world! I remember the Quarter Master who answered my phone call saying to me, "you better say that to the Captain" and passed the phone over. On hearing my news the Captain dropped the phone!'

Chapter 9

From LJC's Cockpit

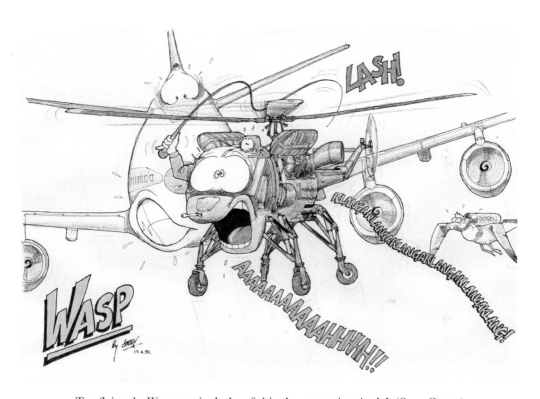

Test flying the Wasp required a lot of altitude - or was it attitude? *(Steve George)*

As I said in my introduction to this book, I actually first flew in a Wasp in 1970 whilst learning to fly civilian light aircraft at Carlisle airport. I then scrounged as many trips as I could whilst a midshipman in HMS *Sirius* in 1972.

However, my first flight to learn to fly the aircraft was on 17 November 1982. I had just returned to the UK from being the Flight pilot in HMS *Andromeda*, flying her Lynx and partaking in a small war some 8000 miles away. In typical RN fashion my appointer had completely forgotten that I had been away for the whole of the year and was actually due rather a lot of leave. Consequently, I was swiftly (too swiftly) sent on courses and then back to Portland to learn to fly the Wasp. I was destined to become the resident Maintenance Test Pilot (MTP) at the air station for the next four years.

I look back on that time as probably the most exciting and professionally rewarding appointment of my thirty years in the Royal Navy.

The role of the MTP is what would nowadays be called Quality Assurance. I flew every machine on the station once a year and put it through the full flight test schedule. The idea was to make sure nothing untoward had crept into the aircraft's performance over the preceding year. Because I was an 'expert' at flight testing and also an independent assessor, it was a good way of maintaining standards. It was also especially important when testing aircraft that had been probably only flown by one person that year, unlike on a squadron where a machine was regularly flown by many aircrew. Often, I would find a fault that was obvious to me, but had slowly crept in so that it hadn't been noticed as it grew worse. I was also often called on to fly aircraft with problems that no one else could diagnose. Those sorties could be real fun - more on that later.

So how did I find the Wasp compared to the Lynx and Sea King that I had previously flown? Two words probably sum up my initial impression - 'basic' and underpowered'. Basic because it was extremely simple, although it did have some complications, like the ability to fly it in manual throttle, which wasn't easy to start off with. Underpowered is a little unfair, as the engine had loads of grunt and it was the transmission that was the limiting factor. I remember lifting into the hover and needing over 90%: torque to do that. I then gently transited forward into the climb at 60 knots, still needing 90% and then, when high enough, accelerating to 90 knots and still needing 90% torque to fly straight and level.

Actually I quite enjoyed flying it as it was a real pilot's machine. There was very little in it to help the poor driver, he had to do it all himself. The autostabilisation system was crude and limited, as was the fairly useless height hold. In fact, unless I was testing these systems, I preferred to fly with them switched out. And it could bite the unwary very hard in several ways. For example, if one was travelling at max speed and you exceeded that even slightly or pulled any significant G, one or all of the rotor blades on the retreating side could stall. If one blade went, a significant thump was felt through the airframe, which was exciting, but easily rectified by slowing down. If more than one went all hell could break loose. On one occasion I was conducting a vibration check test flight at 100 knots and without warning the nose dropped and rolled hard left. I recovered somehow using full rear and right cyclic and with heart thumping, made my way back to the air station, very slowly. When the maintainers checked the aircraft over they found that the witness marks on the shiny parts of the hydraulic jacks were at full travel, something no one had ever seen before!

The Nimbus engine also had a nasty habit of 'surging'. Put simply, surge is when the pressure in the combustion chamber exceeds that at the exit of the compressor and blows all the air back out of the front of the engine. It's similar to a car engine back firing.

It can be caused by several things; damage to the compressor by ingesting something nasty is one common reason for it. Another is pumping too much fuel in at low engine speeds. With some engines it can be very damaging, with the Nimbus, which was quite good at surging under certain conditions, it wouldn't damage the engine, only the pilot's pride. One general flying skill practiced by all helicopter pilots in all types, is a practice autorotation to the hover. The aircraft is flown with the collective fully lowered and the airflow up through the rotors maintaining rotor speed. When at about one hundred and fifty feet the nose is raised to wash off speed and when at about fifty feet lowered again and the collective raised to enter the hover. The Wasp could bite the unwary pilot very easily at this point. The engine needed to be accelerated very gently from low rpm so as the aircraft was being flared, one had to raise the collective just a little to ensure that the engine speed was rising and that the free power turbine was reengaged. Failure to get this right would send the engine into surge. The engine would start to make a violent 'chuffing' noise and absolutely refuse to give any power. By simply stopping movement of the collective, most of the time it was enough to let the engine recover quite quickly. Unfortunately, at this point, the aircraft was descending quite fast towards the ground. If the surge did not cease then at some point the pilot would have to make the decision to pull the lever up anyway to cushion the inevitable impact with the ground.

Being a single-engined aircraft one also had to practice real landings with the engine throttled right back, effectively off. In some ways this was easier than the powered version described above because you knew you were committed from the start. No difficult last second decisions to make. The only problem with the Wasp was that in autorotation it descended quite fast with the aerodynamic properties of a house brick and very little energy stored in the rotors. This meant that at the bottom of the autorotation the flare/level/raise lever to cushion the landing happened extremely fast and there was no latitude at all for getting it wrong. Hard it may have been, but I considered it to be one of the most exacting, exciting and rewarding piece of piloting I've ever done - to quote a well-known film - 'real pilot s**t'.

I qualified on the Wasp on 1 December and then did a short course with the MTP. I was relieving to learn all about the flight test schedule. Much of it was straightforward and pretty standard; fly at various speeds and measure vibration, check engine power output, ensure the handling was correct at max speed and angles of bank and make sure the rotor rpm was controllable in autorotation. All of this was similar to tests I also conducted in the Lynx which I flew at the same time. However, the Wasp had one test that was unique - the dreaded 'height climb', or more properly the 'governor topping check'.

As described earlier, the engine was not required to give all of its 1050 horsepower and was limited to 685hp. However, if one tried to pull this much power at sea level it was still far too much for the transmission to take. The only way to be sure that the engine control system was set up correctly, i.e., that full fuel flow could be achieved without loss of power, was therefore to go Up. The higher the altitude, the less loading on the compressor and the faster it had to go to produce the required power to maintain a given torque. The height climb consisted of flying the aircraft at a steady 50 knots and 100% torque until the 'one hour power' rating of the engine in terms of engine speed and temperature was achieved. One then continued up a further thousand feet and pulled even more power to ensure that maximum contingency power was available and that the rotor speed had not dropped out of limits.

The issue with this test was the heights achieved were always well over 10,000 feet. Military aircraft are not normally allowed above this height unless the aircrew are on oxygen, which the Wasp definitely did not have. Consequently, special dispensation was given to temporarily go up to 12,000 for short periods, which was usually enough. Mind you, my record with a particularly good engine was a shade over 14,500 feet, but I never admitted to that at the time. Another issue which wasn't immediately apparent was why do the test at 50 knots, not 60, which was the normal speed for climbing? The answer was simple, a helicopter's maximum speed limit decreases with height. At 12000 feet it was 55 knots. Should one go much slower than that and it would not be possible to climb at all. Should one start to descend with high power applied, another nasty helicopter feature can occur called 'vortex ring', which can really ruin your whole day. Therefore one can see that at that height rather a lot of care was needed to fly the aircraft as well as read two tiny gauges while on the verge of hypoxia!!

Actually, once you were used to it, it was rather fun, even if being at that height was very alien to most helicopter aircrew. It was always amusing to watch a Sea Harrier fly-past several thousand feet below you and listen to his radio reply when air traffic told him to look up for rotary traffic well above him!

One of my other tasks was to take all the students learning to fly the aircraft through the whole test schedule, as they might well have to do some or all of the tests when deployed. The height climb was definitely a test of moral fibre. I could usually tell how a student was coping by seeing how tightly he was gripping the controls. One thing I never did and now regret, was conducting this test whilst wearing a parachute, which I could have done as they were available from the safety equipment section. My view at the time was that if I suffered a catastrophic failure, then a parachute was of no use and if I could still fly the aircraft then I could land it. It was only just before I finished at Portland that I heard about a prototype Merlin helicopter that suffered a tail rotor failure at 12000 feet and all the crew safely exited via parachute that I realised maybe I had missed a trick.

I spent four years flying the Wasp and enjoyed all of them. However, I did mention that on occasions I was asked to fly problem aircraft. One heart stopping moment was when conducting a height climb at a steady 50 knots and passing 8500 feet the engine started to surge. This should not have been possible and I was expecting the thing to quit on me all the way back to Portland. It didn't but neither did the squadron Air Engineer Officer really believe me. So after some more tethered ground runs he went flying in it with one of the squadron pilots. I got an apology when he returned after his precautionary landing. The engine was rejected.

On another occasion I was asked to fly an aircraft and give it an assessment, but the squadron AEO would not say why. His reason was that he wanted an unbiased opinion. Fair enough. I lifted into the hover and all seemed fine so I transited into forward flight and by four hundred feet knew something was very wrong, but couldn't say what. However, it felt bad enough that I had no desire to stay airborne in it and promptly returned to terra firma. We then had long discussions and made careful checks. I then took it off again at least confident that all the important load bearing parts were in good order. It still felt awful but we conducted a full vibration test on it. The levels were absolutely dreadful. I don't think I've ever seen vibration that bad, yet strangely it didn't feel that rough, just very unresponsive. At that point I sat down with the squadron and we decided to 'rogue' the machine. This was a process where the decision was taken that it would not be cost effective to keep on trying to get it serviceable. By this time the aircraft fleet was going out of service and there were plenty of other airframes around. I may be wrong but I think this is the last time an aircraft has been declared rogue in the Feet Air Arm. The story didn't end there though. The airframe was kept on the squadron, partially stripped and used for training. One day I got a call from the squadron to come and have a look. I was invited to climb up on the transmission deck and give the rotor head a shove. As I pushed hard it suddenly moved sideways. I looked down and could see that the whole gearbox was moving in sympathy. The gearbox in the Wasp is held to the main lift frames with rods, these were also moving. In fact what had happened was that the rivets holding the lift frames to rest of the airframe had pulled and elongated the holes they were fitted in. The net result was that the aircraft's transmission was not connected rigidly to the airframe. No wonder the handling felt awful.

My last flight in command of a Wasp was on 6 May 1986 with John Stratton - who was taking over from me - and lasted one hour twenty-five minutes, which meant we must have done the whole flight test schedule together. I was sorry to say goodbye to the little machine. That said, having flown both Lynx and Sea Kings operationally at sea I wasn't too upset that I'd never had the 'fun' of landing one on the back of a bouncing frigate in the middle of a black night with no horizon.

Fast forward to Friday, 12 August 2017. My co-author, Terry Martin, had been threatening to take me flying in XT 784, his privately owned Wasp, for some time. The day was the first opportunity to take him up on his offer. The plan was to fly from the private field near Winchester, where the machine is kept, to RAF Benson near Oxford, to put the aircraft in a static display along with many other machines for their annual family's day. We were planning to meet up with two army machines, a Scout and Sioux, near Newbury and fly in together in formation. The weather forecast had a cold front moving in later in the afternoon but it was not a very active one.

The aircraft lives in the open at the moment and so the first order of the day was to remove the large number of covers off the aircraft. Terry then cleaned the leading edge of the rotor blades. Being made of steel, they get rusty very quickly. Paint is no solution as it wears off almost immediately. While Terry got on with that I took the time to have a look around the old girl, she looked in good shape. The next challenge was getting in. To do so you have to climb the front undercarriage leg and clamber into your seat. Thirty-one years ago this was a doddle. The passage of time had made it a bit more of a trial, nevertheless, I was soon strapping in and re-familiarising myself with the cockpit layout. The aircraft is fitted with a set of dual controls and instruments which meant I would be able to have a play.

Now, can I remember what on earth this switch is for? *(LJC)*

Terry soon joined me and went through the prestart checks and fired up the mighty Nimbus. The Wasp is a fairly simple machine, in that with one engine and only basic controls it doesn't take long to get it ready to leap into the air, which we duly did. For the trip up, Terry was going to fly and I would just sit and act as an extra pair of eyes. Once cruising north at ninety knots it all started to come back to me, the smell of the machine, the vibration, just the overall ambience. The years slipped away. As we neared Greenham Common the Scout joined us, but the Sioux had had problems and so, as we were getting low on fuel we left the Scout waiting for his buddy and headed off to Benson.

The afternoon at Benson was fun, with some excellent flying displays to watch and quite a few people coming over to look at the Wasp. Questions seemed to fall into two categories, either, 'what on earth is it?' or, 'I used to work on these'. It certainly passed the time.

By half past four it was time to clamber in again and get ready to go home. The weather had deteriorated a little but the cloud base was still well above two thousand feet. The Wasp is now operated under the auspices of the Civil Aviation Authority and as such has several limitations placed on it. One of the most important being that it can only be flown 'Day VMC'. This translates as in daylight and only when you can see where you are going. We departed with the Scout and flew in formation for the first ten miles before he headed off for his base at Middle Wallop and we went off in search of Winchester. It was clear that Terry was a good formation pilot and it allowed me to get some good air-to-air photos of the Scout ahead. It also reminded me how much I actually disliked formation flying in helicopters and was more than happy for Terry to do the hard work. Although 1960s technology, one major change in the aircraft was a modern navigation system. In my day we had a map, the compass and the 'Mark One eyeball'. Terry had a far more accurate system - an iPad. Loaded with aviation navigation software and GPS, knowing where you are and where you are going is far easier (and of course we had the A34 to follow if all went wrong).

So Terry uttered those immortal words, 'you have control'. Another of the CAA mandated limitations to the aircraft is that the autostabilisation system cannot be used. I'm not sure why this is, apparently sometime in the past it malfunctioned in a privately owned machine and so a blanket ban was introduced. Consequently, the aircraft felt rather twitchy, but I had to remind myself that this was how I liked to fly it anyway. This was my excuse for wandering around the sky a little until I got used to it again. However, one thing I immediately noticed was that we were only using about 70% torque to fly at ninety knots. This was because Terry, quite sensibly, does not have the dreadful flotation gear fitted. It all soon came back to me and within a few minutes it was as though the intervening years had disappeared. I always loved flying this little helicopter on clear days over land and the next few minutes passed in what seemed like seconds. We flew down past my old home town of Winchester. My daughter was attending the 'Boomtown' pop festival just to the east of the town so we arranged with Southampton air traffic for a quick trip to say hello. I got some great aerial photos, but sadly my girl was heavily into the music at the time and missed seeing us. We did wave, but from fifteen hundred feet, we couldn't see her waving back for some reason!

All too soon it was time to head back to the field. Finding a small landing strip surrounded by trees in the countryside is no easy matter, even with and iPad to help, so I was quite pleased that I actually managed to spot it before Terry took control for the landing. As the little airfield has trees all around it, a steep and careful approach is needed. However, once we were in the hover on the runway he suggested I take over again. This was the moment I would really find out whether the passage of time had taken its toll. Flying straight and level is one thing. Hovering is a completely different art form. Once again Terry handed over control. For a split second I let the nose wander to starboard, then took charge of the beast. I won't say it all flooded back because it didn't need to. Clearly some things, once learnt, don't get forgotten and I spent a happy few minutes doing spot turns and hover taxying around before landing on. Great fun.

A thoroughly enjoyable day for many reasons and it was really great to know I could still hack it. However, as I thought back over the trip, one thing came strongly back. You literally have to fly the Wasp every second of every minute. There are no systems to help you keep height or heading as in later machines. As there is no stabilisation you cannot take your hand off the cyclic stick. This leaves your left knee to hold the collective in position while you do everything else with your left hand, changing radio frequencies, operating the iPad or looking at the map etc. This was no problem on a short trip in daylight over land.

I never flew the Wasp at sea, although I had plenty of experience doing so in the Lynx and Sea King, so I know exactly what a Wasp pilot would have to cope with. Even though the operational aircraft did have limited stabilisation, it forcibly reminded me what a task it would have been flying to the deck of a ship, at night, in rough weather, with no visual horizon. To all who did that over the years – respect.

Section Two

WASPS IN SERVICE OVERSEAS AND IN RETIREMENT

Chapter 10

The Life Cycle of a Wasp – Phase 2: Born to Fight Again

XT787 - a surviving Wasp that served in both the Royal Navy and Royal New Zealand Navy and still displays in the UK. (*Neil Cave*)

When we think about longevity of service of military helicopters currently still being flown, life expectancy beyond thirty years is not unusual. The Bell UH-1 (Huey) first flew in 1956 and entered service with the US Army in 1960, and they were still flying with the US Army reserves until 2015 after fifty-five years of service in countries all around the world. In the Royal Navy, the Westland Sea King was also in service for just over fifty years (1966 to 2017), and the Westland Lynx is trailing behind only slightly with forty-four years of service and lives on, in part, as the Wildcat. The big difference between these helicopters and the Wasps and Scouts, is that neither of this Westland pair were developed beyond their Mark 1 versions. Having read Larry Jeram-Croft's excellent account of the technical improvements made to the Wasp in Chapters 4 and 5, readers will have noticed that the fundamental helicopter design remained unchanged. There was no increase in size, speed, range, or any other aspects of performance. Clearly the rapid advances in helicopter technology in the 1960s and 1970s dictated that a completely new design (the Lynx) was a more suitable approach, rather than to spend money redesigning the already very outdated Wasp.

In the words of former Wasp pilot Lieutenant Commander Bill McCamy, an exchange pilot from the US Navy, when I asked him, 'At that time, did the Wasp seem antiquated to you?', his reply was:

'When I arrived in UK to transition to the WASP, I had flown TH-57 Jet Rangers (single engine, training command, IFR capable), UH-1B Huey gunships in Vietnam (single engine, IFR capable), and SH-3D Sea Kings (dual engine, IFR capable). My experience with small ships helo ops was limited to Hueys and Sea Kings landing on frigates, cruisers and destroyers. I had not been assigned to small ship flights or done any HS(L) (Helicopter Anti-Submarine - Light) operations (H-2 Seasprite). My career track was HS (Helicopter Anti-Submarine) with the Sea King flying off aircraft carriers in support of the air wing composed of fighter, light attack, medium attack, airborne early warning and fixed wing anti-submarine aircraft. So, the first time I laid my hands on a Wasp, it was quite the experience.

HMS *Leander* Flight Commander Lieutenant Commander Bill McCamy, USN, (third from left) with ship's Flight and Wasp XT787. (*Bill McCamy*)

Westland Wasps had started to be withdrawn from Royal Navy service in the late 1970s, coinciding with the introduction of the more capable Westland Lynx. Given the decision not to invest in a Mark 2 Wasp, it is not surprising that the Lynx was introduced into service to replace the Wasp long before the Falklands conflict in 1982. However, after Argentine forces invaded the Falkland Islands, the ensuing South Atlantic campaign gave the Wasp another shot at fame and adventure. As Larry Jeram-Croft explains in much detail in Chapter 7, it's worthy of note that right up to the Falklands campaign, Wasps were still fully operational on a number of ships, including HMS *Endurance* and the Type 12 Frigates, *Yarmouth* and *Plymouth*. Other Wasps were deployed to a wide assortment of small vessels, and nine Wasp helicopters were en route to the Falklands on the former Italian built container ship MV *Contender Bezant* when the cease fire occurred. The *Contender Bezant* was later purchased by the Royal Navy and renamed the RFA *Argus*, which was extensively modified to become an aviation training and support vessel as well as a primary casualty reception ship. The *Argus* went on to see operational service in the both Gulf wars (Ops Granby and Telic) and off the coast of Sierra Leone during the 2014 Ebola epidemic.

Also in Chapter 7, Larry details the full part played by Wasps during the Falklands conflict, but it's worth summarising here the key events surrounding the first firing of weapons in anger by Wasp crews and the significance of these events in the history of naval aviation.

The story starts with a Wessex helicopter from HMS *Antrim* and a Westland Lynx HAS 2 from HMS *Brilliant,* that had launched a number of depth charges and a Mk 46 torpedo which homed in on, and heavily damaged, the Argentine submarine ARA *Santa Fe*. The sub posed a very real risk to the British Task Force that was steaming towards the Falkland Islands. The *Santa Fe* was finally disabled by two AS12 missiles from Wasps operating from HMS *Plymouth* (XT429, c/n f.9599) and HMS *Endurance* (XT539, c/n F.9566 and XS527, c/n F.9543), the Antarctic patrol ship. The damaged submarine was later run aground by her crew, thus becoming the first casualty of the sea war, as well as the first direct engagement by the Royal Navy Task Force. This was also the first action since the Second World War in which an aircraft had disabled a naval vessel, and it was also the first ever successful attack on a submarine by a helicopter. In many respects, this event is what makes the Wasp unique in Royal Navy history.

Wasp HAS 1 firing an AS12 missile. (*829 Squadron RN (MoD)*)

It was plain to see that after twenty years in service with the Royal Navy, there was still plenty of life left in much of the Wasp helicopter fleet. It's not surprising then, that like the sale of paid-off warships to foreign navies, the Wasps were seen as attractive and cheap alternatives to the new Lynx helicopters. This was especially so, of course, for those countries that had already purchased warships with the small flight-deck design, such as the Leander and Tribal class frigates.

The last Wasp was finally withdrawn from Royal Navy service in 1988 when HMS *Plymouth*, the last of the frigates that the Wasp had been designed for, was decommissioned.

Ninety-eight Wasps in total were procured for the RN from the first flight on 28 October 1962 until the end of the production line. In addition, Saunders Roe (SARO) produced three P.531 prototypes. The Wasp was also a very successful export aircraft for the UK, with twenty-seven being sold direct from Westland factories to foreign navies, as well as many retired Wasps, after being struck off charge by the Royal Navy. These helicopters were exported to The Netherlands, Brazil, Indonesia, Malaysia, New Zealand and South Africa. An impressive 125 Wasps, plus the three P.351s, were built, making 128 aircraft in total.

New Zealand

Due to the structure and capabilities of the Royal New Zealand Navy (RNZN) in the 1970s, RNZN rotary wing pilot training was provided by the Royal New Zealand Air Force (RNZAF) and the Wasps were initially flown by naval pilots whilst being serviced and maintained by RNZAF personnel. In subsequent years, pilots came from exchange programs between the two services, but also between the RNZN and RN Fleet Air Arm, these included (the then) Lieutenant Tony Ellerbeck in 1977, who went on to become famous for his attack on the ARA *Santa Fe*.

There was little consistency in the association between individual Wasps and the RNZN fleet of warships, and helicopters were rotated as the various naval vessels were assigned and re-assigned duties and when they were being repaired or refitted. Like their Royal Navy sisters, the RNZAF/RNZN Wasps often had code numbers painted on the nose and sides of the tail boom. These two or three digit codes were the ships' pennant numbers used by each ship's Flight. All British Commonwealth naval ships at that time used the same system of coding, thus making co-operative manoeuvres easier in the event of allied action in wartime, but also, of course, for the many peacetime joint operational exercises that took place. For the RNZN, these operations included patrols and service in the Persian Gulf (especially when the Royal Navy was busy in the Falklands conflict), and peace keeping duties in Bougainville, Papua New Guinea, after the civil war in the 1990s.

A total of nine Wasp helicopters (NZ3901 to NZ3909) were operated for the Royal New Zealand Navy between 1966 and 1998. Nicknamed affectionately as the 'paraffin pigeons', these birds were purchased to provide anti-submarine (ASW) capability and the same sort of general support for New Zealand's Leander class frigates as undertaken when the same ships were in RN service (occasionally on the very same ships). However, there were also some interesting additional tasks undertaken under Kiwi command, such as aerial agricultural spraying on Raoul Island in 1975.

The first two aircraft (NZ3901 and NZ3902) were purchased in 1966. NZ3901 was immediately assigned to the new Leander class frigate of the Royal New Zealand Navy, HMNZS *Waikato*, but was lost after ditching in the Hauraki Gulf, between Auckland and the Coromandel Peninsula, in 1973.

The third Wasp, NZ3903 (c/n F.9757), was delivered in 1971, but it too was lost in 1973, in the Waitemata (Auckland) harbour, also after ditching due to engine failure.

The fourth Wasp, NZ3904 (originally XT417, c/n F.9587), was borrowed from the Royal Navy to compensate for those earlier losses, but returned to the UK in 1974, and was eventually purchased by the RNZN in 1977. Sadly, NZ3904 was later written off in 1992 when it crashed after a tarpaulin was drawn up into the rotor disc while landing at Taupo, in the centre of the north island of New Zealand.

After delivery of the newly acquired frigates, HMNZS *Southland* and HMNZS *Wellington*, four further Wasps were purchased and arrived in 1983 for immediate work-up at sea, and to build a larger training capability. To ease the problem of spares, at about the same time, the Royal Navy released two further Wasps (XS536 and XV622) for cannibalisation, and seven more attrition airframes were acquired between 1985 and 1989, one being broken down for spares and the remaining three going into storage. The final active Wasp to serve with the RNZN (XT782) arrived in 1983 as an intended parts source, but was later rebuilt using elements of both NZ3901 and NZ3904. It finally entered service as NZ3909 in 1994.

On 12 March 1984, NZ3907 (previously XT435, and later G-RIMM) suffered an engine failure at Hobsonville airfield, Auckland. Flown by an experienced exchange Royal Navy helicopter instructor, NZ3907 suffered a catastrophic failure of the free turbine bolts just as the pilot was nearing completion of a torque turn manoeuvre. In a less than ideal flight attitude, altitude and speed, he managed to perform an engine off landing without causing harm or injury to himself or others, but the Wasp was completely written off after the very heavy landing, with category 3-4 damage to almost every part of the machine. Perhaps surprisingly, NZ3907 was extensively rebuilt from parts cannibalised from XS536 and XS622, the attrition airframes purchased in 1982. This helicopter eventually became my first Wasp purchase after it was returned to the UK in 1998, and remarked as XT435.

NZ3905 (previously known as XT787 and now flying as G-KAXT back in the UK) was my second Wasp purchase, and the fifth individual Wasp that I had flown. The stories of XT787 and XT435 continue in Chapters 11 and 12.

Formerly NZ3907, still flying as G-RIMM in the UK. (Loop *magazine*)

Wasps were maintained by ground crews of Number 3 Squadron RNZAF and proved to be respected and long-serving helicopters for the RNZN. They supported numerous tasks and roles, as well as taking part in the Armilla Patrol in the Persian Gulf during the 1980s. In fact, despite the retirement of most Wasps in 1996, two continued in service until 1998, after an admirable thirty-two years in service. HMNZS *Waikato*, the ship that had first operationally deployed the Wasp, was herself decommissioned that same year.

As a final show of might, in 1997, a formation of Wasps performed a fly-past, marking the arrival of the new ANZAC-class frigate, HMNZS *Te Kaha*, with its far more capable Kaman SH-2F Seasprite helicopters, and the end of active service life of the Wasp was in sight.

The Captain's barge, RNZN Wasp in the South Pacific off the coast of New Zealand. (*RNZAF*)

Of the retired RNZN Wasps, NZ3906 (c/n F.9570, ex XS543) was passed to the RNZAF museum at Wigram air base near Christchurch, and NZ3902 (c/n F.9679) was originally displayed at MOTAT (the Museum of Transport and Technology) in Auckland, but moved, in 2010, to the RNZN Museum at Torpedo Bay near the Devonport Naval base on the north shore of Auckland harbour.

Three further Wasps, including the gutted remains of NZ3901 (c/n F.9678/ XS532 - marked '406') and 'NZ3912' (c/n F.9559)/XS553 - marked '457') were sold to Don Subritzky of Dairy Flat, north of Auckland. As mentioned earlier, NZ3901 ditched in the sea in 1973, but was recovered from the Hauraki Gulf, and the RNZN spent a lot of time reconditioning it. I believe this airframe may be one of two sold on to a private buyer in Sydney, Australia. It is likely that at least one is now approaching a return to flight.

Several Wasps in flying condition were purchased back by Westland in the late 1990s and were destined to be restored to flight and registered for civilian use in the UK.

What I didn't know at the time was that two, NZ3907 (XT435) and NZ3905 (XT787), were both to come in to my ownership a decade later.

Although the current status and location of all the New Zealand Wasps cannot be verified, the following summary traces the fates of these helicopters until the trail of each aircraft runs dry.

NZ tail registration	Construction number	RN tail registration	History
NZ3901	F.9678	(none)	Delivered new from the Westlands factory in October 1966, NZ3901 suffered engine failure and ditched into the Hauraki Gulf, Auckland, while operating from HMNZS *Canterbury* on 7 April 1993. Some parts were used to build NZ3909. The remains were acquired and stored with Don Subritzky of Dairy Flat, Auckland, and may now be in Sydney, Australia undergoing restoration.
NZ3902	F.9679	(none)	Delivered new from the Westlands factory in October 1966, marked as '430' and had a long service with the RNZN. After its active service finished in 1988, NZ3902 was given to the RNZN museum and loaned to MOTAT museum in Auckland. In 2010, it was moved to the newly build RNZN museum at Torpedo Bay, Devonport.
NZ3903	F.9757	(none)	Delivered new from the factory in late 1971 and carried the '460' markings. It had a short life after engine failure at only 400hrs, followed by a ditching in Waitemata Harbour, near Bean Rock on 30 November 1973. The written-off salvaged remains were taken to Devonport for initial damage limitation and then storage. See story below.
NZ3904	F.9587	XT417	XT417 was loaned by the Royal Navy from 1974 to 1975 and again from 1977 to 1979 (to replace the losses of NZ3901 and NZ3903). It became a permanent acquisition in September 1979. Unfortunately, this Wasp was written off when a tarpaulin was sucked into rotor blades at Taupo airport on 20 November 1992. NZ3904 was later stored at Devonport Naval Base in damaged condition.

NZ tail registration	Construction number	RN tail registration	History
NZ3905	F.9669	XT787	Another ex-Royal Navy Wasp, XT787 enjoyed long service in the RNZN as NZ3905 from 1982 until 1997. NZ3905 was returned to Westlands in the UK in 1997, sold on to Kennet Aviation, restored to flying condition and registered as G–KAXT. It was sold to Terry Martin in 2012 and is still flying in the UK as a historic display aircraft.
NZ3906	F.9570	XS543	Wasp XS543 entered service as NZ3906 in 1982. This helicopter had a long and uneventful service life until retirement in 1995. NZ3906 was donated to the RNZAF museum at Wigram, near Christchurch, in 1998, where it remains on display.
NZ3907	F.9605	XT435	NZ3907 was ex-Royal Navy XT435, which was transferred and entered served with the RNZN in 1983. It spent part of its operational life wearing a high conspicuity orange colour scheme due to its long peace-keeping duties in Bourgainville Island in Papua New Guinea. After completion of its NZ service, NZ3907 returned to Westland in the UK, and then on to Kennet Aviation for restoration to flight. It has since been operated under private ownership as G–RIMM in Royal Navy colours.
NZ3908	F.9663	XT781	Formerly XT781, NZ3908 was delivered in 1983 and served for five years. On retirement in 1998, NZ3908 returned to Westland in the UK, after which it was acquired by Kennet Aviation in 2003, restored to flying condition and registered in the UK as G–KAWW. It was subsequently sold in 2005 to a private buyer in South Africa (see below), having returned to Royal Navy colours and been marked as XT781.

NZ tail registration	Construction number	RN tail registration	History
NZ3909	F.9663	XT782	As described above, NZ3909 was a 'Frankenstein' made up from elements of two written-off Wasps, NZ3901 and NZ3904, plus the attrition frame, XT782. The composite NZ3909 entered service in 1994, but served relatively briefly, returning to Westlands in the UK in 1997. It was placed on the UK CAA register by Kennet Aviation in 2005 as G–KANZ with, interestingly, the original XT782 registered date of manufacture (1966) and construction number (c/n F.9664). G–KANZ remains in Royal New Zealand Navy colours and wearing the serial NZ3909. This Wasp was sold to a private buyer in the UK.
NZ3910	F.9544	XS528	In Royal Navy service, XS528 spent most of its career in trials and development work at Boscombe Down until finding fame in the UK BBC television series '*Warship*' in 1975. This Wasp was purchased and collected from the UK by a RNZAF C130 Hercules in 1985 and transported to Hamilton and held in store as a spare aircraft, but allocated the tail number NZ3910. On withdrawal from service in 1987, NZ3910 was acquired by a private buyer in Auckland, NZ.
NZ3911	F.9598	XT428	XT428 was purchased from the Royal Navy in 1985 and delivered for use as a spare aircraft, or for aircraft parts.
NZ3912	F.9559	XS532	XS532 was a troubled helicopter when serving with the Royal Navy and had a history of several minor and one major accident requiring extensive rebuilding. This aircraft was sold to the RNZN in 1985 and was allocated the tail number NZ3912 and held in store as a spare aircraft until withdrawn from service in 1987. The remains were acquired by Don Subritzky after withdrawal from service. This aircraft may now be in Sydney undergoing restoration.
(not assigned)	F.9563	XS536	Delivered in 1982 for provision of spare parts. Stored at Woodbourne air base and used for the rebuild of NZ3907.

NZ tail registration	Construction number	RN tail registration	History
(not assigned)	F.9717	XV622	Another troubled helicopter with a history of several significant accidents in Royal Navy service, XV622 was purchased and delivered in 1983 for provision of spare parts and used for the rebuild of NZ3907.
(not assigned)	F.9577	XS566	XS566 was delivered to the RNZN in 1989 for use as a spares source.
(not assigned)	F.9585	XT415	XT415 was another unfortunate Wasp, having experienced more than its fair share of misfortunes in Royal Navy service. It was transported to the Falkland Islands in 1985 to replace one of HMS *Endurance's* Wasps, only to be purchased by the RNZN in 1987 as another source of spares, and subsequently stored at Hobsonville in Auckland.
(not assigned)	F.9602	XT432	XT432 was used as a casualty evacuation helicopter during the Falklands conflict (1982), operating from HMS *Hydra* with Red Cross markings applied. Purchased by, and delivered to, the RNZN as a source of aircraft spares in 1989.
(not assigned)	F.9729	XV634	After twenty years of service in the Royal Navy, XT634 was purchased and delivered, along with XT432, in 1989 as a source of aircraft spares.

The '*Wings over New Zealand*' website is an excellent source of information and dits from former RNZN/RNZAF Waspies and engineers. The following account of the aftermath of the ditching of NZ3903 was posted by 'Camtech' on 8 Feb 2010:

'I can recall the aftermath of NZ3903 crashing into the Waitemata Harbour. After the aircraft was recovered back to Devonport, there was a mad rush to preserve as much of the electronics as possible and much of the instrumentation was hauled out and dumped into fresh water tanks. I had the job of recovering the autopilot system a few days later when it was brought over to Whenuapai. After a lot of work drying the parts out, spraying them with WD40 and cleaning them up, we put the system together and managed to get a basic autopilot functioning. Some components were damaged in the crash, but most were working, so we were able to build a test bench for the Mk28 by incorporating the bits we had, plus some homemade panels and electronic wizardry (purloined from a set of ex Royal Navy publications) and saved many thousands of dollars. The test bench was still in use in 1981 when I left Whenuapai.'

RNZN Wasp formation on retirement from service. (*RNZAF*)

Perhaps the last word about the Wasp's retirement from naval service should come from the equally retired, but still very active, Rear Admiral Sir Terry Loughran, a most kindly gentleman who openly showed a passion and affection for the Wasp when we met at a Navy Wings fund-raising event in London and subsequently at RNAS Yeovilton Air Day in 2017. His delight is clearly visible in the photograph.

'I had my final encounter with the Wasp, when as Flag Officer Naval Aviation (FONA), I visited the RNZN Fleet Air Arm which boasted, at that time, four Wasps. Needless to say I was taken on an aerial tour in one flown by the Flight Commander, who, somewhat ambitiously, suggested we finish off with an Engine Off Landing - "for old time's sake"! Having moved on some twenty years from Mombasa*, I could see the impact of FONA reducing the Orbat of the RNZN FAA by 25% in one afternoon and generously declined.'
[* see Section one, Chapter 8)

The author (TM) with Rear Admiral Terry Loughran visiting Wasp XT787 with his wife, Philipa, at RNAS Yeovilton Air Day in July 2017. (*Terry Martin*)

Netherlands

The requirement for an anti-submarine helicopter in the Royal Netherlands Navy (*Koninklijke Marine*) came about after a fire aboard the aircraft carrier HNLMS *Karel Doorman* in 1968. After the fire, it was decided that the cost of the repair was too high and planning was started for her withdrawal from service in the early 1970s. The date was set to coincide with the arrival of long-range maritime patrol aircraft that were to take over the ASW (anti-submarine warfare) role of the HNLMS *Karel Doorman*. Part of the decision also included an order for twelve Westland Wasp AH-12A helicopters to be operated in the anti-submarine war role from six Van Speijk class frigates.

The introduction of the Wasp program started in the spring of 1966 as a group of Dutch pilots and engineers were detached to the Westland factory in Yeovil for an introduction to the Wasp. Immediately after successful completion of this introduction course, the first three Wasps were deployed to RNAS Culdrose for initial flying training. Further training was completed by the Dutch Navy 860 Squadron at De Kooy Naval Air Station (NAS). A complete squadron of twelve Westland Wasp AH-12As were then delivered between November 1966 and June 1967. An additional one extra Wasp was ordered and delivered in 1974 as a spare for attrition purposes.

The land base during the operational life of the Westland Wasp was at De Kooy airfield, to the south of Den Helder, a naval airfield under the name *Maritiem Vliegkamp De Kooy* (Maritime Aviation Site De Kooy). 860 Squadron was converted to a helicopter unit on 4 Oct 1966 and it became the parent unit for deployments to the Van Speijk Class Frigates. During the latter half of 1974, there were also a number of ships flight attachments to the Royal Navy's helicopter base at Portland.

The Westland Wasp was primarily flown in the ASW role, but it was also utilised for SAR and transport tasks. The last of the Dutch Westland Wasps were eventually replaced by the much superior Westland Lynx.

The replacement was gradual with phased retirement starting after the introduction of the very first SH-14B Lynx in October 1978. Most had been withdrawn from service in December 1980, and the very last of the Dutch Wasps were eventually paid-off in 1981.

Of the thirteen Westland Wasp AH-12As purchased by the Koninklijke Marine, three had been written off, and the remaining ten were refurbished by Westland and sold to the Indonesian Navy, where they were flown, in part, from former Koninklijke Marine Van Speijk class frigates.

One Westland Wasp helicopter is preserved at De Kooy NAS. Interestingly, this example never actually saw service in the Netherlands. It is former Royal Navy Wasp, XT795 marked as '235', the first Wasp delivered to the Royal Netherlands Navy.

Displayed as 235/K at De Kooy naval air base, Wasp c/n F9677 is actually XT795, a former Royal Navy helicopter that did not see service in the Koninklijke Marine. (*Maritiem Vliegkamp De Kooy*)

Indonesia

After refurbishment at the Westland factory in the UK, the Indonesian Navy (*Tentara Nasional Indonesia-Angkatan Laut*, abbreviated to TNI–AL) purchased ten retired and restored former Dutch Wasp helicopters. The Wasps were operated by 400 Squadron (RON 400) from Juanda Naval Air Station and, when at sea, they were embarked on the Indonesian Navy's former British Royal Navy Tribal class frigates and former Koninklijke Marine (Dutch Navy) Van Speijk class frigates.

The Van Speijk class ships were modifications of the British Leander class frigates built for the Royal Netherlands Navy in the 1960s. The British design was the quickest solution in order for the Dutch to replace elderly destroyer escorts and to take up responsibility for the NATO patrol duties of the decommissioned anti-submarine warfare aircraft carrier HNLMS *Karel Doorman*. These ships were modernised in the late 1970s and all six vessels were sold to the Indonesian Navy between 1986 and 1989 and remained in service as the Ahmad Yani class of frigates. Britain's Tribal class frigates were renamed the Khristina Tiyahahu Class.

Former Dutch Van Speijk class frigates

Dutch Frigate	Dutch Pennant Number	Purchased	TNI–AL (Indonesian) Name	TNI–AL Pennant Number
Van Speijk	F802	1986	*Slamet Riyadi*	352
Van Galen	F803	1987	*Yos Sudarso*	353
Tjerk Hiddes	F804	1986	*Ahmad Yani*	351
Van Nes	F805	1986	*Oswald Siahaan*	354
Isaac Sweers	F814	1987	*Karel Satsuit Tubun*	356
Evertsen	F815	1989	*Abdul Halim Perdanakusuma*	355

Former British Tribal class frigates

British Frigate	British Pennant Number	Purchased	TNI–AL (Indonesian) Name	TNI–AL Pennant Number
HMS *Zulu*	F124	1984	*Martha Kristina Tiyahahu*	331
HMS *Gurkha*	F122	1989	*Wilhelmus Zakaria Johannes*	332
HMS *Tartar*	F133	1984	*Hasanuddin*	333

Although none of the Indonesian Wasps had previously served in the British Royal Navy, they were all former Royal Netherlands Navy helicopters that were made in the same construction line as the Royal Navy Wasps. As such, it is useful to trace individual aircraft by their construction numbers (c/n). The letter 'F', preceding a four digit number starting with '9', indicates that the Wasps were built at the Fairey factory in Hayes, Middlesex (near to London Heathrow airport). Fairey was a subsidiary of Westland, and took over the role of development of the Westland Wasp from the original design authority, Saunders-Roe (SARO). All Wasps built at the Hayes factory were initially transported by road to White Waltham airfield, near Reading in Berkshire, for their first flights.

The ten former Dutch Navy AH-12A Wasps were delivered to Indonesia from April 1981 onwards. The initial batch of four (HS-430, HS-431, HS-432 and HS-433) were dispatched direct from the Netherlands to Surabaya and the remaining six were refurbished at Westland's factory at Weston-Super-Mare before later delivery to Surabaya during late 1981 and 1982.

NL tail registration	Construction number	Written-off or sold by Dutch Navy	Indonesian tail registration
235	F.9680	w/o 27-01-1978	
236	F.9681	Sold	HS-430
237	F.9682	Sold	HS-436
238	F.9683	Sold	HS-437
239	F.9684	w/o 27-01-1978	
240	F.9685	Sold	HS-435
241	F.9686	w/o 28-11-1968	
242	F.9687	Sold	HS-439
243	F.9688	Sold	HS-434
244	F.9689	Sold	HS-431
245	F.9690	Sold	HS-438
246	F.9691	Sold	HS-432
247	F.9765	Sold	HS-433

All Indonesian Wasps were grounded in 1998. The Indonesian and Malaysian navies were the last military operators of the Wasp.

Indonesian Wasp HS-434, formerly Koninklijke Marine Wasp 234, now at Juanda. (*Peter de Jong*)

Royal Malaysian Navy

The Wasp's entry into service with the Royal Malaysian Navy (*Tentera Laut Diraja Malaysia*, known at the TLDM) was very late compared to the other nations that procured the aircraft. The first delivery of former Royal Navy Wasps to the TLDM occurred in April 1988 and the second batch arrived two years later in May 1990. The Royal Malaysian Navy formed 499 *Skuadron* (squadron) in 1988 to operate the small ship's Wasp Flights at KD Rajawali, Lumut Naval Base, Perak. Unfortunately, the helicopters had a relatively short career and were being phased out just ten years after the last Wasp was delivered. Full withdrawal from service was completed by September 2002.

Much of the early days of Malaysian naval helicopter operations was witnessed by Richard Garton who wrote this fascinating account:

'During the final few months with Euryalus Flight a signal was received asking for volunteers to form a Loan Service Team to set up an Air Wing in Malaysia. Having no idea what this was about, I made some enquiries and found that LT Steve Leggett was forming a team, and currently CPOAEA(M) Chris Burrows was one of the team, he was an old acquaintance, as was Steve on 829 as AEO. After a great deal of thought and consultation with my wife we decided if selected to give it a go. I was lucky to get the chance and the rest as they say is history. We left on the 18 April 1988, a date which has stuck in the mind ever since. The event became a once in a lifetime opportunity for both me and my family.

'The first wasp arrived from Port Klang to be delivered to the converted ship dry dock area, where we would start to rebuild these aircraft for the Tentera Laut Diraja Malaysia Naval Air Wing 499 Squadron. [The first one was the only one to be painted in a light grey finish.]

'Wasp 499-02 became the first helicopter to land on board a Malaysian warship at sea and eventually all six Wasps were put back together. We all worked tirelessly in 30° plus heat to achieve this. We were also training ground crew on all the aspects of aircraft engineering, from refueling, firefighting, ground equipment and aircraft maintenance. A huge task, none of the junior rates spoke English.

'I was invited to remain in Malaysia when the first team's time was up and a second team arrived to take up the reins. I studied and passed my Charge Chiefs board on 2 May 1991 and left Malaysia with great regret on 23 July 1992 after more than four years. Shortly after my return to UK the Malaysian Navy purchased six more Wasps, which became the foundation of their Air Wing.'

LT Daryl Whitehead and CPOAEA(M) Richard Garton in between engine adjustments with the first delivered Malaysian Wasp in June 1988. (*Richard Garton*)

Malaysian Wasp MA-499 Wasp at Museum. Note: it is still marked as XT784 behind the rear door.
(*Malacca Maritime Museum*)

The following table summarises the initial purchase of the Wasps and some detail of the fate of a few, but detail of any other survivors is lacking.

Royal Navy registration	Construction number	Malaysian registration	Purchased	Comments
XV632	F.9727	M499-01	Mar 1988	Written off/destroyed 1991.
XT785	F.9667	M499-01	Aug 1992	Attrition replacement for ex XV632. Withdrawn from service 26 September 2002.
XV636	F.9731	M499-02	Mar 1988	Withdrawn from service 26 September 2002.
XT421	F.9591	M499-03	Mar 1988	Withdrawn from service 26 September 2002.
XT784	F.9666	M499-04	Aug 1992	Instructional airframe at Malaysian Aviation Training Academy, Kuantan. It was later transferred to the Malaysian Air Force Museum in Kuala Lumpur.

XT783	F.9665	M499-05	Aug 1992	XT783 was due to be purchased by the SAAF as '98', but never delivered because of the international arms embargo, so it was instead sold to the Malaysian Navy as M499-05. Withdrawn from service 26 September 2002.
XV626	F.9721	M499-06	Aug 1992	Withdrawn from service 26 September 2002.
XT426	F.9596	M499-07	Aug 1992	On display at the Royal Malaysian Navy (TLDM) Malacca Maritime Museum, Malaysia. Withdrawn from service 26 September 2002.
XT429	F.9599	M499-08	Aug 1992	Withdrawn from service 26 September 2002.
XT790	F.9672	M499-09	Aug 1992	Withdrawn from service 26 September 2002.
XT779	F.9661		Aug 1992	(For spare parts?)
XT791	f.9673		Aug 1992	(For spare parts?)

The story of a Malaysian Wasp: M499-08

XT429, c/n serial F.9599 was built in 1965 and delivered on 1 June 1965 to the Royal Navy. She served on HMS *Vidal* as '408' between 1968 and March 1970 and was attached to HMS *Plymouth* in 1982 and took part in the famous attack on the Argentine submarine, ARA *Santa Fe*. She was withdrawn from Royal Navy service in 1988, and quickly sold to the *Tentera Laut Diraja Malaysia* (Royal Malaysian Navy) as M499-08, until final withdrawal from service in late September 2002. Surely this aircraft must have been one of the last few Wasps 'in uniform' anywhere in the world?

M499-08 may well have been the same aircraft that Peter Taylor (HMS *Vidal* Flight) refers to in the following story:

'In early 1969 I was drafted to Vidal Flight – no aircraft had been assigned to the Flight at that time – in the interim we were assigned to an HQ Wasp known as the MAD cab – this was a Wasp modified to carry a Magnetic Abnormality Detector on a winch boom mounted on the port side of the aircraft – the detector was shaped like a 250KG bomb – the front port seat was reversed and the system operator sat there – the theory being that the aircraft could track submarines from the distortion they caused in the earth's magnetic field. As Vidal Flight we looked after this Wasp for three months until we embarked on the *Vidal* with our own aircraft and set off for nine months in the Gulf. On our return the MAD Cab had disappeared.'

One surviving Wasp, M499-07 formerly XT426 (c/n F.9596) in the Royal Navy (1965 to 1992), is still on display at the Royal Malaysian Navy (TLDM) Malacca Maritime Museum, Malaysia. Another, M499 formerly XT784 (c/n F.9666) may also survive, although it's location is uncertain after discussions about transferring the airframe from the Malaysian Air Force Museum in Kuala Lumpur to the Malacca Maritime Museum.

Brazil
The *Força Aeronaval da Marinha do Brasil* (Brazilian Navy) operated the Wasp as the UH-2 and UH-2A after taking delivery of three helicopters direct from Westlands in April 1966 and a further eight ex-Royal Navy helicopters in 1977. *1º Esquadrão de Helicópteros de Emprego Geral* flew these Wasps from the former US Navy's Gearing and Allen M. Sumner class destroyers and the British built Niterói class frigates.

The Brazilian ship *Defensora*, a Niterói class frigate (F41) carried the last two Wasps to Brazil in 1977 on its maiden voyage from the Vosper Thornycroft shipyard in Southampton, to Rio de Janeiro.

One surviving Wasp, N-7039, formerly XT433 in the Royal Navy (1965 to 1978), is still on display at *Campo Dos Afonsos*.

Brazilian Wasp N-7039, formerly XT433 in the Royal Navy, is still on display at *Campo Dos Afonsos*. (*Terry Martin*)

This table summarises the eleven Wasps purchased by the *Força Aeronaval da Marinha do Brasil* (FAMB).

Royal Navy registration	Construction number	Brazilian registration	Delivered	Comments
None	F.9614	N–7015	20 Apr 1966	UH-2 version. Code '15'.
None	F.9615	N–7016	20 Apr 1966	UH-2 version. Code '16'. Written off 15 July 1967 and replaced by XS476.
XS476	F.9542	N–7016		Pre-production airframe built at Hayes. G-17-2. Second UH-2 Wasp to bear this FAMB serial after previous loss/write-off.
None	F.9616	N–7017	20 Apr 1966	UH-2 version. Code '17'.
XT419	F.9589	N–7018 N–7036	1977	G-17-1. Written off as N-7036 on 21 November 1977.
XS564	F.9575	N–7019 N–7037	1977	G-17-22.
XV633	F.9728	N–7038	1977	G-17-21.
XT433	F.9603	N–7039	1977	G-17-6. Displayed at the *Museu Aeroespacial*, Campo Delio Jardim de Mattos /Campo dos Afonsos near Rio de Janeiro.
XS530	F.9557	N–7040	1977	G-17-7.
XT792	F.9674	N–7041	1977	G-17-8.
XS542	F.9569	N–7042	1977	G-17-30. Written off 06 December 1982.

South Africa

The South African Navy was the largest export operator of the Wasp, having ordered a total of eighteen Wasps direct from Westland Helicopters. The first batch of ten helicopters arrived in 1963, but, of a second order for a further eight helicopters, only six were delivered in 1973 due to the international arms embargo placed on South Africa during the apartheid regime. However, the South African Air Force (*Suid-Afrikaanse Lugmag*) managed to acquire a former Bahraini Police Unit Scout helicopter which was used as an instructional airframe. All the aircraft were allocated and flown by 22 Flight South African Air Force, from their base at Ysterplaat. The unit subsequently became 22 Squadron, Maritime Command in 1976 and the Wasps were operated from the President Class frigates such as SAS *President Kruger*. The Wasp fleet was withdrawn in 1990 and eventually replaced by the Westland Lynx.

South African Air Force Wasp helicopter '92'. (*Terry Martin*)

Construction number	South African registration	Delivered	Comments
F.9550	81	1963	Written off 16 Jun 1964.
F.9551	82	1963	Preserved, SAAF Museum at AFB Swartkop.
F.9552	83	1963	Written off on 25 Nov 1971 near Luanda.
F.9553	84	1963	Written off 18 Feb 1982, sank while operating from SAS President Kruger.
F.9554	85	1963	Displayed at SAAF Museum, Durban and has been loaned to Simonstown Navy Museum.
F.9555	86	1963	Ditched in the sea off the South African west coast and written off 25 Sep 1964.
F.9753	91	1973	Withdrawn from service March 1992 and transferred to New Zealand in 1996 by Aeromotive (Hamilton Airport) along with Wasp '92'. Used as spare parts for restoration of '92'. This helicopter may have ended up in Texas, USA (see below).
F.9754	92	1973	Registered as ZK-HOX, but in 1996 was transferred to New Zealand and rebuilt to ground running standard. Some parts from Wasp '91' were used (see above). It did not fly in NZ but around 2001 it was shipped to Thruxton, UK. There it was restored to flight and registered as G–BYCX.
F.9755	93	1973	Displayed at SAAF Museum satellite, AFB Ysterplaat.
F.9756	94	1973	Accident near Cape Point. Written off 5 December 1979.

The two Wasp helicopters that were ordered but not delivered were originally coded '97' (became Royal Navy Wasp XT782) and '98' (became Royal Navy Wasp XT783).

Another Wasp (XT781 c/n F.9663), formerly restored to flight by Kennet Aviation in the UK and registered as G-KAWW, defied the natural order of things and was imported into South Africa from the UK in the early 2000's. Now wearing the ship's code '426', she is registered as ZU–HAS and was based at Durban Virginia airfield and flew at air shows in South Africa until 2007. Her current status is unknown but she is thought to be grounded and based in the Natal.

Three other Wasps have survived in the Republic of South Africa. Wasp '90' (c/n F.9659) and Wasp '96' (c/n F.9763) are both on display at the South African Air Force Museum at AFB Zwartkop and another Wasp '93' (c/n F.9754), is preserved with the SAAF Museum Historic Flight South African Air Force Ysterplaat, Cape Town.

In tracing the fate of the remaining former South African Wasps, it seems that two were exported to New Zealand, by an American citizen from Texas. One (Wasp '92') later appeared on the UK civil register as G-BYCX and is still flying in private ownership. The other (Wasp '91') disappeared from trace.

In attempting to locate SAAF Wasp '91', the following intriguing story unfolded. A mysterious 'medical' helicopter had crash landed in Denison, Texas, after an engine

South African Air Force Wasp helicopter. (*Cliff Ibell*)

failure on take-off. The press release, below, is accompanied by a photograph of a sad looking flattened Wasp with collapsed undercarriage oleos, but wearing the same shade of blue-grey paint as used by the South African Air Force/Navy. Strangely, this Wasp had 'RESCUE' painted along the tail boom, and yet the Wasp would never have been appropriately equipped or registered for use by a civilian medical or rescue service, so the mystery deepens.

Medical Helicopter Makes Emergency Landing on City Street
(Source: http://www.nbc5i.com/news/4549195/detail.html)
POSTED: 9:45 am CDT May 31, 2005
No Injuries Reported in Hard Landing
DENISON, Texas

No serious injuries were reported when a medical helicopter with two people aboard made a hard emergency landing on a busy Denison street. The pilot told police that he was lifting off Monday from a helipad on Morton Street, just west of downtown Denison, when he lost engine power.
The Westland Wasp helicopter landed hard, right-side-up, on the busy street. Parts from the helicopter hit a nearby car, but the family inside was not injured. The impact damaged the chopper's tail, rotor and landing gear. The Federal Aviation Administration will investigate on Tuesday.
Residents near the helipad say they've been complaining to the city about the noise and wind from the helicopter's take-offs.

Helicopter Makes Hard Landing
UPDATED: 9:52 am CDT May 31, 2005

A vintage military helicopter made a hard landing at Morton and Maurice Streets in Denison after its engine failed. Denison police say the private helicopter took off from a parking lot, then crashed a short time later. Two people were inside the helicopter when it made the rough landing, but authorities say they escaped with only minor injuries. Police say a part of the helicopter flew off when it hit the ground and the piece of metal hit a car passing by. A woman and her two children were inside the car and they also escaped with minor injuries.

Chapter 11

The Final Part of the Wasps' Life Cycle – Phase 3: Gentle Retirement

By 2000, most of the remaining Wasps in service around the world had been finally retired to museums, with others being used for fire/rescue practice, and even for target practice. A small number were returned to Westlands because of embargos on weapon sales that were often enshrined in the original purchase contracts when the Wasps were sold on by the Royal Navy between 1984 and 1988. Even the briefest of web searches identifies the outcome and often the current status of all the Wasps and Saro P.531s that were released to service. In addition, Lee Howard's magnus opus, *Fleet Air Arm Helicopters since 1948* (Howard L., Burrow M., and Myall E., Pub Air Britain, 2011) is undoubtedly the definitive one-stop reference for tracking those airframes that served in the Royal Navy, and is gratefully used as a prime source for the following list of Wasp survivors.

United Kingdom surviving Wasps still flying.

RN registration	Construction number	Current registration	Other registration	Other markings	Current status
(None)	F.9754	G-BYCX	92		G-BYCX, a former South African Wasp Mk 1B is privately owned and based at Thruxton aerodrome in Hampshire and still flies marked as SAAF '92'.
XT420	F.9590	G-CBUI		'606'	G-CBUI, a Wasp HAS.1 (was RN serial number XT420) is privately owned and flies from Thruxton in Royal Navy markings as XT420 in markings of 829 NAS, HQ Flight at RNAS Yeovilton.

RN registration	Construction number	Current registration	Other registration	Other markings	Current status
XT435	F.9605	G-RIMM	NZ3907	'430'	G-RIMM (was also RNZN NZ3907) is privately owned and still flies in the final colour scheme of XT778 with the banded wasp's tail.
XT787	F.9669	G-KAXT	NZ3905	HMS *Endurance*	G-KAXT, a former Royal Navy (XT787) and Royal New Zealand Navy (NZ3905) Wasp HAS.1 is privately owned in Hampshire and, as a frequent visitor to air shows, is flown in Royal Navy south Atlantic camouflage scheme wearing the badge of HMS *Endurance* and its original tail number of XT787.

G-BYCX, SAAF '92'. (*Terry Martin*)

XS527 at Cobham Hall storage facility of the Fleet Air Arm Museum, RNAS Yeovilton. (*Howard Curtis*)

XS568 at DSAE HMS *Sultan*. (*Terry Martin*)

United Kingdom surviving Wasps recently registered as 'No Flight', but with potential to return to flight.

RN registration	Construction number	Current registration	Other registration	Other markings	Current status
XT781	F.9663	ZU-HAS	NZ3908 G-KAWW		HAS.1 (XT781) was on the UK Civil Register, in Royal Navy markings, but sold to a private buyer in South Africa in 2005. Possibly in Richmond, Natal.
XT782	F.9664	G-KANZ	NZ3909		G-KANZ, a former RN (XT782) and RNZN (NZ3909) Wasp HAS.1 was restored by Weald Aviation and is now in RNZN markings as NZ3909.

XT431 at the Bournemouth Aviation Museum. Aircraft restorer Rob Ellis with the author after discovering a photo of himself flying the Wasp on the display board. (*Terry Martin*)

XT439 in private storage in Hertfordshire. (*Alan Allen*)

United Kingdom surviving Wasps on display or storage.

RN registration	Construction number	Current registration	Other registration	Other markings	Current status
XS527	F.9543	(Static only)			Wasp HAS.1 XS527 is stored and sometimes displayed at Fleet Air Arm Museum, Yeovilton. This Wasp served on HMS *Endurance* during the Falklands conflict of 1982 and took part in the raid on the ARA *Santa Fe*.
XS529	F.9556	(Wreck)			After retirement XS529 moved to Predannack and was used by the fire training school. It was sold to the House of Fear film studio in Redruth in 2008, but the company was dissolved in 2012 and the current location of this airframe is not known.

RN registration	Construction number	Current registration	Other registration	Other markings	Current status
XS539	F.9566	(Unknown)			Preserved and seen at Fleetlands RN repair facility painted in 1982 colours as '434' HMS *Endurance*. Took part in the attack on the RA *Santa Fe*. Current location unknown.
XS567	F.9578	(Static only)	A2719	'434'	Former HMS *Endurance* Flight Wasp HAS.1 XS567 is on display at the Imperial War Museum Duxford.
XS568	F.9579	(Static only)		'441'	On display by DCAES HMS *Sultan* (mobile display)
XS569	F.9580	(Static only)			Ex-Fleetlands Apprentice School. Ex-XS569 and A2717. Now thought to be on display at Hermeskeil – Flugausstellung, Germany.
XT423	F.9607	(Unknown)			Initially preserved in the Falkland Islands after ditching and Cat 5 loss in 1985. Now possibly in the UK but location unknown.
XT427	F.9597	(Static only)			Wasp XT427 was originally purchased by the Flambards Theme Park in Helston, Cornwall, but, in 1999, was transferred to the Fleet Air Arm Museum, Yeovilton where it is held in storage.
XT431	F.9601	(Static only)			Wasp XT431 was initially on display outdoors at the Gatwick Aviation Museum but bought by a private collector and loaned to the Bournemouth Aviation Museum around 2012 and restored to better display condition, although it remains outdoors.

RN registration	Construction number	Current registration	Other registration	Other markings	Current status
XT434	F.9604	(Static only)	G–CGGK	'455'	XT434 is at Breighton Airfield under private ownership (The Real Aeroplane Company). Ex-RN 829 Sqn and latterly DARA Fleetlands Apprentice School. XT434 remains on the UK civil register as G–CGGK and marked as '455' of HMS *Ariadne*, and is awaiting long term restoration, hopefully to flying condition.
XT437	F.9607	(Static only)		'423'	Wasp HAS.1 XT437 is held by the Boscombe Down Aviation Collection at Old Sarum Airfield as '423' of HMS *Diomede*.
XT439	F.9609	(Static only)			Former 829 NAS Wasp HAS.1 XT439 was retired to Cranfield Institute of technology and later moved to Bruntingthorpe. It is now privately owned and stored in Hemel Hempstead, Hertfordshire.
XT443	F.9613	(Static only)		'422'	Wasp HAS.1 XT443 is on display at The Helicopter Museum, Weston–Super–Mare as '422' of HMS *Aurora* (1981-82).
XT778	F.9660	(Static only)		'430'	Wasp HAS.1 XT778 is held in storage by the Fleet Air Arm Museum, Yeovilton as '430', HMS *Achilles*.

RN registration	Construction number	Current registration	Other registration	Other markings	Current status
XT780	F.9662	(Instructional airframe)		'636'	Delivered to the Royal Navy (703 NAS) in 1966 and given the side number '636' which is still evident on the airframe. In 1989 it was designated for Ground Instructional use and was Gate Guardian at RNAY/DARA Fleetlands (now Vector Aerospace) in Gosport. It was later gifted to Fareham College and now resides with the college's successor, CEMAST (Centre of Excellence in Engineering, Manufacturing and Advanced Skills Training) on the site of the former RNAS at Lee-on-Solent. A fitting place to rest and yet still provide good education for aspiring aircraft technicians.
XT788	F.9670	(Static only)	G-BMIR	'474'	Wasp XT788 served with HMS *Zulu* and took part in the Falklands conflict. Parts of the helicopter came from G-BKLJ, which was previously 5X-UUX, and G-17-2. After retirement, as G-BMIR, it was based in Devon, UK and displayed at various locations as a focal point for charity collection. The owner was involved in a legal action and the aircraft was later reported to have moved to South Yorkshire Aircraft Museum, Doncaster Airport, but not listed in current inventory. It has now been traced to another private owner at Storwood in Yorkshire.

RN registration	Construction number	Current registration	Other registration	Other markings	Current status
XT793	F.9675	(Wreck)	G–BZPP	'456' (HMS *Yarmouth*)	Wasp HAS.1 XT793 was privately owned and stored at Thruxton in Royal Navy markings as '456' HMS *Yarmouth*. The remains of XT793 now reside at the Boscombe Down Aircraft Collection following the helicopter being written off after accident in 2010 at RNAS Yeovilton. Accident report: AAIB Bulletin: 7/2011.
XV625	F.9720	(Static only)		'471' (HMS *Phoebe*)	Former 829 Squadron, on HMS *Phoebe* Flight as '471', and later served at RNEC Manadon and RNAS Lee-on-Solent. It was later restored to static condition at DSAE HMS *Sultan* and sold to Withams in 2014. Auctioned several times, but failed to reach a rather high asking price and was eventually sold in 2017 to a private buyer in New York for less than a half the original reserve price.

XT435 (G-RIMM) at North Weald. (*Terry Martin*)

G-KAXT flying over HMS *Queen Elizabeth* at Portsmouth Naval Base. (*Adrian Balch*)

Of this record of survivors, the list of Wasps still flying, being refurbished or renovated back to flying condition is small. Their post-retirement stories are often sad, due to accidents, incidents and projects that failed whether due to lack of budget or paucity of spares, but there are also some shining examples of Wasps that are still flying over fifty years after they first entered service with the Royal Navy. It is a credit to the original design and manufacture that these machines can still be maintained, serviced, refurbished, and sometimes rebuilt, in order to pass all the criteria deemed essential to be considered airworthy by the relevant aviation regulatory authorities.

In the UK, the Civil Aviation Authority (CAA) considers all vintage and veteran aircraft as special cases. The Wasp and Scout pair both have agreed maintenance schedules and special rules applied in order that these helicopters can be placed on the civilian aircraft register. The UK Ministry of Defence (MoD) has the power to authorise the continued use of military colour schemes, markings, and registration marks as long as they are historically accurate and representative of the type in service.

Naturally there are restrictions and limitations to the way the helicopters can be flown (for instance they can only be operated during day/visual meteorological conditions - VMC), and weapons systems, as well as some other features, are either removed or disabled. Pilot training is a straightforward conversion to type, but all the current pilots are either ex-military or have had some serious 'type differences training' by some very experienced former RN and army instructors. The famous UK display pilot, John Beattie, has led the field in training and examining 'wannabe' Wasp and Scout pilots since the late 1990s, and he also trains and examines the few of us who have a Display Authority (DA). Fortunately, John has also future-proofed the ongoing succession of the Westland twins by passing on his knowledge and skills to the next generation of instructors and examiners that will help us all to keep flying for as long as possible.

So why do we do it? Why do otherwise sensible and rational grown men (so far, only men, no women) pay large sums of money to keep 50-year-old helicopters flying? And why do they take such delight in flying single engine helicopters, well known to have appalling autorotation characteristics and with a less than perfect safety record? Talking to my fellow Westland pilots, I hear phrases like, 'It's part of history', 'where else could I buy a jet engine helicopter at that price', 'It turns heads wherever I go', 'It's a beautiful helicopter to fly' and 'It's a classic'. I must admit that all of these reasons occurred to me back in 2000 when I bought a half share in my first Wasp, but my motives have change over the years as I've learned more about the helicopter, it's place in history, and the people who flew in, maintained, built, or marshalled/handled these beautiful machines.

My own story has taken a different path and has been, firstly, influenced by a love and respect for history, and, secondly, sadness that the unique Wasp helicopter has not been properly recognised for its significant place in the history of naval aviation. I'm still often asked how I ended up buying such an expensive 'man toy', especially since I don't have any previous relationship with the Royal Navy. To put this in perspective, the following text is extracted from an air show 'interview'.

'In November 2012, Kennet Aviation sold XT787 to Terry Martin, a former Royal Air Force doctor and pilot who now maintains her in a historic camouflage paint scheme and is proud to keep alive the memory of this distinguished first generation military jet helicopter and to represent the many crews who served in Westland Wasps during more than thirty years of naval service. Interestingly, in a sense, XT787 became truly tri-service for a while, being flown by Terry, a former RAF Wing Commander, and being based at the Headquarters of the Army Air Corps at Middle Wallop in Hampshire until August 2015. And, as for Terry, how does an RAF doctor end up flying a Navy helicopter?: "I joined the RAF as a medical officer and learned to fly fixed wing aircraft before a posting to the helicopter training base at RAF Shawbury where I converted to Gazelle. By the time I was posted out of Shawbury, my medical career had taken precedence over flying even though I did manage to keep up some 'gash' hours on Pumas in postings to both Germany and Belize. Much later, as HEMS [Helicopter Emergency Medical services] programs were being developed in the UK, I worked as a doctor in the newly established London Air Ambulance and felt the passion to return to flying. I bought a half share in my first Wasp (XT435/ NZ3907) in 2000 and then purchased XT787 outright in 2012. It's a real privilege to keep this warbird flying and to honour those that flew in Wasps during the cold war and the Falklands campaign"'.

My first Wasp

XT435 had respectable careers in both the Royal Navy and the Royal New Zealand Navy, as NZ3907. At almost the end of her service career, NZ3907 operated from the Leander class frigate HMNZS *Canterbury* during the periods of civil unrest on Bougainville Island in Papua New Guinea. For conspicuity and recognition, she was painted in an almost total all-over high visibility red scheme resulting in the nickname 'orange sprat'. She was never repainted during her remaining RNZN service, and was delivered back to the UK in the same colour scheme when I purchased a half share in 2000. That Wasp became G-RIMM, a very unfortunate registration mark, but it was insisted on by the owner of the first half share - a chap called Grimshaw. I recall he couldn't (or wouldn't) understand my reason for wanting to change the registration! We did change the colour scheme though and at least with UK Ministry of Defence approval we were able to remove the offensive G-RIMM mark and replace it with her former true registration mark under RN service, XT435. Grimshaw, who also chose the new RN persona for XT435, decided to dress her up as XT778, a former HMS *Achilles* Wasp (the original of which is still in the Fleet Air Arm Museum at RNAS Yeovilton in the UK), which, for its final flight with the RN, was given the accolade of yellow painted stripes along the tail cone to make it much more convincing as a 'wasp'! However, one further insult was to plague this poor Wasp. No, it wasn't the painted tail cone – the stripes set this Wasp apart from others and they fascinate people who often asked why that paint scheme was applied. The next insult derives from this particular Wasp's reputation. She had caused some ongoing despair to her crews and engineers whilst on HMS *Achilles* Flight and so was affectionately, but perhaps unfairly, nicknamed 'Sleazebag'. To be true to history, Grimshaw had the name 'painted' on the nose. How deeply upsetting to be called 'GRIMM Sleazebag'!

XT435 carried the ships number '43' on the nose, and I chose to fly her with a newly designated call sign 'C-CAT-43', pronounced 'Sea Cat Four Three'. Much more respectable I thought!

[CCAT is the acronym for a training program I developed in the 1997 at about the same time as NZ3907 was retiring from service, and Sea Cat missiles were retrofitted to small frigates during the service career of Wasps used by both Navies, although not actually carried on the helicopters of course.]

Sadly G-RIMM continued its habit of causing grief and frustration, and I had a few problems and challenges with her before we finally parted company in 2005. For some strange reason, never truly diagnosed, she had a knack of shedding Perspex panels – the windows. It always happened on the starboard (right) side and they 'fell off' either the door or the nose 'bubble'. Fortunately these panels were never lost over urban areas, and no damage or harm came to any third parties, but the cause of the problem was a mystery, even though I always put it down to a mixture of vibration and decay in the rubber window seals.

Talking of seals, and recalling that old adage, bitterly put about by fixed wing pilots, that, 'a helicopter is a loose arrangement of 3000 parts rotating around an oil leak', G-RIMM did succumb to a well-known Wasp issue, wherein smoke is seen coming from a vent in the top of the Nimbus 103 engine after flight - profuse at first and then diminishing as the engine cools. This phenomenon is easily recognised by Wasp and Scout engineers and was quickly diagnosed by an 'old salt' who was refuelling G-RIMM at the Middle Wallop Army Air Corp base, not long after I bought my share. 'Looks like you've got a blown vestibule seal in the rear turbine', he said cheerily in the knowledge that he knew something that I didn't.

[The relationship between pilots and aircraft engineers is a very unique and very strange one. Engineers believe that pilots are always the cause of the damage or 'illness' that has befallen their cherished machines. Comments like, 'What have you done to it?' and 'It was fine when it left maintenance', or 'Didn't they tell you not to do that?' are all very well, and often said in jest, but can cut to the quick for the poor sensitive newbie pilot!]

Despite all the angst, as my first Wasp, XT435 taught me a lot, and there is, and always will be, a small place in my heart for the helicopter that opened my mind to the concept of 'keeping history alive and flying'.

XT435 (G-RIMM) dressed as XT778, 'Sleazebag', representing the 'wasp tail' colour scheme worn during XT778's final flight from HMS *Achilles*. (*Terry Martin*)

Chapter 12

The Story of One Wasp in Active Retirement

XT787 rolled off the production line at the Fairey division of Westland Helicopters at Hayes in Middlesex on 10 January 1967 and made its first flight at nearby White Waltham on 19 January 1967. In her Royal Navy career, XT787 operated on frigates HMS *Leander* and HMS *Rhyl*, as part of 829 Squadron, and also later at Portland with 703 Squadron, as a fleet reserve aircraft.

A short history of Wasp helicopter XT787. (Construction number F.9669)

06 Feb 1967	XT787 was delivered to Royal Navy Fleet Air Arm.
28 Sep 1982	NZ3905 was delivered to Royal New Zealand Navy.
09 Apr 1998	Although NZ3905 was withdrawn from service with RNZN in 1997, all Wasps were officially retired on 09 Apr 1998 and this helicopter was sold back to its manufacturer, Westland Helicopters, in the UK.
05 Mar 2002	G-KAXT was registered on United Kingdom Civil Aircraft Register.
10 Jun 2011	G-KAXT/XT787 was again flying in Royal Navy colours and given display of Registration Mark Exemption by the MOD. She was, by then, marked-up as the Wasp of HMS *Endurance* in South Atlantic camouflage.
01 Jan 2018	Total flying time: 3,062 hours.

XT787 spent the first nine years of her life as a reserve machine in storage. She wasn't assigned to a ship until 1976 and her first service pilot on her first ship of the Royal Navy was not a Royal Navy officer. To clarify, let's revisit Lieutenant Commander (now retired Commander) Bill McCamy, USN, to explain in his own words:

'In March of 1976, when I was a relatively senior LT, I was called by my detailer and told it was time for me to go back out to sea or to DC (egads!!!). I was offered a couple of rather non interesting jobs and then the WASP PEP exchange was opened to me. Over the next twenty-four hours I spoke with about thirty-five others who had some knowledge of the Exchange Program and specifically the WASP exchange. Following the success of Jack Cassidy as the first USN WASP pilot, the two follow-on USN pilots were not so successful. So, when I started my inquiry about the WASP/PEP program, these disqualified pilots' story was shared with me, over and over, and "failure is not an option" was mentioned a time or two by my contemporaries and seniors. Bottom line, I decided to take the appointment and give it my best shot - besides, how much fun would it be to take my whole family over to UK!!

'Leaving the US in July 1976, I was told by my "handlers" to get over to 703 Squadron as soon as possible to get started with the transition to the WASP. I did just that, and, unbeknownst to the Senior Pilot of 703 Squadron, Mike Mullane, I showed up quite a bit early - they weren't ready for me to start any training as my 703 replacement class was not going to be starting until after the summer break, i.e., September. So, I was told to, "throttle it back" a bit, get settled in to housing, enjoy southern UK, and, oh by the way, let's do your SE drills, get outfitted with UK flying gear, and go out to Culdrose to do a special flying evaluation with C.O. Standards in a Gazelle. Once this was done, and successfully, I might add, I returned to Weymouth and just hung out until my class convening date in early September.'

XT787 flown by a Yank in the USA. (*Bill McCamy*)

Lieutenant Commander McCamy contributed the photograph above in which he generously describes XT787 as 'our Wasp'. In his own words:

'Here is a picture of our Wasp taken in November 1978 while I was on the Group 7 Deployment and *Leander* was in Mayport, FL. This picture is actually taken at NAS Jacksonville while I was giving my brother Tom, an air force transport pilot, a briefing on the WASP, so I could take him for a spin around the pattern. Tom had never been in a helicopter and was pretty excited about this event. During that time I also took the local Flag Officer, RADM Robert Carius, for a ride to include some autorotations and low flight across the airfield. Admiral Carius was a VS pilot (S-2 Trackers and S-3 Viking) so he knew something about anti-submarine warfare, but from a fixed wing perspective.'

Bill has been very complimentary about the Royal Navy and insists that the RN was ahead of the US Navy in terms of small anti-submarine helicopters operating off small ships. At the time, though, he was less enthusiastic about the Wasp:

'I believe the RN was the forerunner in small ships helicopter operations and the USN took from the RN what it could to start HS(L) in the early 70s. Of course we expanded the mission and improved the helicopter platform tremendously – SH-60. Today, the whole helicopter organization is completely different and I would have to reach out to the USN helicopter world to find out exactly how they operate – new ships, new helicopters, greatly expanded helicopter mission.
    'To say that the Wasp seem antiquated would be an understatement. Single pilot, over the sea at night, 400ft altitude, positive control, minimal IFR capability, limited fuel capacity, and hands on/manual approach to a VFR deck landing was a new order of flying for me. Don't get me wrong, it was exciting, exhilarating, and very challenging – which was right up my alley.'

It wasn't an easy start for Bill. His Flight Commander's monthly report for June 1997 reveals just a tad of frustration in his new role!

Flight Commander's monthly report: Leander Flight. June 1977.

This is the first entry for LEANDER since 19 Dec 1976. The Flight basically reformed 21 Feb 1977, but without an aircraft and a ship in refit the officialdom of flight reformation was somewhat lacking. However, we are well and together even though a Yank, Lieutenant Commander Bill McCamy, USN, is at the controls.

During the latter stages of spring, the ship was rededicated and then began her post-refit sea trials, Now that the summer solstice has passed, the ship is still doing her sea trials and it looks like she'll be at it for a while. Captain Mike Clapp and trusty crew are anxiously awaiting the completion of SAT (Air) so that all of us can begin operating as we should - together.

Late June found the Flight Commander and the SMR 'driving' over to Fleetlands to pick-up our long overdue, unserviceable airframe. Once back in Portland we frantically made it 'S' and returned HMS *Falmouth's* budgie, as it had been on loan to us for the ORI work-up. XT787 is a very young aircraft and obviously needs many more hours on the airframe before she realizes that she ain't supposed to vibrate so much. The SMR, AA1 'Fritz' Heritier is assured and confident that the Flight can sort this one out, once given the chance following the ORI in July. All in all, things are looking good for a successful start of this Flight commissioning sometime in the near future.

W.C. McCamy
Lieutenant Commander
United States Navy
Flight Commander
Leander Flight

The ship's Flight monthly reports are fascinating relics of history that reveal more about daily life in naval aviation than can normally be read from textbooks. From my perspective as a mere Royal Air Force officer, life at sea never really interested me, and yet I have nothing but admiration for the brave and adventurous souls who made a career out of landing and taking off from tiny spaces on the back of moving targets as the ships heave and sway in all sorts of weather and lighting conditions. But it's clear from the time-capsules that are the reports of the men who flew those missions, that life was a fascinating mixture of adventure, frustration, fun, camaraderie and rarely fear. Take this next example, for instance. Bill McCamy's report delivers an absorbing snapshot of a ship at work from the viewpoint of the ship's Flight:

Flight Commander's monthly report: Leander Flight. July 1978.

Curacao is hot in the summer but is bearable due to a warm northerly breeze. It is also dusty, unsophisticated and, if you're a gambler, a loser. However, the fourth of July was celebrated in grand style with Harvey Wallbangers and American-style nosh, courtesy of the Flight Commander.

Sailing on the seventh, we carried on flying despite rough seas and limited visibility. The ninth was reserved for transiting the canal and it was quite hot, humid and muggy. Lots of mosquitos, bugs and interesting sights along the way, as well as the majesty of the canal, made for a really neat experience. Once in the Pacific we got on with more HDS, F5 SOOTAX'G, and a few love days to upgrade our tans. Budgie 'Uribus' mysteriously developed an 'additional' hole in the tailpipe and needed a quick welding, which could only be done on board *Blake*. It was arranged and carried out on a glorious day, but would you believe it took four hours to complete a one and a half minute weld job? The hangar and flight deck had to be totally shifted and was some sight, as well as a monumental headache for 820 Squadron.

Arriving at Long Beach, Ca, a day early due to ship problems, we disembarked to Los Alamitos and were met by some rather astonished natives. They were army mechanics who had never seen a Wasp, much less heard about it. We got on quite well with them from the outset and spent the rest of the month transiting from Naval Support Activity Long Beach to AFRC Los Alamitos daily (which is not such a good arrangement). The Flight also took some leave and saw the sights of the south-west USA and the Flight Commander spent nine days on a rubber raft floating down the Grand Canyon (Sierra Hotel) with half of next month alongside, what will August bring but more beautiful weather and lovely ladies to keep everyone happy.

W.C. McCamy
Lieutenant Commander
United States Navy
Flight Commander
Leander Flight

Every pilot, crewman, engineer and mechanic takes a pride in 'their' aircraft, no less so than in the tight team that makes up the ship's flight, who quickly learn to work cohesively and harmoniously together in their very own band of brothers. The monthly reports demonstrate the camaraderie well and it is a phenomenon that civilian pilots can only dream about and aspire to. The same applies to the ease of access to both skilled resources and also to spare parts in the Royal Navy. For an item that might cost the civilian owner of a Wasp perhaps half a year's salary, the Royal Navy had the luxury of being able to take expensive spares straight of the shelf. And if one didn't work, it could be thrown away and yet another quickly sourced to replace it. The following report by Bill McCamy's replacement on HMS *Leander* ship's Flight (Lt A.P.G. Davies) nicely describes the procedures as repairs don't go exactly right:

Flight Commander's monthly report: Leander Flight. March 1979.

A particularly difficult month for the Flight, still disembarked at Portland. With embarkation date looming on the horizon, 476 was placed unserviceable when cracks were discovered on one of the Inlet Guide Vanes. The engine was hastily changed over a weekend, but proved very difficult to set up, eventually being rejected by the MTP when it surged badly at height necessitating a precautionary landing.

A further engine change was carried out again over a weekend and the ship was warned we would not be able to arrive as planned. This engine, too, was rejected – after many hours of work on the ground – when it was found impossible to set up for a test flight.

Yet another engine was produced and this time was quickly cleared for test flying, only to discover several faults in the torque meter system. Another engine change appeared to be on the cards at this stage, but fortunately things took a turn for the better and at the eleventh hour 476 eventually passed its maintenance test flights.

All in all a very trying month for all the Flight personnel, whose overtime pay, had they been in civilian employment, would have been enormous. However, morale remained gratifyingly high and the end result means that at the time of writing embarkation on the second of next month is definitely on the cards.

A.P.G. Davies
Flight Commander
Leander Flight

XT787 in maintenance in 2017 at North Weald. (*Terry Martin*)

Not long after the cessation of hostilities in the Falkland Islands, XT787 was finally struck off charge from the Royal Navy in October 1982. Because of her excellent condition and low hours (679:40 total flying hours in the Royal Navy) XT787 was transferred to New Zealand where, until 1997, she served as part of the Royal New Zealand Air Force, but in service with Royal New Zealand Navy as NZ3905.

In New Zealand service, NZ3905 took part in many operations and exercises in the South Pacific, but one rather surprising event was to give her a unique place in history. To quote from the pilot, Lt John Adams (RN exchange pilot):

'On 24 March 85, and against all the rules, I landed the right front wheel of her on the top of Mount Cook, at 12,350 Feet. I know that no other Wasp had ever done this, but why unrepeatable? Well a few years later, about 70 million tons fell off the top and it's now 32 feet shorter.'

I found the corroboration for this story in the New Zealand press media:

'Aoraki/Mt Cook has shrunk 30 metres as the summit reshapes after the massive rock-ice collapse in 1991. Work to measure the height of the mountain was done by an Otago-led climbing expedition last November and analysis of high accuracy GPS data obtained during the climb has confirmed the new height. The readings reinforce new aerial photography-based calculations by Otago National School of Surveying researcher Pascal Sirguey and Masters student Sebastion Vivero, with support from GNS Science and New Zealand Aerial Mapping.

'Dr Sirguey says the discrepancy between the old height of 3754m (estimated from aerial photography immediately following a massive rock-ice collapse on 14 December 1991) and the new height of 3724m can be explained by a two-decades long reshaping process affecting the remnant of the originally thick ice cap.

'"By carefully studying photos taken after the collapse, it appears that there was still a relatively thick ice cap, which was most likely out of balance with the new shape of the summit ridge," he says, "as a result, the ice cap has been subject to erosion over the past twenty years".'

By all accounts, NZ3905 was busier in RNZN service than she was during her career in the Royal Navy. In her ten years of service down under, she accrued twice the number of flying hours than she had in the previous two decades. But life for this particular Wasp didn't end there. On being withdrawn from RNZN service in March 2002, NZ3905 was sold back to Westlands and was subsequently bought by Tim Manna's historic aircraft collection at Kennet Aviation where she was refurbished, adapted for civilian use (new VHF radio and GPS; disabled radio altimeter, autopilot and SAS; removal of flotation devices), and registered as G-KAXT.

With MoD approval, G-KAXT was given permission to be re-marked as XT787 again, and repainted in the South Atlantic camouflage scheme of Wasp XS527. This was the famous helicopter of HMS *Endurance* Flight (829 Squadron) which fired two AS12 missiles that severely damaged the Argentine submarine the ARA *Santa Fe* at Grytviken in South Georgia in May 1982.

The camouflage paint scheme is a very frequent question at air shows, especially from former RN personnel who don't believe that any Wasp ever flew in such markings. Nevertheless, photographic evidence from the Falklands conflict reveal various different patterns as the ice blue colour variably turned to green. From these old photos, it appears that the camouflage pattern was toned down at some stage. My best guess at the time was that the Wasp was probably used in support of land ops after the troops disembarked on the Falkland Islands and so the light shaded markings would have really stood out. It then made sense that the 'ice blue' areas of camouflage were concealed with a darker colour and later painted over with green. In summary, the change surely came about as the Wasps were moved from maritime to shore-based operations. As I discovered during a fascinating conversation with John Bibby at the RAF Cosford Air Show in 2016, this theory is actually not too far away from the truth. John was there at the time, serving on HMS *Endurance*, and he was involved in the decision-making. Here are his own words:

'The original camouflage that was applied to the aircraft meant that the aircraft was too easily seen once the season changed and snow started to collect close to the shore. The solution was to have the aircraft approach the ship at say 20 feet above the water with its anti-collision light off and we would line the edge of the flight deck and try to 'spot' the aircraft as it approached. I remember this being done on the last sortie each day. The A&E (airframe and engine) trades were responsible for any paint spraying and they did a very good job of it, adding a bit more "snow" as the season progressed! For the 1982 season we had three different A/C, we commenced with XT418 and XS527, one of which came to grief on a South Georgia beach (with the then Governor of the Falkland islands and his wife on board!). No one was hurt. This was due to a "wind switch" as the A/C came into land. Whichever one crashed it was replaced by XS539.'
John Bibby

For history lovers and the doubters who question the accuracy of the Wasp's markings, this, an old photo taken in May 1982 (credited to the MoD), is said to describe the arctic camouflage pattern as 'zebra-like'. I'm not sure I agree, but you can clearly see that XT787 is modelled on these markings.

XS539 in original camouflage pattern, May 1982. (*MoD*)

A more modern photograph, taken in 2017, shows XT787 at 1000ft over the Solent, south of the former Royal Navy Hospital at Haslar (Gosport). The photo clearly demonstrates how well XT787's camouflage disrupts her outline even over urban and rural England!

XT787 flying over Haslar in September 2017. (*Adrian Balch*)

I have never ceased to be amazed how much fascination and respect for the Wasp still abounds in those who once worked with, or flew in, these dynamic and feisty little helicopters. Even more amazing, though, is the respect that I often see from people who are too young to have ever seen them in service. Here is an example from a blog I wrote on Friday, 12 August 2016.

Amusing conversation on the air band this afternoon after I was told that ATC was closed and I was making a 'blind' call to anybody who may have been on frequency. It went something like this…

Me:	'Wallop Traffic, this is Wasp helicopter X-ray Tango, rotors turning on delta for heli west departure'.
Wallop Tower:	'X-ray Tango, this is Wallop Tower, wind two zero zero at ten knots. Be advised there is one vehicle on the airfield.'
Me:	'Apologies Wallop Tower, I thought you were closed'.

Wallop Tower: 'We are, but there's still a vehicle on the airfield.'

(At this point I spot that the only other aircraft in the vicinity is a low level Royal Navy Merlin helicopter transiting on the north-west boundary of the MATZ)

Topcat 1:   'Wallop Tower, this is TopCat1 to the north of the field'

Wallop Tower: 'Topcat1 this is Wallop Tower, we closed ten minutes ago, but you have a Wasp helicopter about to depart to the east'.

Topcat 1:   'A Wasp? You mean like a Navy version of a Scout?'

Wallop Tower: 'Affirm'

Topcat 1:   (pause) ... 'Blimey!!!'

Me: 'That sounds like admiration!'

Topcat 1:   'Wow! I haven't seen a Wasp in years, but I can see you on the ground now!'

Big smiles all round and a beautiful take-off to the east in great viz and fantastic late afternoon sunshine as the Merlin continued its journey to the south-east in the distance. #historicwasp

Chapter 13

Almost the End for XT787

XT787 after emergency landing near Salisbury in September 2016. (*Terry Martin*)

Like cats - perhaps Sea Cats? - Wasps also appear to have nine lives. After several significant incidents during her Royal Navy service, XT787 suffered a catastrophic failure whilst on an intended short flight in 2016. This is a story worthy of inclusion because it describes a rare helicopter emergency that has apparently not been reported before. The story demonstrates, perhaps, the complacency of trouble-free flying and the effect on response to events after an emergency is declared. However, the story has drawn a lot of attention from many quarters (CAA, AAIGB, RN, RAF and GASCO, to name a few) because of its uniqueness, but also because the human factors have been closely scrutinised. I have reproduced an abbreviated version of what was published in the GASCO flight safety journal in 2017, and which appeared as 'blogs' as, and when, events unfolded.

To set the scenario, I was flying XT787 (G–KAXT) from AAC Middle Wallop to RNAS Yeovilton, to take part in an event celebrating the seventieth anniversary of Alan Bristow's first ever helicopter landing on a small ship at sea. The sky was blue from horizon to horizon and there was only a whisper of wind. I was cruising at 1,200 feet to the west of Salisbury, with a basic air traffic service being provided by Boscombe Zone.

The following blog entries describe the incident and the days, weeks and months taken to rebuild XT787 and restore her to flight.

Friday, 23 September 2016 at 13:26 UTC+01
WASP DOWN

Sad to say X-ray Tango didn't make it to Yeovilton. Midway between Alderbury and Compton Abbas I detected some vibration in the collective lever and then discovered that I had lost collective pitch control. That means I couldn't climb or descend! The rest of the story merits telling later, but I'm currently waiting for a recovery truck to remove the helicopter from a field near Bishopstone. Nobody was injured, the helicopter is still upright, but there was some damage which looks expensive at first glance. I'll keep you posted. #historicwasp

Saturday, 1 October 2016 at 14:59 UTC+01
The story of the incident on 23 September.

Lots of you have asked. Here is part 1 of the story about the emergency that befell X-ray Tango recently, which I hope will interest you and may even give aircrew and engineers alike some food for thought.

Friday, 23 September 2016 was a beautiful late summer's day. Visibility was unlimited, and the sky was blue and almost cloudless. I was flying XT787 in the cruise at 1000ft and in straight, level and balanced flight at a speed of 80knots. The flying controls had all been behaving normally and all temperature and pressure gauges were 'in the green'. Ironically, I was en route to RNAS Yeovilton to join in the celebration of the seventieth anniversary of Alan Bristow's first helicopter landing on a RN ship. A few miles south-west of Salisbury I felt a two to three second vibration in the collective lever and soon discovered I had a total collective pitch failure.

Finding I could neither climb nor descend was a little disconcerting, as I was above hilly and rising ground. Fearing this event may be the first part of a greater mishap, I opted to turn away from the undulating hills ahead of me and prepare for a precautionary landing as soon as possible. I made a 'PAN' call to the air traffic controller at Boscombe Zone to announce intention to land asap. A 'PAN' call is like a 'MAYDAY' call but less urgent, i.e. used for emergency situations that are not immediately life threatening, but do require assistance from someone on the ground. A serious aircraft system failure that requires an immediate route or altitude change falls in to this category.

I soon found what looked like a suitable flat site in the nearby valley of the River Ebble (Chalke Valley), a somewhat small sports field adjacent to a larger flat field with low lying crops and no visible fence or barrier between the two. The chosen site was opposite a village, so I'd be sure of responders in the event that the landing didn't go well, but far enough away to minimise risks to others. I noticed a small play area but it was school-time and there were no children anywhere to be seen. There was time for a few circuits and to do some slow speed handling checks. This was valuable time. As I cruised in a figure of eight around my selected safe site, I had time to brief my crewperson, Gail, who secured the cabin whilst I focused on trying to figure out how I was going to descend and land safely without collective pitch control. Of the options that were running through my head, I considered converting from governed to manual throttle, but the main rotor RPM was tending to over-speed so I decided initially to fly by attitude, i.e. to decay some rotor energy and forward speed. I found that decaying the NR and pulling the nose up would give me a gentle rate of descent and also slow my forward speed, so after a final check of temperatures and pressures, RRPM, height and airspeed, and with no alarms or attention-getters, I made another radio call to Boscombe Zone to ensure I was still on radar and to inform the controller that I was making my final approach. The approach, landing, and my reflections, will follow in part 2. #historicwasp

Saturday, 1 October 2016 at 16:26 UTC+01
The precautionary landing.
The story continues. Part 2.

Before committing to the approach, I checked that the selected site was still the best option and that there were no people, animals or other obstructions to a clear landing area. I eventually converted to manual throttle at about 500-300ft for the final approach to the field. In doing so, and taking account of a flare at the bottom of the descent, I underestimated my 'glide' range* and landed about 5m short of the sports ground. The landing wasn't particularly heavy, but without ability to cushion, and a very low forward speed, the first wheel to touch caused a significant 'oleo-bounce' and there followed a couple of seconds of bouncing between all four corners as I shut down.

(* TM: 'glide' range is a tongue-in-cheek description of the angle at which the Wasp descends under these circumstances.)

The large oleos on the Wasp were designed to be useful when landing on heaving decks in very rough seas. The Wasp also therefore has a 'negative' pitch (actually just a lower pitch called 'superfine') used to pin it to the flight deck whilst the flight deck crew lash/lock the helicopter down. On the one hand the oleos clearly mop up some of the kinetic energy of the landing, but they also caused the bouncing, which seemed to resonate and grow remarkably quickly. This may have been exacerbated by the rear wheels being 'toed inwards' which is designed to prevent the Wasp rolling out of control in a roll-on landing.

With the marvels of modern GPS technology, my on-board iPad, fitted with Airbox Runway HD, plotted the whole thing. By exporting the file to Google Earth, I saw an enormous amount of detail recorded every five seconds of the flight. From these data, I've calculated that my descent rate was only 170ft/min, hence the landing wasn't particularly heavy, but, of course, without collective pitch, I couldn't cushion the landing and I certainly couldn't take advantage of superfine pitch to counter the bouncing. The data also showed that my forward speed was 11kt. That's only about 12.6mph, but, with the rear wheels toed in and dense vegetation on the field, the Wasp couldn't roll forward to dissipate the energy, which probably exacerbated the bounce.

Unfortunately, after what should have been a good landing, the bounce immediately tipped the nose up and the tail rotor dug in to the ground. The subsequent rapid yaw to the right felt like being in a human centrifuge (I know, I've done that in my RAF days) and almost caused a roll-over, so I was fighting the instability to keep us upright for a few more seconds whilst I throttled down and shut off the fuel (HP cock). As the rotors wound down, all focus was on neutralising cyclic control to keep the main rotor tips from contact with the ground. Everything settled quite quickly, we were down on all four wheels and nobody was injured. I completed the shut-down checks properly before Gail and I safely made our exit. In retrospect, there are other possible ways this emergency may have been resolved, but hindsight is always 20/20 vision. Unfortunately, since foresight is always preferable, this wasn't really possible as complete collective pitch failure is one emergency that doesn't feature in the Wasp training manual, operating procedures, or even in the Annual Skills Test. It's that rare! #historicwasp

(TM: I discovered later that this particular emergency had never happened to a Wasp previously, and, at the time, I hadn't heard of it occurring in any other helicopter type.)

Saturday, 1 October 2016 at 16:37 UTC+01
Digging deep to deal with the emergency Part 3.
    Some people have asked if I felt fear or panic. In all honesty, I can truly say that I was too busy trying to work out what the problem was, and then what I could do to

get safely back to mother earth – I had no time for panic. I had to focus and not be distracted, there was a lot going on inside the helicopter and I also needed to keep my eyes outside because of the potential for harm to others or their property. My day job is as an anaesthetist and intensive care/emergency medicine specialist, working much of the time in an air ambulance. Wearing that hat, I've spent many years dealing with emergency life-threatening events that need quick decision making followed by precise and rapid interventions. I learned long ago not to waste energy on panic or unfocused thoughts. Perhaps that helped me on the 23 September 2016, but, having a crewperson who kept her cool and didn't distract me, as well as an instant response from an excellent air traffic controller who let me get on with the flying, both must surely have helped enormously.

As it turned out, XT787 is repairable, nobody was injured, and collateral damage was minimal and confined to only a very small area of root crops. I'm hoping that makes it a reasonably good precautionary landing. Again, thank you to you all, for your verbal, text, and actual physical help, support and care. I'll continue to post X-ray Tango's progress over the coming weeks.

Quote from *'Fatal Traps for Helicopter Pilots'* (by Greg Whyte)

In my first edition copy of this fascinating book by Greg Whyte, there is no mention of loss of collective pitch control, but the following quote is interesting:

'Have you ever thought about what you are going to do when a serious mechanical problem develops during a flight? Given half an hour and a committee to thrash out all the options, you would probably come up with the right answer. Unfortunately, it's noisy, lights are flashing, horns are blaring and people are looking genuinely apprehensive. You have seconds to make a decision. While doing so you must control the aircraft. It's no time to reflect on your decision to take up flying. There are glaringly obvious things that you can embark on right now – education, practice, training, prior thought.'

This is good advice and guidance I have followed seriously since the incident at Bishopstone.

Saturday, 1 October 2016 at 11:07 UTC+01
X-ray Tango in hospital.

With thanks to Don Baggett, Anthony Draper (who ensured a safe shelter for XT last weekend), Wiltshire Aircraft Maintenance (Rangers recovery) from Popham, and Pix, Dave and Josh, the lads from Weald Aviation, XT arrived back in Essex without further damage. Engineers from the AAIB, CAA and the loss adjusters met with me and Weald Aviation's senior engineers yesterday (Friday, 30 Sep), exactly one week after the incident. The photo shows XT being dissected to reveal the damage, starting initially with the search for cause. A panel was removed from the rear of the cabin to reveal the pitch linkages under the gearbox. In one photograph the failure of the collective pitch rod can clearly be seen where it would normally sit inside the semi-aperture of a metal plate 'guide'. The next photograph is of an intact pitch linkage assembly for comparison. The failed component was sent for metallurgy tests to try and establish if this was a materials failure or if there may have been a preceding event that resulted in the fracture. Clearly we all want to be sure that any risks can be identified to protect all the other flying Wasps and Scouts. #historicwasp

XT787 being ambulanced home for some TLC. (*Don Baggett*)

Wasp being dissected to find the cause of the collective pitch control rod failure and the hidden damage. (*Weald Aviation*)

After recovery of XT787 from the incident site back to North Weald in Essex, the helicopter was comprehensively assessed and evaluated as a potential rebuild project. In addition to the original failure of the collective pitch control rod, deep within the gearbox, the initial cause was discovered to be a dry universal joint. In effect, the control rod failure was secondary to a universal joint failure that had occurred in the cyclic control circuit due to lack of lubrication and a build-up of corrosion deposits. The full Air Accident Investigation Board report (AAIB Bulletin: 6/2017) is available at: https://assets.publishing.service.gov.uk/media/591c30aaed915d20f800001c/Westland_Wasp_HAS1_G-KAXT_06-17.pdf

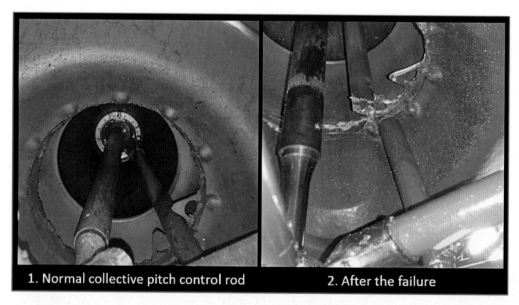

1. Normal collective pitch control rod   2. After the failure

Before and after views of the collective pitch control rod showing the failure. (*Weald Aviation*)

Unfortunately, the damage was not limited to the gearbox, much more damage occurred after the tail rotor struck the ground during the emergency landing. Clearly, the tail rotor itself was destroyed and that hurt! It was a brand new replacement only a month earlier! Along with the tail rotor blades, the repair necessitated acquisition of a whole tail rotor assembly, including angle gearbox and transmission. As the design intended, the tail rotor strike was followed by a failure of the tail rotor drive shaft. This weak link is designed to prevent the shock of the strike spreading back through the transmission and onward to the gearbox and engine. However, the free end of the fractured drive shaft, whilst continuing to rotate as the energy decayed, cut through structures within the tail cone that were hidden from view at the time. So, in addition to drive shafts and control cables, there was also structural and cosmetic damage to the tail pylon and to the cone itself, as well as transmitted damage to the torque meter, a fuel pump and one of the cabin roof panels.

Naturally, a lot of structures needed to be NDT'd (non-destructive testing) to ensure that they remained airworthy. All in all, the situation was beginning to look much more expensive than I first thought. The photograph of the Wasp immediately after landing certainly didn't reveal the whole story. Nevertheless, despite all the damage, I decided to bite the bullet and go ahead with approval to start the restoration and rebuild.

New spares for most of the rebuild were acquired after the kind intervention of Tim Manna, owner of Kennet Aviation. Actually, it's more accurate to describe the spares as 'zero hours', or 'previously unused', as all the 'new' spares currently available were, of course, manufactured over thirty-five years earlier. The one thing we couldn't find was an unused tail cone, but the Chief Engineers at Weald Aviation, Dave Horsfield and colleague Fran Renouf, were unfazed by the challenge. In fact Dave was ecstatic at the prospect of a Cat 4 rebuild which, he told me, was, 'real repair work, just like (he had done) in his time as an RAF engineer' at the major maintenance base at RAF St Athan, and so it was agreed. With new (zero-hours) spares and a rebuild of the tail cone, the restoration and rebuild was to start without delay, the aim being to be flying again in time for the 2017 summer air show season.

XT787 during the rebuild of the tail cone. (*Weald Aviation*)

XT787 during the rebuild, making acquaintance with XT435. My first and second Wasps together in the same hangar! (*Weald Aviation*)

Stepping forward a few months and, although there had been many challenges to resolve en route and the delays seemed to go on forever, the end result was worth waiting for. The 'return to the air' first flight test went extremely well and occurred, by chance, as another special aircraft was inbound to Weald Aviation, plus, the date fell on a very special anniversary!

Thursday, 15 June 2017 at 23:08 UTC+01
XT787's FIRST FLIGHT IN 2017.
We've received some really nice photos taken by Matt Smith (Weald Aviation) showing X-ray Tango's return to flight. By pure coincidence, my first Wasp (XT435) was inbound to North Weald with John Beattie and Graham Hinkley at the controls whilst XT787 was flying. This could be the only photo in existence with these two stablemates in the air together.

Possibly the only photo in existence showing both XT787 and XT435 in the air together at the same time since leaving New Zealand. (*Weald Aviation*)

A FITTING TRIBUTE

The surrender of Argentine forces brought an end to fighting in the Falkland Islands, effective at 2359 hours ZULU on 14 June 1982 (2059 hours local). The Wasp is one of the very few remaining types that served in the Falklands War and yet is still flying today. We're proud that XT787's return to the air coincided with the thirty-fifth anniversary of the first day of freedom and peace in the Falkland Islands. This campaign was both the Westland Wasp's swansong and also her entry into the history books for the attack on the Argentine submarine, the Santa Fe. #historicwasp

The summer weather in 2017 had started well and I was sad to have missed the first three air show bookings in our busy summer schedule, but there was much to do before XT787 was ready to display again.

Friday, 23 June 2017 at 21:32 UTC+01

THE EAGLE HAS LANDED

Well, not quite, but the Wasp has! X-ray Tango was handed over to me at North Weald this morning. There she was, waiting to spring to life on the apron outside Weald

Aviation whilst I took an engineering handover from Pix. All systems working fine, new radio is so much of an improvement on the previous model, the sun was shining and the 1hr 10min flight was a delight. Many thanks to all the engineers who have worked so hard to rebuild XT over the past nine months. Yes, it has been EXACTLY nine months to the day since the emergency landing in Bishopstone on 23 September 2016. A nine month gestation. XT787 has so many new parts that this really was a rebirth. I'm also very grateful to Sally, the ATC tower controller whose dulcet tones welcomed us back to Hampshire, and I really appreciate the welcoming party - Matt (test pilot), Chris (photographer), the duty fire crew, and to all the spectators who watched me approach, hover taxi to parking and the eventual landing. A great day for the logbook. #historicwasp

After returning the insurance cover to full flying activity, acquiring the usual MoD indemnity document, and studying recent changes to the CAA guidance on air show performance and local air law/air traffic updates, I embarked on a short period of re-familiarisation flying and self-testing in preparation for my return to display flying, it was great to run through XT787's display routine for examiner John Beattie and it felt event better to be the recipient of a brand new display authority (DA) for the remainder of the year.

Friday, 7 July 2017 at 23:44 UTC+01
ANOTHER GREAT DAY!
After polishing the rotor blades in glorious sunshine, then filling the tank at Middle Wallop, it was good to catch up with Air Traffic, Flight Ops, as well as the fuellers. A cuppa and short rest to brief and plan the evening's events, and it was soon time to get back in to the air for the short flight to Bishopstone for our 'thank you' fly-past. It was so nice to see some of the villagers on the sports field, outside the pub, and in the streets of the village.

Thank you to the kind and generous Bishopstonians. From Wiltshire we flew south-west to the coast of Dorset at Weymouth, where we joined up with a Skyvan packed full of photographers intent on enticing X-ray Tango closer and closer to take some amazing air-to-air shots with the beautiful Dorset coast as background. I'd asked permission for us to fly over the now closed former RN Air Station at Portland since it was the home for almost every Wasp in RN service at some time in its life-cycle.

Permission was granted for us to transit the danger areas and regulated airspace south of Chesil Beach and I spent a glorious twenty minutes formating behind (line astern) and beside (echelon left and echelon right) the chunky, box-like Skyvan photo-ship at 2000ft.

After all that excitement, we made our way steadily across the beautiful Dorset and Somerset countryside to land back at Yeovilton in readiness for tomorrow's Air Day. Thus we completed the journey that we started on 23 September 2016 that ended prematurely in a field at Bishopstone opposite the village pub!

It's fantastic to be flying again. #historicwasp

XT787 proudly flying over the former Royal Navy Air Station (HMS *Osprey*) at Portland where she spent much of her service life. (*Aviation Photocrew*)

For the last step forward in time, what better way to celebrate the first anniversary of the incident than to fly back to Wiltshire? This was a beautiful late summer's day with blue skies and light winds. A perfect day for a flight past Stonehenge and over the beautiful green and Neolithic countryside south and west of Salisbury Plain.

Friday, 22 September 2017 at 10:32 UTC+01

The anniversary.

Saturday 23rd September 2017 will be exactly one year since X-ray Tango's emergency landing at Bishopstone and we're heading back to Wiltshire! I'm aiming to land at the Bratton Showground at 10:00 for the 'Bratton at War' event. For those attending, please be vigilant and follow the instructions of our ground crew, especially if you're too near to the HLS. Keep good control of your children and pets and stay away from the ground wash, which can create flying objects of any discarded rubbish, or even intentional items placed on the ground within about 50 yards/m of the landing site. For anybody who lives near the low-level corridor, westbound along the A303 from Cholderton, then north on the A36, and east of Warminster and Westbury, do listen out for that Nimbus 103 and give us a wave as we fly over. #historicwasp

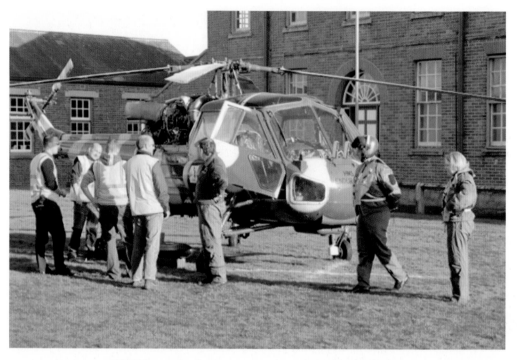

XT787 on static display at an event in 2016. (*Richard Noyce*)

Chapter 14

Civilian Pilots Flying Rotary Warbirds

The author (TM) flying XT787 over southern England in 2016. (*Chris Parsons*)

ABC News commentary by Harry reasoner during the Vietnam War, 16 February 1971:

Helicopter pilots.

You can't help but have the feeling that there will come a future generation of men, if there are any future generations of men, who will look at old pictures of helicopters and say, 'You've got to be kidding'. Helicopters have that look that certain machines have in historical drawings. Machines or devices that came just before a major breakthrough. Record changers just before the lightweight vinyl LP for instance.

Mark Twain once noted that he lost belief in conventional pictures of angels of his boyhood when a scientist calculated for a 150-pound man to fly like a bird, he would have to have a breastbone 15 feet wide supporting wings in proportion.

Well, that's sort of the way a helicopter looks.

The thing is, helicopters are different from airplanes. An airplane by its nature wants to fly, and if not interfered with too strongly by unusual events or incompetent piloting, it will fly. A helicopter does not want to fly. It is maintained in the air by a variety of forces and controls working in opposition to each other and if there is any disturbance in this delicate balance the helicopter stops flying, immediately and disastrously.

There is no such thing as a gliding helicopter. That's why being a helicopter pilot is so different from being an airplane pilot, and why in generality airplane pilots are open, clear-eyed, buoyant, extroverts. And helicopter pilots are brooders, introspective anticipators of trouble.

They know if something bad has not happened it is about to.

The famous helicopter display pilot, Dennis Kenyon, and the author (TM) flying XT435 over the Needles, Isle of Wight. (Loop *Magazine*)

A View from the Pilot's Seat

Sitting on board, I'm always reminded of the Wasp's naval heritage and their links with military flying in the cold war years. It's not just that fabulous 'Spitfire' smell of leather and oils that is so iconic of vintage aircraft, but it's also an acute awareness that this chunky warbird is no lightweight helicopter. Empty, she weighs in at 3,250lbs (1474kg) and, with a MAUW of 5,550lbs (2517kg), this leaves a very useful 1043kg for fuel and payload, and yet she still has more than enough power to comfortably lift this extra ton in weight. On top of that, I have to climb up to get in to the driving seat of this compact warbird, and I look down at the world even before leaving the ground. That's why I started this paragraph with the words 'sitting on board' and not 'sitting in'. There's a definite feeling of, 'this helicopter means business'. She really is a sub killer.

Renowned helicopter display pilot Dennis Kenyon is a convert to this fabulous warbird helicopter. After flying my first Wasp (XT435/NZ3907/G-RIMM) on a gusty day over the cliffs of the Isle of Wight in 2006, he wrote:

'Even with full fuel, two up, and a HOGE hover, we could comfortably hold station a whisker under max continuous torque. A little feature I welcomed was the discreet klaxon sounding in the Bose headsets as we approached 100% power, avoiding a constant reference to the instrument panel when one's attention needs to be well focussed outside.'

Pilots who trained on the Scout sometimes complain about the skittish hover taxi in high winds. It's true the Wasp lacks some stability (the Scout has a tailplane) and the tail rotor runs out of authority quicker than expected. Take-offs can appear a tad untidy in a wind shear, as the aircraft fish tails during translational lift. However, I have to say, the few 'Waspies' (former navy pilots) that still maintain currency do manage to make the insect-like helicopter (with its lanky dangling 'legs') look very graceful indeed.

The Wasp is a sturdy machine which gives a marvellous sense of being surrounded by something substantial. However, it does come with warnings on the box. The small rotor disc means that an engine failure results in a rapid decay of main rotor RPM, and leaving it too late to lower the collective will only end in tears. Even then, all that weight means the autorotation is more akin to dropping an armoured car out of the back of a C130 Hercules with no parachute. Engine-off landings (EOLs) are very interesting indeed! Having said that, the undercarriage suspension was developed for landing on heaving decks at sea, and is very forgiving on land too.

Fantastic fun to fly, the Wasp is manoeuvrable, responsive, and more agile than it looks. In the right hands it can compete with much more modern helicopters on the air show display circuit. One thing it is not, however, is fast. Best cruise speed is 85 to 95 knots and anything faster burns so much more fuel that it doesn't seem worthwhile. The relatively slow speed means long distances equate with long flights. However, the Wasp burns about 450lb (260 litres) of Avtur (JetA1 fuel) per hour and holds 1250lb (760 litres) in a full tank, so a two hour flight can cover up to 220 miles and still leaves a healthy reserve in the tank on landing.

Naturally, there are limits imposed on flying Wasps on the civilian register. For instance, flying in IMC (instrument meteorological conditions), and at night are forbidden, as are 'aerobatics'. In addition, civilian Wasps have less frequent 'eyes on' by technical experts, and we (pilots) have less opportunities to train, and therefore fewer opportunities to learn from other, more experienced pilots, than compared to military aircrew. Clearly, being privately funded and counting the cost of every minute in the air, making the most of every flying hour is paramount.

There are mitigations and some solutions to these limitations. In the period 2016 to 2017, the UK Civil Aviation Authority responded to a number of accidents and incidents involving ex-military aircraft by instigating thorough investigations of these events and by revising and/or re-writing the regulations pertaining to maintenance, general flying and air show displays of vintage ex-military aircraft. Obviously, we must follow these Civil Aviation Authority (CAA) rules and regulations to the letter, and also maintain a dialogue with the regulators and engineers with regards to incident reporting and propagation of safety information that is relevant to the type. In my own case, after the loss of collective control incident, the following essential interventions were imposed by the CAA to protect others who fly similar types:

1. The CAA issued Emergency Mandatory Permit Directive No 2017-002-E, applicable to UK-registered Westland Wasp and Scout helicopters, to perform a visual check of the condition of the universal joint and introduce periodic lubrication of the joint.

2. The issue of Safety Recommendation 2017-012 in which it recommended that, for ex-military aircraft on the UK civil register, the Civil Aviation Authority requires maintenance and overhaul tasks to be reviewed in the light of the expected aircraft utilisation and calendar-based time limits introduced where appropriate. Where such calendar-based time limits already exist, these should be reviewed to ensure that they are appropriate for the aircraft utilisation.

Further to official advisory recommendations and changes to legal regulations, it pays to be vigilant and prepared for any event at any time. Flying over populated areas, dense woodland, open stretches of water and mountainous topography, are all dangerous in the event of an engine failure and these areas must be considered as sterile on the navigational charts and should never be flown over by helicopter pilots who rely on only one engine. Arguably, helicopter pilots – who fly mostly under VMC (visual meteorological conditions), and predominantly under an altitude of 2000ft – must be more aware of the weather than those who fly under radar control and under instrument flight rules (IFR) or at high altitude. All in all, the cockpit of a single pilot, single engine helicopter flying at low-level in marginal weather is a busy place.

Getting to know the helicopter in every possible way is important. I have been fortunate to meet ex-RN/military aircrew, engineers, ground crew, designers, and all sorts of people with expert knowledge of the Wasp, and they all have something to offer a pilot who never 'went to sea'. Many of these kind people have shown their enthusiasm and keenness to support this particular Wasp and, by creating the Westland Wasp Historic Flight in 2016 and an associated volunteers' group a year later, I have witnessed an immense and amazing outflowing of fervour and passion for XT787, and for both Wasps and Scouts in general. Over the months, these kind people have demonstrated their ardour for the whole concept of keeping history flying by freely giving their time in all manner of ways. I have met so many ex-servicemen, from many nations, who have worked on, or with Wasps, during navy service. Their stories and knowledge have helped me better understand the difficulties and the joys of flying the Wasp operationally.

I have learned much about the technical aspects of the helicopter itself, as well as about the roles of flight deck personnel, engineering and technical support staff, crewmen and pilots, not least from my co-author of this book, retired Commander Larry Jeram-Croft, a former maintenance test pilot of this very aircraft type. As well as specific facts, figures, dates and dits, I have picked up so much more that makes my flying safer and happier, for instance, these tips are invaluable:

- Use every flight as a training flight. Cover at least one aspect from the LPC per flight.
- Set targets and be tough on myself. Set questions and rehearse emergencies.
- Don't ever skip on daily, weekly and scheduled maintenance.
- Whatever it costs, ignore budgets when affordable and, when not, look at ways to gain financial support. Safety must always come first.

- Within the bounds of safety, consider ways of bringing the significance of the Wasp to the public eye. Find innovative ways of keeping living history alive.
- Always use the Annual Skills Test (formerly LPC) as an extension to the teaching.

This is from my blog of 29 September 2017:

Thanks to my very patient examiner (John Beattie), who took me through the steps to complete my annual skills test at Compton Abbas today. That's done for another year, but I've re-learned the importance of practice, and of thinking 'safety' on every flight. My next job is to write 'what if' cards. I'll pick one out before every flight and it'll help me to revise all those urgent actions that may be needed unexpectedly at any time. Something very useful to make the most out of the day when you wake up and the rain is falling through the low cloud and thick mist.

Whilst on the subject of the weather, there's no doubt that flying inadvertently into bad weather can be fatal, but, on the other hand, at least a helicopter can be landed in small spaces that a fixed wing aeroplane could never possibly get into. The helicopter offers extra escape possibilities even after potentially bad earlier decisions or unexpected weather deterioration. However, this advantage may also be a peril in itself, as many helicopter pilots have come a cropper by overestimating their abilities to fly the chopper in such circumstances. The concept of the 'hard centred cloud' is drummed in to all pilots during training, yet there is a depressingly frequent number of accidents every year of controlled flight into terrain (CFIT), in which an airworthy aircraft, under pilot control, is unintentionally flown into high ground, a mountain, water, or an obstacle.

The weather in the UK is notoriously changeable and internationally known for consistently low cloud and poor visibility, with a significantly high risk of precipitation most days of the year. Here is a blog describing just such a day:

Tuesday, 2 August 2016 at 18:35 UTC+01
X-ray Tango is safely home after an interesting flight back from North Weald yesterday evening. As the weather started closing in it was a race to get back to base before the cloud base dropped below 500ft. All started well, but five minutes to the west of North Weald the GPS stopped working. No problem, I know my way round north London and the Home Counties 'with my eyes shut'. Well, that's okay, but the cloud base was already 1,400ft and the sky looked darker in the distance. No drama as the viz was good 'underneath' and the rain was only a drizzle. By the time I reached the south of

Reading, the rain was pounding at the windscreen, wipers looking like manic sloping eyelashes, and the cloud base dropped to 1,000ft. Scudding around under the clouds can be a lot of fun, but it does mean all the other VFR air traffic is compressed into a smaller block of airspace, and the low altitude means that radar and radio contact is tenuous at best. Add a hill or two with cloud for a hat, plus the necessary 'go-round' diversions and the paucity of landmarks in the central part of rural Hampshire, and my focus was definitely outside of the cockpit. Great flight though! Just over an hour, good old-fashioned eyeball and map navigation, some not-too-low level flying around a beautiful part of the country and X-ray Tango was on home ground again. Happy days! #historicwasp

Naturally, extra sets of eyes, scouring the sky for other aircraft, helping with navigation, or simply commenting on the weather, all helps flight safety. The Wasp is a single pilot aircraft, but that's not to say that the accompaniment of working 'crew' cannot be embraced. This turned out to be a great advantage of creating the volunteer group in 2017. Here is one example of where the skills from a former professional helicopter pilot came to be quite useful:

Friday, 18 August 2017 at 23:30 UTC+01
What a storm!

Taking advantage of a day of mostly blue skies, and the coincidental calls from two of the Wasp's Band of Volunteers (BoVers) to help with some daily maintenance, a refuel, plus some filming, it seemed like a great idea to take the BoVers for a hover. It takes a while to teach the BoVers to remove all the covers, and by the time I was doing the pre-flight checks, the sky turned very dark grey, with interesting spears of bright yellow light closely associated with extremely loud and deep rumbling noises. 'Take cover', cried the BoVers, and we sat patiently for the torrential rain to turn to drizzle and the sky to turn back to blue – all helped of course, with the latest app for weather radar. There's a hole in the Cu-Nims, pointed out Neil Knowles, one of the BoVers – an interesting chap who seems to have had many careers, but still reminisces about his years flying the Lynx in the Army Air Corps. I was impressed with his uncanny powers of weather prediction (helped by that lovely little app, of course) so we waited out the storm. Immediately the rain stopped and the wind died down, Chris Parsons showed off his new toy – a very neat and tiny drone that proceeded to buzz round the Wasp like an even smaller insect, apparently filming and snapping photos of the rest of us working. Soon after, we were climbing aboard and firing that gorgeous Nimbus engine in to life. It was a ten minute flight to EGVP, and we arrived just as the thunderstorm warning was lifted. That meant the bowser team could refuel the thirsty Squirrels that were patiently waiting on the dispersal. I landed nearby, and it was soon X-ray Tango's turn for replenishment, 271 litres later, with the chit signed, it was back in, fire up and depart back to our farm strip as the next black cloud chased us all the way. A great day – taking a helicopter veteran flying and reliving that nostalgia with him, plus the company of an excellent photographer and general all-round aviation buff, made for a very pleasant afternoon. All that was left to do was clean the blades, put the covers back on, etc. #historicwasp

XT787 covered for the harsh British weather. (*Terry Martin*)

Chapter 15

The End of the Life Cycle – Representing the Glories, Successes and Triumphs of the Past

I have always had an interest in history and a passion for all things aviation, so the opportunity to purchase and fly a warbird was never likely to have passed me by, and of course, new projects always open new doors with new opportunities waiting on the other side. It was with this in mind that I first responded to the request for the Wasp to be flown to an air show - not, of course to do a flying display at that stage, but simply to take place as a static exhibit alongside other vintage aircraft. That was in 2001, at Abingdon, the former RAF station where I first learned to fly with the RAF's University of London Air Squadron. From my perspective, this show was a success and a lot of fun. I wasn't aware of how much the Wasp was loved and revered by aviation enthusiasts, history buffs, and former servicemen alike. The day was spent talking to so many interesting and interested spectators and I knew I was doing an important thing, just by bringing the Wasp to the show. This single event awoke a realisation that I could help keep history alive and also pay respects to the crews that flew, and those that still fly, in dangerous conditions at sea, in all weathers and with all the risks incumbent on flying over the sea.

Over the following years, I offered the services of Wasp XT435 (G-RIMM) initially, then later, other Wasps that I had access to, such as XT420 (G-CBUI), XT793 (G-ZBPP) and SAAF '92' (G-BYCX), thanks to friends and colleagues who allowed me to rent their aircraft whilst mine was unavailable and before I purchased XT787 (G-KAXT).

The big occasion that opened my eyes to what was possible, was an amazing aircrew and ground crew reunion event in 2008 that offered me the privilege to fly with a large number of former serving RN personnel who had worked with, or flown in, Wasps, as the following blog explains:

Friday, 25 March 2016 at 10:49 UTC
Camaraderie, reunions and reminiscence.

Wasp crew reunion at RNAS Yeovilton, 12 April 2008. What a fantastic day! Three Westland Wasps flying non-stop all day, dozens of ex-aircrew and ground crew flown for about fifteen minutes each. Lots of memories, stories shared and wide smiles. It was a great privilege to be there and to meet some amazing people. I was flying XT793,

*but XT787 was also there, four years before I bought her. I thought I'd show a photo
(thanks to Lee Howard) of XT787 and XT420 in formation over the air traffic control
tower at Yeovilton. Lee was doing all the hard work, photographing from the rear bench
seat with the door open – lots of noise and only a lap belt to keep him in! He took some
amazing shots. I had the easy bit, all I had to do was fly straight and level! Here's a link
to a really nice article by Duncan Chase, with a lot of info on the event, and nice pics –
including the famous photo at BAM, of me flying XT793 straight towards the camera.*
http://www.airsceneuk.org.uk/airshow08/477wasp/wasp.htm

Two of the three ship formation at the Wasp crew's Reunion at RNAS Yeovilton in 2008. (*Lee Howard*)

Over subsequent years, XT787 made appearances at various events, mostly associated
with Royal Navy charities, museums, or Royal Air Force family's open days. Locations
included the Royal Marines Museum in Eastney, Portsmouth; Explosion Museum
at Priddy's Hard, Gosport; The Defence School of Aircraft Engineering (DSAE),
HMS *Sultan*, Gosport; Royal Navy Air Stations Culdrose and Yeovilton; RAF stations
Benson, Odiham, Coningsby, Cosford and Shawbury; and the Army Air Corps base at
Middle Wallop. I made several offers to represent the history of the Fleet Air Arm's
rotary wing fleet to the Fly Navy Heritage Trust (FNHT) and was very happy to

eventually receive an invitation from Rear Admiral Tom Cunningham for XT787 to join the Naval Heritage aircraft community in May 2016.

After discussions with Commodore Jock Alexander (CEO) and Commodore Bill Covington (Sea Vixen [G-CVIX] team leader for the Fly Navy Heritage Trust) at RNAS Yeovilton, I was delighted to announce that XT787 was confirmed as the first rotary wing Associate aircraft of the Fly Navy Heritage Trust, although I decided that the Westland Wasp Historic Flight would still continue to be its own 'brand'. XT787 would enjoy the opportunity to be 'on parade' with the Sea Vixen, Swordfish and others, including the aircraft of the Royal Navy Historic Flight, but does not receive any funding or support from the Royal Navy or its charities.

However, I was convinced of the value and kudos of being associated with the official RN heritage organisations and that the improved exposure would increase awareness of the importance of the Wasp in the history of rotorcraft development, its valuable role in early helicopter anti-submarine warfare, and the value of its swansong appearance in the Falklands conflict of 1982.

The next opportunity to show off X-ray Tango came along only a few months later with the launch of the new brand name of Royal Navy aviation heritage, 'Navy Wings'. This was my blog of the day:

Friday, 1 July 2016 at 18:00 UTC+01
NAVY WINGS will be officially launched tomorrow (Sat, 2 July 2016) at the Yeovilton Air Day. What was once 'Fly Navy Heritage Trust' has become 'Navy Wings'. Perhaps the biggest change that most folks will see is the gradual addition of more and more historic FAA aircraft to the 'fleet', and they will be actual fliers! I'm very proud that XT787 was the first privately owned aircraft to join the Sea Vixen in this new venture, and it's still the only representative of rotary wing RN aircraft in the collection. But I don't expect this to last long. Bring on the Gazelle, Wessex and even Sea King and Lynx! Come along and find out more about Navy Wings at Yeovilton on Saturday, or look at the new website: http://www.navywings.org.uk/ *And, while you're there, take a look at the Wasp page:* http://www.navywings.org.uk/aircraft/all-aircraft/westland-wasp-xt787/
#historicwasp

The next challenge in my quest for recognition of the gallant Wasp was to educate a new generation of aviation enthusiasts some of whom had perhaps never heard of the Wasp, or had simply not known of the Wasps superb service record. The opportunities trickled in slowly at first, but I was soon receiving requests to lecture and present both the history of my Wasp, but also of the development and service life of Wasps in general. The fascinating thing was that these events were attended by so many old salts from the Royal Navy and others who had flown or worked with Scouts in the British Army Air Corps and my lectures soon became very interactional as I leaned on the assembled experts to chip in with their own stories and memories. This is my blog written the day after my second guest lecture:

Friday, 22 April 2016 at 15:39 UTC+01
Education – Spreading the word (My presentations and meetings)
Thanks to all who came to listen to my presentation 'Doctors with Wings' at the Boscombe Down Aviation Collection at Old Sarum on 21 April. You were a lovely audience, great participation, and your generous appreciation was humbling. For those who missed it, this was an excuse for me to wax lyrical about the journeys taken by both XT787 and by me, through a timeline that demonstrated the amazing helicopter ancestry from Count Juan de la Cierva's autogyros, through the SARO Skeeter, and Scout, and on to Westland's development of the Wasp from the early P.531 and 'Sea Scout'. All this occurred within fifty miles of Old Sarum – including the UK's first cross country flight by a rotary wing aircraft (Cierva in 1927, from Eastleigh to Farnborough). That's Hampshire – my part of the world – and so, for those who had the strength to listen for the full hour, I also talked about how I came to fly, how I met my first Wasp, and also about my life's work with air ambulances in Africa, New Zealand, the Middle East, and all over the UK. Some asked about how all this can be distilled into one lifetime and I talked about the good fortune I've been blessed with and the great opportunities I've seized that allowed me the privilege to have at least three careers at all times through my adult life. Thanks for listening guys! Blue skies are coming (think positive), Terry.

The Wasp's popularity seemed to be growing so fast that it was difficult to keep up. Thinking of new ways to keep the supporters interested has led to a wide range of news items, correspondence threads, spectator participations, and the eventual formation of the Westland Wasp Historic Flight Volunteers Group. This blog is an example of keeping the interest going. It received a significant number of replies and maintained a debate for over two months:

Monday, 11 April 2016 at 19:32 UTC+01
Naming aircraft.
It's customary to name 'planes, and I was wondering what name I'd choose for X-ray Tango. Aircraft, like ships, are traditionally 'female' ('God bless her and all who sail in her') and, anyway, XT lived on a ship for much of her active duty. So – it has to be a female sounding name. BUT – she's feisty. She's been to war and she's aimed a few shots (or

at least she represents a Wasp that did). She's also cute (beauty's in the eye of the beholder) and yet, at the same time, rugged. What a dilemma! This baby 'flies like a butterfly and stings like a bee' (or, in this case, wasp) and trying to find a name worthy of her is not going to be easy. Help me choose a name. There's a flight on offer if your suggestion is used.

Of course, the other way to draw in crowds, teach them about the glorious history and create income for the ex-serviceman's charities, whilst commemorating the past triumphs and achievements and celebrate the courage of the spirited and expert aircrew of former decades, is to display the Wasp actually flying. Air shows and other events had been targeted since 2015 but, in that year, I decided that I could do more than a simple fly-past. It was time to study and practice for my Display Authority and the legendary John Beattie offered to take me through the process. By early 2016, both XT787 and I were ready for the summer season with a full 3D show planned and practiced accordingly.

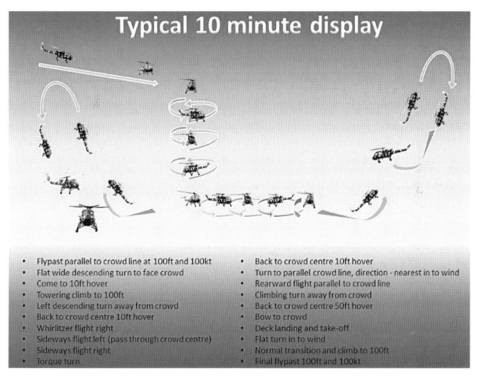

Typical 10 minute display

• Flypast parallel to crowd line at 100ft and 100kt	• Back to crowd centre 10ft hover
• Flat wide descending turn to face crowd	• Turn to parallel crowd line, direction - nearest in to wind
• Come to 10ft hover	• Rearward flight parallel to crowd line
• Towering climb to 100ft	• Climbing turn away from crowd
• Left descending turn away from crowd	• Back to crowd centre 50ft hover
• Back to crowd centre 10ft hover	• Bow to crowd
• Whirlitzer flight right	• Deck landing and take-off
• Sideways flight left (pass through crowd centre)	• Flat turn in to wind
• Sideways flight right	• Normal transition and climb to 100ft
• Torque turn	• Final flypast 100ft and 100kt

XT787 air show display plan. (*Terry Martin*)

One of the greatest joys of display flying is meeting the spectators and hearing what they have to say. Sometimes they come over just to say hello and to have a photo taken with the Wasp, and sometimes even with the pilot! At other times, the really zealous ones will pass the time by asking the most esoteric questions, and they sometimes even try to catch me out. Small children can be great fun - they always want to know where the guns are and why the engine doesn't have a cover, so I'm always well prepared for suitable answers and stories to pad out the explanations in a simple way. My favourite visitors, though, are the elderly chaps (no ladies yet, sadly) who served with the Wasp Flights, or as engineers, or who were involved in the design, manufacture, or trials of the aircraft. Sometimes, these gentlemen had simply seen Wasps on the ships in which they served. But every single one of them has a story to tell and I love to hear them. During a long hot day on the flight line at a show, it is also a welcome relief to let somebody else do the talking for a while and I often invite these gentlemen to stay and talk to the other visitors - and most happily agree! Here is a typical busy show day at RNAS Yeovilton's Air Day in 2017.

Sunday, 9 July 2017 at 17:03 UTC+01
Yeovilton Air Day 2017.

Another great show. Even though X-ray Tango wasn't on the flying display programme this year, it was great to be invited to the static display and to be parked right outside the Navy Wings sales marquee and beneath the banner showing the Wasp in fine company with the Sea Vixen, Sea Fury and Swordfish. We had dozens, if not hundreds, of inquisitive visitors who all braved the searing heat to stop, reminisce, chat, share stories and photograph X-ray Tango in the Somerset sunshine today.

I've attached photos of two very special gentlemen who both have a special history with Wasps in the Royal Navy. The first was Rear Admiral Terry Loughran, accompanied by his lovely wife Phillipa. Terry first flew Wessex helicopters with the Royal Navy, but quickly graduated to the Sea King. He was later surprised, therefore, to be selected as a Wasp Flight Commander in 1973, but soon learned to love and respect these agile and spirited little helicopters during his two years on Tribal and Leander class frigates. He was delighted to be back in the cockpit after all those years.

The second gentleman was former NAM (Navy Aircraft Mechanic) Frank 'Fred' Mills (who proudly gave his service number without hesitation) and stated that he was a member of 700 Squadron, based at Yeovilton in the early 1960s, when the SARO P.531 predecessor of the Wasp was being flown on trials. His claim to fame was that it took him only forty-five minutes to change the engine on the P.531, but the paperwork took two and a half hours. Now this might be a fisherman's tale, but I queried it and he insisted - only three quarters of an hour to take one engine off and put another one on! Of course it helps that there are no cowlings over the engine, but it surely was a superb effort. Thank you to all the many other people who visited us in the heat of the day. It was amazing to chat to you all and to share your passion for the wonderful Wasp.

Rear Admiral Terry Loughran revisiting the Wasp after more than thirty years. (*Terry Martin*)

NAM Frank Mills reliving his days as a P.531 mechanic, photographed at RNAS
Yeovilton Air Day, July 2017. (*Terry Martin*)

The air shows are not always glorious days with sunny skies, and they're often quite exhausting, especially the larger events. Some events are very well organised with catering and refreshments available for those who struggle to find time to evade the spectators for long enough to take some sustenance. Occasionally things don't go quite to plan. Here, for instance, is my blog about a day that didn't turn out the way I expected it to:

Sunday, 14 August 2016 at 22:19 UTC+01
Search and Rescue - Not quite the day I was expecting!

There was an incident today at Herne Bay during the air show. A Tiger Club Turbulent, with an engine problem, ditched in the bay at around 15:35, exactly as I was running in towards for my display. I was told to hold, but soon realised that an incident was unfolding so, instead of displaying I asked ATC if the Wasp could assist. I was sent out to the approximate site (which was out of view of the Flying Display Director and air traffic assistant) and asked to verify if the pilot or wreckage could be seen. I searched the sea in expanding box style and then spotted the small blue aeroplane on the beach. By the time I transmitted the sitrep, emergency vehicles were arriving along the beach and I was tasked with hovering near the aircraft to act as a locator beacon for incoming vehicles, boats and HEMS helicopter. By that time I could see the pilot was alive and reasonably well enough to stand and walk, and reports were coming back on the radio that he had been rescued. Youtube and news reports told the story of a ditching very close to the shallows, but the Turbulent overturned and the pilot was submerged. Members of the crowd waded out and righted the aircraft, pulled out the pilot and then dragged the aircraft back to the beach! Marvellous effort by all. First reports are that the pilot has only minor injuries - thanks to his decision to ditch very near to the beach and the very quick rescue by spectators. The aircraft looked intact too. The show was suspended for about an hour so the only 'display' that I did was the search pattern along the beach and initially further out to sea. Once 'Helimed' (Kent HEMS) arrived on scene, I handed over the airspace and did one fly-past in front of the show crowd as I departed back to Maypole aerodrome. Something different! A very survivable incident nicely managed by the pilot and courageously aided by the spectators. I don't know what the CAA will make of it, but I hope they don't go overboard (no pun intended). Anyway, the complete day's flying was superb, the weather was perfect and I met some nice folks at Maypole and Lashenden. There's not much of the Wasp on YouTube, but whilst you're looking at the ditching videoclips, you can just see or hear X-ray Tango on these two…

https://www.youtube.com/watch?v=k0dIspQB66U
https://www.youtube.com/watch?v=Nl9X3IqspFk

The story was much better one year later.

Saturday, 19 August 2017 at 23:35 UTC+01
To Kent and back.

One of the disadvantages of displaying at a coastal event is not being on the ground to see the rest of the show. Today was a little different. I and my crew of two (Gail and 'BoVer' Cliff Ibell) were hosted by Andy and his team at Maypole, a delightful airstrip only a few miles south of Herne Bay. After my display slot at 15:30, I returned to Maypole field to pick up the crew, but also to watch the air show sky from a great distance. Then, out of the windswept clouds aloft, the beautiful singing of a Merlin engine drowned out the summer birdsong and the chatter of merrymakers and spectators gathered to watch the comings and goings of air show traffic. The unmistakable shape of a Spitfire loomed in to view, flew a low-level pass down the runway, followed by a second, then an amazing and unexpected third. The most moving moment was the rocking wings of farewell as she slipped skyward towards the horizon en route (one imagines) to protect the skies of Britain from invaders over the nearby channel. Truly amazing. Our own private show! Thank you to Andy's team for the hospitality and family atmosphere at Maypole field. It was good to see the classic cars there too.

Thanks also to the nice folks at Lashenden who accepted us for a refuel and offered tea, refreshments and friendship, as well as an invitation to return anytime. How about an invite to next year's show guys? I can do two in a day easily! The flight back facing into a western sun was brilliant in both senses. The uninterrupted blue sky, with cotton fluffy white buds of clouds, contrasted well against the carpet of shades of green that was the South Downs. If only every day could be like this. Of the Band of Volunteers and crew, Gail is now an expert on the Wasp daily chores, and is doing brilliantly with her nav and operation of the comms in flight. She's also a creditable trainer and manifester for newer BoVers. OTOH, Cliff was a little disappointed about the cabin service during the day's flying, but he was still smiling when we were putting X-ray Tango back under wraps for the night, so I don't think he really missed the G&T and inflight movie. #historicwasp

XT787 showing her top whilst climbing towards a torque turn in the display. (*Chris Parsons*)

On a more serious note, there are a lot of preparations to be done before a flying display. Plans, timings, layouts and rules must be learned precisely. On the day, there will be a compulsory briefing to cover all of the above, plus much more such as weather, restrictions, air law, potential conflictions, radio frequencies, and, of course, any last minute changes to the previously promulgated instructions. A visit to RAF Shawbury's family's day in 2017 is typical of most air shows.

Saturday, 5 August 2017 at 10:50 UTC+01
Typical Air Show Day.
    Having arrived at Shawbury just as the airfield opened, the immediate next item is 'where do I park?' It's important to know whether the Wasp needs to park with

the other static displays, or if there's a separate area for aircraft that take part in the flying display. My arrival at Shawbury was at 08:10L ('L' is local time to avoid confusion with 'Z' or 'Zulu' time. which is aka GMT aka UTC, i.e. one hour earlier than BST British Summer Time - confused??). The pilot's display briefing (an essential and legal requirement) was due at 08:45, so there was just enough time to visit facilities, grab a coffee, and prepare for the briefing. After a thorough presentation of the met (weather actuals and forecast), and a review of the display program, timings, rules and regulations, there followed an opportunity for questions and clarifications from all present. At Shawbury, X-ray Tango was parked in an area that could be accessed by the public, but easy enough to be closed off when it was my turn to move back on to the airfield to display. So, it was back to the Wasp in preparation to meet the public. My display slot was 10:10 to 10:20, and after checking with the ground crew about clearing the public from the area, I was soon back in the cab, running pre-flight checks and requesting 'engine start' from air traffic control (tower frequency). Prior to start, I checked again that the area was completely clear and safe for me launch. The next radio call I made was a request to position away from the static park pending the clearance advice, 'Wasp you are cleared to display', which came at exactly 10:10. The display was 'spirited' to say the least. The forecast wind was 18kt gusting 25kt, direct on to the crowd line. That makes it important to constantly fly with a sharp eye on the 150m and 230m marker boards in order not to be blown too close to the crowd. All went well but I wished I could have heard the commentary as I always do. One day I'll be organised enough to ask somebody to record it for me. The remainder of the day was spent back in the static park (after landing a safe distance away and finding four strong helpers to push X-ray Tango back in to the spectator area). Parked behind a Puma - the Wasp looks quite small! It's always a lot of fun talking with the public. Some folks just want to have their photo taken in or outside the Wasp, some want to know what a Wasp is/does/did/etc.., and then there are those who have flown Wasps, worked on them or with them in the Royal Navy. I have learned so many interesting, and occasionally amusing, stories from these lovely people. The Shawbury day was no exception. I learned a lot, and seeing a Wasp flying again brings joy to so many people. That is the real reward for taking part in these events.
#historicwasp

Wasp 'squadron' at the Wasp Crew Reunion, Yeovilton 2008. (*Lee Howard*)

The Volunteers Group

Throughout these pages I've often talked about the Westland Wasp Historic Flight's volunteers group. These enthusiastic supporters of our aims and objectives are all keen to offer a little of their spare time to help with daily maintenance, keeping Wasp XT787 shipshape and sometimes even more complex and technical jobs for those with an engineering background, especially those who are current licenced engineers. We've had a few meetings for like-minded people to get to know more about the Wasp and the challenges we face in trying to keep her flying and maintain her in good condition despite all the ravages of the British weather. Volunteers with aircrew skills are soon in the cockpit and relearning old skills, and the ground crew ride in the back for flight experience and on-board training.

The first group of volunteers were, in fact, former Fleet Air Arm aircrew. It was a beautiful day to be in, and flying over, the Hampshire countryside, and the volunteers were rewarded with a day of memories, helped by the evocative smells and sounds of the Wasp. Before, between, and after the two short flights, the air was full of Jackspeak and Navy banter, as if the old salts had never lost touch with each other, despite some who had never met during RN service and two hadn't seen each other in seventeen years. It was a lot of fun, but not all fun! There were rotor blades to de-rust and lubricate, covers to put on the irregular and complex shape of the helicopter, and some general tidying before the day was done. Nobody complained, and the former aircrew did a half good job – a great start! It was a privilege to meet these guys and I welcome them to the Wasp 'band of brothers'. It was also nice to surprise them when I did my usual trick of jumping 'up top', to refuel the Wasp myself. 'Great to see the pilot doing the refuel', was the comment I heard as the mateys watched agog!

Aircrewman Gail Barkes organising the volunteers group and shows how it's done – at work on XT787 (*Terry Martin*)

Those same aircrew volunteers stepped in to help with our first non-aircrew volunteers group full day of training at Old Sarum in October 2017, in which twenty-two individuals successfully qualified as ground crew that can now act in support of the flying team at air shows with such tasks as landing site surveys, constructing a helicopter landing site, crowd management, marshalling, and embarkation/disembarkation of passengers.

This and future similar events are designed to train new volunteers, and for updating and re-engaging existing volunteers who support Westland Wasp XT787 for its charitable work on behalf of MoD good causes (such as Help for Heroes) and for

Navy Wings (Fly Navy Heritage Trust). It wasn't long before the first volunteers were put in to action as this last blog recounts:

Saturday, 23 September 2017 at 18:46 UTC+01
Beautiful day in Bratton.

Wasp volunteer Ray Hatch took a step back in history and re-acquainted himself with the Westland Wasp today, on the 23 September 2017, by joining the crew for a visit to the 'Bratton at War' event, near Westbury, in a beautiful part of Wiltshire. With thanks to Salisbury Plain Ops and Boscombe Radar, we transited the low-level route around the south of the danger areas on the Plain. After a cloudy start, we had a fantastic view of Stonehenge, with hardly a person in sight, although there were dozens of cars parked nearby (something to do with the autumn equinox perhaps?). The sky gradually cleared as we passed Yarnbury Castle, and by the time we approached the Westbury White Horse, there wasn't a cloud in sight anywhere. Just beyond the white horse monument and, with the event showground in sight, we made a gentle circling approach to look at the landing area to ensure it was safe. Another Wasp volunteer, Derek Priest, had previously conducted a site survey for me, and discussed the best layout with the show organisers. Derek marshalled us in perfectly and his small group of willing ground crew kept the area clear until the engine was off and rotors had stopped. The volunteers did very well indeed. #historicwasp

There is still more to be done. If my Wasp, or any others, are to continue flying and displaying for the public, we need supporters who can help. For instance, the job isn't over when the public leave the air show. Apart from reviewing the flight plan for the return journey, checking the departure slot with air traffic control, and finding a little sustenance and fluid before the flight (it can be difficult to find time to eat and drink during busy shows), the Wasp needs to be checked for flight (yes - again, before every flight), and there may be a need to reposition the fixed and lockable undercarriage in the 'flight over land' mode. The fuel requirement has to be calculated, the refuelling bowser has to be booked (and may well be busy with a lot of other aircraft waiting to depart) and then there's the actual refuelling itself. There's quite an art to refuelling a Wasp, so it's better that I do it myself rather than rely on people who haven't been trained on Wasp/Scout peculiarities, but this is something that can be learned in the future. Overfilling through the conical filler results in an enormous overflow of spurting JetA1 (Avtur) kerosene. Underfilling may mean an unscheduled extra fuelling stop. Getting airborne is often delayed because of queuing aircraft all wanting to get home as soon as possible, but, once up and away, it's once again time to relax and enjoy the flight after a good day's work.

Final words

It is always a real joy and privilege to fly the Wasp and I never take for granted that I have a significant piece of history under my control whenever I fly. The opportunity to display this unique helicopter to the public is humbling, and the experience of teaching youngsters about the Wasp's history, as well as listening to older generations when they share their stories and experiences is fulfilling.

As Larry Jeram-Croft mentioned in his final chapter of section one of this book, he did fly Wasp XT787, around thirty years after he last flew a Wasp in operational service. He wrote of his joy and, as I read his words, I wondered who was having the most fun at the time. Perhaps him because of his initial relief and then glee as he found his way around a trusted old friend – a helicopter which he had pushed to its limits three decades ago? Or was it me, because I could make this reunion happen, and I was there to witness the sheer thrill of aviation once more emerging from a man who thought, only a few weeks earlier, that he would never fly again? We'll never be able to measure those emotions, as the moment has now passed, but one thing is certain, the Westland Wasp is an amazingly unique and very special helicopter that demands a lot from its pilots, but returns the favour with the joy that is felt when master and helicopter work as one.

XT789 – still flying, still thrilling the crowds. (*Chris Parsons*)

Annex A – Glossary of Terms

Acronym	Translation	Meaning
AEO	Air Engineer Officer	The LJ-C's profession.
AAW	Anti-Air Warfare	A defined role for a warship with area anti-aircraft missiles such as Sea Dart.
AEW	Airborne Early Warning	Any airborne system that can detect attacking aircraft and give warning.
AMCO	Air Maintenance Control Office	The engineering hub of a squadron or ship's flight.
AS12	An air-to-surface missile	Carried by the Wasp helicopter and used during the Falklands War on the Argentinian submarine *Santa Fe*.
ASUW/ASV	Anti-Surface Warfare/ Anti-Surface Vessel	Two terms meaning the same thing that changed over time.
ASW	Anti-Submarine Warfare	
ATC	Air Traffic Control	
AUM	All Up Mass	The total mass of an aircraft at any time.
AUW	All-Up Weight	The total weight of an aircraft at any time – changed to 'mass' to be more correct.
BAS	British Antarctic Survey	
BOST	Basic Operational Sea Training	The workup package of training for ships entering the fleet.
CAA	Civil Aviation Authority	The UK governing body for all civil aircraft.
CASEVAC	Casualty Evacuation	Term used for helicopter sorties to conduct medical transfers. Also MEDEVAC.
DIDTAC	Detect Identify Destroy Tactics	More commonly referred to as 'Death in the Dark tactic'. The use of flares to illuminate a target before firing air-to-surface missiles - primarily used by the Wasp.
FCU	Fuel Control Unit	The hydro-mechanical system used to control fuel into a gas turbine - analogous to a car's carburettor.
FISHHEAD	Slang	A term of endearment used by naval aviators for their seamen officer friends.

Acronym	Translation	Meaning
FOD	Foreign Object Damage	A generic term for anything going into a gas turbine engine and causing damage.
FOST	Flag Officer Sea Training	The organisation that works up ships when they enter service now based in Plymouth.
FOTI	Fleet Operational Tactical Instruction	Instructions on how to deploy and use various weapons and systems.
FPB	Fast Patrol Boat	Generic term for any small, high speed and armed military vessel.
GOONSUIT		Slang term for the immersion coverall worn by naval aircrew when the sea temperature is less than 15 degrees - similar to a diver's dry suit.
GPMG	General Purpose Machine Gun	7.62 millimetre belt fed machine gun used by all the British services.
HAS	Helicopter Anti-Submarine	A title given to an aircraft to identify its primary role.
HCA	Helicopter Controlled Approach	A method of returning to ones ship using the aircraft's own radar.
HDS	Helicopter Delivery Service	Generic term for any helicopter flight delivering stores, whether internally or in underslung loads. See also VERTREP.
IFP	Instrument Flying Practice	Generic term for aircrew training and continuation flying to enable them to fly in IMC (see below).
IFTU	Intensive Flight Trial Unit	First unit to be equipped with a new aircraft in the Fleet Air Arm so that it can be evaluated.
ILS	Instrument Landing System	A radio system that lets the aircraft know its height and range from the runway to allow it to land in bad visibility.
IMC	Instrument Flying Conditions	Defined conditions when aircrew are flying solely on instruments.
LACM	Leading Aircrewman	
MEDEVAC	Medical Evacuation	Generic term for any aircraft sortie to evacuate a medical emergency. See also CASEVAC.
MLA	Minimum Landing Allowance	The minimum fuel state an aircraft must have at final land on. Going beyond this may result in engines flaming out.
MPA	Maritime Patrol Aircraft	Normally a modified commercial airliner. The RAF used to operate the Nimrod - based on the Comet airliner - until they were scrapped in the latest Defence Review.

Acronym	Translation	Meaning
NASU	Naval Aircraft Support Unit	An organisation at a Naval Air Station that conducts deeper maintenance and modification than can be conducted on a squadron.
NATEC	Naval Aircraft Technical Evaluation Centre	Based at the air station at Lee-on-Solent, the NATEC was responsible for many elements of specialist engineering such as vibration and helicopter oil analysis.
NATIU	Naval Aircraft Trials Installation Unit	Now defunct – but an organisation based at the air station at Lee-on-Solent that managed and conducted trial modifications of aircraft.
NAVOCFORMED	Naval On Call Force Mediterranean	A temporary force in the Mediterranean from several countries that operated together to gain experience of NATO operations.
NGS	Naval Gunfire Support	The act of spotting the fall of shot of naval guns to correct their aim. Can be done by observers from the ground or in aircraft.
ODM	Operating Data Manual	A publication relevant to a type of aircraft listing all its performance data.
OOW	Officer Of The Watch	The officer in charge on the bridge of a warship.
OP	Observation Post	A military outpost designed to keep surveillance over a given area.
PNR	Point Of No Return	The point in an aircraft's journey when it will no longer be possible to turn around and land elsewhere.
PVA/ELVA	Poor Visibility Approach/ Extremely Limited Visibility Approach	Normally an emergency procedure to recover to one's ship when the visibility has reduced below safe minima. A combination of radar control, flares being dropped into the wake of the ship and other techniques. During the Falklands War it became almost the normal daily procedure used by helicopter crews.
QHI	Qualified Helicopter Instructor	A pilot who has completed the instructors course, then employed on a training squadron, or as a senior member of a regular squadron.
RAE	Royal Aircraft Establishment	The civilian research organisation based at Farnborough and Boscombe Down, as well as elsewhere. Changed to become the Defence Research Agency DRA and then privatised and now known as QinetiQ.
RAN	Royal Australian Navy	
RFA	Royal Fleet Auxiliary	Ships used to support the RN Fleet, i.e. oilers, stores, ships, etc. Painted grey but run to Merchant ship rules.

Acronym	Translation	Meaning
ROE	Rules Of Engagement	The rules provided by Command that give the freedom to use weapons at any given time.
S126	A naval form	Raised to account for lost stores. Not popular!
SAM	Surface-to-air Missile	
SAR	Search and Rescue	
SARBE	Search and Rescue Beacon	A small radio fitted to aircrew life vests that produces a radio signal on the emergency frequency to allow survivors to be located.
SAS/SBS	Special Air Service/ Special Boat Service	The UK's two Special Forces cadres.
SHOL	Ship Helicopter Operating Limitations	The limits to which a particular helicopter can operate to with a specified type of ship. Mainly consisting of ship's pitch and roll limits and wind speed and direction - represented graphically.
SIGINT	Signal Intelligence	Intelligence gathered though analysis of the enemy's radio traffic.
SLR	Self-Loading Rifle	For many years the UK standard rifle for all three services: 7.62 millimetre and twenty rounds fired single shot.
SMR	Senior Maintenance Rating	The Chief Petty Officer in charge of the maintenance of any ships flight.
SQAVO	Squadron Aviation Officer	Frigates and Destroyers are organised into squadrons and the senior ship's staff take on extra responsibility for the ships in their squadron. The Flight Commander of the senior ship is therefore the Squadron Aviation Officer.
STUFT	Ships Taken Up From Trade	Generic term for any merchant ships chartered by the MOD during operations.
TEZ	Total Exclusion Zone	The 200 mile zone around the Falklands imposed by the British at the start of the Falklands War.
VERTREP	Vertical Replenishment	Generic term for transferring stores to ships by helicopter, normally as underslung loads.
VMC	Visual Metrological Conditions	Defined conditions when aircrew are able to operate visually.
WAFU	Slang - and Varied!! Often - 'Wet and Effing Useless'	A term of endearment used to describe aviators.
WIGS	West Indies Guard Ship	Until replaced by APT (N) this was the generic term for any ship operating in the Caribbean.

Annex B – A Dummies Guide to Flying a Helicopter

Although this book is about one specific type of helicopter, the detail of how one is flown is generally only really understood by those who actually get to play with them. Whilst it is obviously not possible to teach someone how to fly one from the pages of a book, in this section the author will attempt to provide just a little more in the way of explanation and maybe bust a couple of myths in the process, as well as providing some more detail about the Wasp.

Nomenclature

'Helicopter speak' uses some common phrases that are not at all obvious to the layman.

The use of the letter 'N' has particular significance to helicopter pilots; it means various forms of rotational speed:

Nr – the speed of the main rotors.

Nf – the speed of the Free Power Turbines – these are the turbines at the back of each engine that are connected to the transmission.

Nc – in the case of the Wasp – the speed of the gas generator (turbine).

Torque – this is a key measurement. The transmission of a helicopter is driven by the power output of its engine/engines. However, for aerodynamic reasons the rotor speed (Nr) of a helicopter needs to be kept fairly constant. It is actually torque that damages a rotating component and so, rather than a power gauge, a helicopter has a Torque gauge (or several – one for each engine) which, as the Nr is constant, is effectively proportional to the power output of the engines. As torque is the damaging factor for the transmission it is the most useful measurement for the pilot to ensure he flies safely.

Collective – this refers to anything that happens to all the rotor blades the same amount. Collective pitch is the amount of pitch applied by the pilot's collective lever. The more applied, the more lift generated, but the more Torque is needed to keep Nr constant.

Cyclic - this refers to anything that happens to the rotor blades as they go round in a circle. The Cyclic stick used by the pilot will change the pitch of the blades where he wants them in order to manoeuvre the aircraft. For example, if he pushes the stick forward, the angle of blades at the rear of the aircraft is increased and that ahead is decreased. The net effect is to tilt the rotor disc forwards and the aircraft will drop its nose.

Yaw - as collective pitch is applied, the fuselage of a helicopter will attempt to turn in the opposite direction to that of the main rotors (torque reaction). This Yaw is counteracted in most helicopters by a tail rotor. The pitch of this rotor is controlled by rudder pedals.

Autorotation - contrary to popular myth, a helicopter will continue to fly without engine power. If the pilot lowers the collective lever to the bottom in forward flight, the aircraft will start to descend (often quite rapidly), but the air now flowing up through the rotors keeps them turning to the extent that the pilot may well have to apply some collective pitch to keep their speed under control. This is called autorotation and consequently all the flying controls will still operate normally. In the case of an engine failure the pilot will enter autorotation and fly the aircraft to a safe area, normally at a speed of about 70 knots or so. When close to the ground he then pulls up the nose to wash off speed, which also has the effect of reducing his rate of descent. When almost down, he then levels the aircraft and pulls the collective lever up to cushion the landing - this will slow down the rotors, but enables a safe and controlled landing to be undertaken. In the Royal Navy this was only practiced in single engine helicopters, the Wasp and Gazelle. With twin engine aircraft, the autorotation phase is practiced - but only to a powered hover.

Getting it started
One of the worst sins committed by novelists is when the hero jumps into an unfamiliar helicopter and starts it up. Strangely, any experienced pilot put behind the controls of a 'burning and turning' helicopter would almost certainly be able to lift into the hover and fly away. What he would NOT be able to do is get the machine going in the first place. This is because nearly every machine will use a totally different set of switches, cocks, levers, gauges, controls etc. to manage the process. Add into the mix different numbers of engines with differing types of control systems, different stabilisation and flight control systems and one can see how complicated life can become. If you have a

set of the startup check lists you could probably figure it out in slow time once all the switches etc. have been located, and you can understand what they do of course.

So, given that learning to fire the thing up is going to be an issue which cannot be addressed here, outlined below is a very simplified routine for getting a Wasp 'burning and turning':

Walk around the machine and check all is secure and all blanks have been removed. Then jump in and do up your straps. Operate the flying controls over the full range and look at the blades to move correspondingly.

Before engine start, all the internal switches need to be made. Ensure the rotor brake is on.

Next, the flying instruments and warning panels are checked before moving to the lower centre console to turn on the radios and other electronics.

When ready, signal ground crew that you are ready to start the engine. Operate the engine start switch and simultaneously open the engine High Pressure (HP) cock. Wait for the engine to light up and monitor the JPT to ensure it stays in limits and that the oil pressures rise.

With the rotor brake on, the rotors don't move.

When satisfied all is well, centre the cyclic and bottom the collective. Turn on the anti-collision light and signal to the marshaller that you want to start the rotors. Check all is clear and release the rotor brake. Gently open the throttle on the collective lever to accelerate the engine and rotors until Nr is stable at 420 rpm

You are now set for the pre-take-off checks and off you go – easy isn't it?

Flying a Helicopter

So now you are at a thousand feet flying along at 100 knots. Your three controls are what you use to keep straight, keep level and maintain speed.

The cyclic stick will bank the aircraft and raise and lower the nose. Unlike a fixed wing aircraft, all helicopters are inherently unstable. This means that if you displace the cyclic in any direction the helicopter will continue to diverge in that direction unless corrected by the pilot. In a fixed wing aircraft, it will tend to self-correct without intervention. In addition, when a manoeuvre is initiated in a fixed wing machine, for example a turn, once the aircraft is at the desired angle of bank then the stick is returned to the central position. In a helicopter the stick has to be held into the turn to hold the bank. This is surprisingly intuitive, unlike the instability issue. Nearly all modern machines have some form of automatic stability built in to make life easier. Normally, this uses gyros to sense aircraft movement and feed in corrective signals. The Wasp has this – but can be flown 'stab out' - and many preferred it out (including the author). Helicopter instructors also like it out to build up piloting skills (and make their students sweat).

The collective lever in you left hand is used to maintain height, and in conjunction with the cyclic, maintain speed. The cyclic is used to select an aircraft attitude and the collective adjusted to maintain height. If the attitude is right then the speed will be also. If not, small adjustments will get it right.

The rudder pedals are used to balance the aircraft when turning and can also be used to make small heading changes.

The Wasp has two other helpful functions from the AFCS. On the rudder pedals are two switches which are closed when the pilot has his 'size tens' on the pedals. When he takes his feet off, the switches make and the AFCS automatically maintains the heading the aircraft was on when his feet were removed.

There were also height holds and when pressed will move the collective to maintain whatever height the aircraft was at when selected. One is driven by the radar altimeter, which only reads up to 1000 feet, and the second is driven by the barometric altimeter, which is less accurate, but can work at all heights.

So, our helicopter pilot can now turn, change speed, and climb and descend. Now, he has to learn to hover.

Hovering is literally like learning to ride a bicycle, in that it seems impossible at first and then it suddenly 'clicks'. The previously described controls still work in the same way as in forward flight, but everything is very sensitive and every control input has an effect which has to be countered by one of the others.

For example; if the aircraft starts to descend slightly, the collective needs to be raised. This increases the torque reaction, so the rudder pedals have to be adjusted to keep the heading steady. Unfortunately, the tail rotor is not at the same height as the main rotor, so increasing the thrust from it will tend to make the aircraft roll slightly. This means the cyclic has to be corrected and so not all the lift is working in the same direction and therefore the collective needs adjusting - you can see where this goes! It's quite fun watching a student for the first time (as long as you have already mastered the art) and its quite obvious, even from the outside, when the penny drops.

Now you can fly forwards and hover - you're a helicopter pilot. Nope. That's just the start. Helicopters are complicated and the systems in it will need managing and you will have to learn how. Then you will need to be able to cope with all the emergencies it is liable to throw your way. This is where simulators come into their own, as all sorts of horrible emergencies can be practiced that would be far too dangerous in a real machine. Many hours will be needed in training before anyone is safe to fly a helicopter. The big danger is 'getting behind the machine' i.e. letting it fly you, not the other way around.

A famous quote from an instructor to his student – *'Blogs, you are the safest pilot I've ever encountered. You're so far behind the aircraft, it will have crashed, burned and the fire will have gone out before you arrive at the scene of the accident!'*

So that's what's needed right? Wrong. Once you can fly the beast and cope with all it can do to you on a bad day, you now start to learn how to use it. In a private aircraft, that may simply be learning to navigate from A to B. In something like the Wasp, it is a fighting machine with a plethora of tasks The pilot's main task will be to fly the aircraft, but crew cooperation with the observer is a key part of being operationally effective. A worked up Wasp crew will work together and share the load of navigating, using the radios and firing weapons. It is often observed by passengers that a good crew rarely speaks to each other, as they know exactly what each are required to do before it needs to be said. Of course, in the Wasp and other naval helicopters, there are lots of secondary tasks like deck landing, load lifting, SAR, collecting the mail and getting ashore before anyone else, but some of those are skills that come naturally! Oh, and some 'non aviators' will also say that aviators are expert at using their 'pits' (beds) and they would be right. After all, we need at least eight hours rest a day – and what we get at night is a bonus.